F
574
.D4
P26
1970

Parkins, Almon
Ernest, 1879-1940.

The historical
geography of
Detroit

DATE			

THE HISTORICAL GEOGRAPHY
OF DETROIT

BY
ALMON ERNEST PARKINS, Ph.D. , 1979-1940

KENNIKAT PRESS
Port Washington, N. Y./London

KENNIKAT PRESS SCHOLARLY REPRINTS

Dr. Ralph Adams Brown, Senior Editor

Series on
MAN AND HIS ENVIRONMENT
Under the General Editorial Supervision of
Dr. Roger C. Heppell
Professor of Geography, State University of New York

THE HISTORICAL GEOGRAPHY OF DETROIT

First published in 1918
Reissued in 1970 by Kennikat Press
Library of Congress Catalog Card No: 77-118422
ISBN 0-8046-1371-0

Manufactured by Taylor Publishing Company   Dallas, Texas

KENNIKAT SERIES ON MAN AND HIS ENVIRONMENT

PREFACE

ON July 24, 1701, a fleet of some two dozen canoes carrying Frenchmen and Indians, entered the Detroit River on a mission that was to introduce civilization into the Great Lakes region nearly one hundred years in advance of British-American progress from the Atlantic seaboard. One hundred persons—fifty uniformed soldiers, some twenty farmers, artisans, and traders, the remainder a few women and children[1]— had come to plant an outpost of French power and influence in the wilderness about the Great Lakes.

Forty-nine days before, they had left the head of the LaChine Rapids near Montreal. Fearing to give umbrage to the ever watchful Iroquois about the shores of Lake Ontario and Lake Erie, they had chosen the "No thern Route." Up the Ottawa they toiled, against the swift currents, around the many rapids, and thence by lakes, and rivers, with many portages, they reached Georgian Bay and later Lake Huron. After a voyage of over seven hundred miles they entered the "Strait,"—"Détroit," in the language of the French. Down this they swept, passing many islands, and on across Lake St. Clair to the upper course of the Detroit River.

They selected a commanding site for their fort on the right bank of the river, for this post was to control the traffic of the Upper Lakes. Grain and seed

---

1. *Magazine of Western History*, II, 55 (Griffin).

and tools were brought, for these settlers were to found a colony which should be a permanent nucleus of French power and influence in the Lakes region. The colony thus established was the beginning of the present Detroit.

There are few other cities in America that have taken so long and so prominent a part in the history and development of the sections in which they are situated. Detroit was fifty-three years old when the British began their fort at Pittsburg, hundreds of miles in advance of civilization. It was ninety-five years old when Moses Cleveland laid out the city that bears his name on Lake Erie. Detroit celebrated its centenary in the year that the Holland Land Company plotted the city of Buffalo at the mouth of Buffalo Creek. The first log cabin in Indianapolis was not erected until 118 years after the French began the city on the "Straits." And Detroit had been making history 129 years when the Illinois Board of Land Commissioners surveyed the site of Chicago, the great metropolis of the interior.[2]

Detroit was founded as an outpost of French power, and a center for French commerce in the Great Lakes region. Its position near the crossing of the French and British lines of advance into the interior gave it a prominent place in the long struggle between these two nations for supremacy in America. Victories at Duquesne and Quebec made the British supreme, and Detroit came under their control. In the Indian revolt of 1763, against the assumption of the control of the Great Lakes by the British, Detroit was considered

2. *Magazine of Western History*, II, 571 (Griffin).

the seat of British power and was called upon to withstand the attacks of the major part of the Indian forces. During the Revolutionary War, it was an outfitting point from which British and Indian expeditions were dispatched to harass the American settlers in the Ohio Valley. Several attempts were made by the Americans to organize expeditions against Detroit. Its isolation was a chief factor in preventing any definite action. According to the terms of the Treaty of Peace of 1783, Detroit, with the other trading posts of the, Lakes, was ceded to the United States, but the importance of these posts to the fur-merchants of Montreal was undoubtedly the reason for their retention by the British for thirteen years. Their final delivery to the United States in 1796 came only after a second treaty had been made and Wayne's victory seemed to have stripped the British of their Indian allies. The general policy, however, which actuated the retention of the posts was not abandoned by the British until after the War of 1812.

In the War of 1812, Detroit was the chief center of the control of the Indians and of the fur trade of the Upper Lakes. It was, therefore, the center of the struggle between American and British forces. Surrendered to the British in 1813, it was reoccupied by the troops of the United States the following year.

Under both French and British influence Detroit was merely a military and trading post. For one hundred years its growth was retarded. The real development did not begin until the early part of the nineteenth century when the American frontier began to envelop it, and it became an integral part of the

United States. Since then few cities have enjoyed
so rapid a growth. In 1830 Detroit was the fifty-
third city in size in the United States. In 1910 it
stood ninth.

Within the last decade or two, the rapid growth in
population, manufactures, building construction, commerce, and other items that indicate a healthy growth,
show that it has not yet reached its final rank among
the cities of America.

*   *   *   *   *   *   *   *   *   *

Such in brief is the story of the founding of Detroit
and a sketch of the more important events in its subsequent history. This brief sketch and the more
detailed discussion which follows indicate the dominance of Detroit in the historic events of the Lakes
region for so many decades. "Egypt is the Nile, and
the Nile is Egypt," is a saying among the Egyptians,
indicating the great importance of the Nile in the life
of that cradle of civilization. With a similar thought
in mind one might say, considering the early history,
"The Lakes region was Detroit, and Detroit was the
Lakes region." For more than a century Detroit was
almost the only civilized spot in the vast area about
the Great Lakes. The reader should keep this in
mind, if, in the reading of the following pages, he is
tempted to consider, at first thought, some of the
historic and geographic material to be extraneous to
the discussion of Detroit.

*   *   *   *   *   *   *   *   *   *

Historical Geography, as the term has come to be
understood by American geographers, is a study of
the history of a region as affected by the geographic

environment.   Geography is concerned with the influ-
ences of physical environment on life,—plant, animal,
and human.   Historical Geography is concerned with
the study of the influence of environment on man,
mainly in the past.

In this thesis, *The Historical Geography of Detroit*,
the chief endeavor will be to indicate the influence of
the topography, the waterways, the soil, the climate,
mineral resources, plant life, animal life, and aboriginal
human life upon the activities of the Europeans and
their descendants who came to occupy the Great Lakes
region, and more especially the region about Detroit.
The point of view is economic, for in the economic
development of a region the influence of environment
is most evident.   In the economic development of
Detroit two environments must be recognized: a forest
environment, the sole work of Nature, and an agricultural, commercial and industrial environment, in
which civilized man has put to his own use the natural
resources and forces.   The former was characterized
by extensive forests, abundant game, furnishing
furs and food, and fish in plenty, all furnishing man
with shelter, food, and clothing at close hand
with a minimum of labor.   Such an environment
tended to prolong the savage stage of culture; and so
strong was its influence that civilized man, when he
marched into the wilderness and severed the lines of
frequent communication with the more civilized seaboard settlements, found himself overwhelmed with
its influence and living the life of a savage.   The
second environment is one of progress.   It is the
result of a transplanted civilization in contact with

rich natural resources. Civilized man makes far different demands upon the resources of his environment than did the Indian. Moreover, in the economic development of the region, as man passed through the various stages of lumbering, agriculture, commerce and manufacturing, he made different demands at different times. The greater density of population and higher standards of living demanded a more complete use of nature's resources. In civilized economy man removed the forests and came to utilize the sustaining power of the land to a fuller extent than did the Indian. He unearthed the treasures of the mines, increased the value of his products by adding skill in their production, lengthened and deepened the waterways and with steel and steam shortened time-distances on land, thereby greatly extending his sustaining area, and widened his markets. The Great Lakes environment during the Indian, French, and English regime was far different from that under the Americans.

The plan of presentation of the material in the thesis follows that of the historian, and not that of the geographer. This seemed to the writer the only feasible arrangement. In writing the historical geography of a large area with diverse topography, climate, soil, and other resources, and of an area whose main lines of historic development are well known, the weaving of the material about the geographic elements of the environment would be feasible. But in tracing the influence of geography on the economic development and growth of an urban group, whose history is little known, the necessity for continuity of thought and richness and fullness of treatment seemed to the writer to demand a chronological arrangement of material.

The writer's interest in the subject grew out of the patriotic feeling he naturally bore to his native State and its metropolis, and especially out of a desire to ascertain, if possible, the factors, geographic or non-geographic, immediate or distant, in the recent phenominal rise of Detroit as a manufacturing center. This led him into the romance of the city's history, of the part taken in its growth and economic development by the Indian, the Catholic missionary, the early French officials, the *coureur de bois*, and the pioneer farmers, sailors, railroad builders, and business men. To all these factors in the long development and slow growth, his studies in the field of modern geography have given an interest and meaning not experienced by a collector and recorder of mere facts.

Most of the historic material has been secured from original documents, manuscripts, papers, journals and reports, a complete list of which is found in the bibliography appended. The libraries of the University of Chicago, the John Crerar and Newberry libraries of Chicago, the Chicago Public Library and that of the Chicago Historical Society, the Detroit Public Library and a few private collections have all been carefully searched.

Special acknowledgments are due Prof. H. H. Barrows of the Department of Geography of the University of Chicago for his interest, his painstaking reading, and helpful suggestions in the preparation of the manuscript. The writer wishes also to thank Professors Salisbury, Goode, and Tower, and his fellow students in the Geographic Seminar of 1913 and 1914, at the University of Chicago, before whom a few of the chapters were read, for their interest and criticism.

CONTENTS

CHAPTER I

CHAPTER II

CHAPTER III

CHAPTER IV

CHAPTER V

CHAPTER VI

CHAPTER VII

Introduction
Detroit located on a till plain
The topography of Southern Michigan
Topographic features result of glaciation
Character of till
The beach ridges
The Detroit moraine
Boulder belts
Drainage of plain
Water power in Detroit region
The lower courses of rivers drowned
Soils of the Detroit region
Mineral resources
    Clay
    Limestone
    Salt

CHAPTER VIII

Population statistics for one hundred years
Deterrent factors in growth in early decades of nineteenth century
Factors in westward movement of population
    Michigan lands made known in East
    Indian titles extinguished
    Change in land laws, 1820
    States to south "filling"
    Improvements in transportation
    Economic changes in New England
    Wandering habits of pioneers
    Emigration to Detroit and Michigan, 1820-30
Detroit in 1827
Detroit in 1837
The boom period, 1837-39
Effect on growth of Detroit and Michigan
Nativity of people at Detroit, 1850
Rivals of Detroit—Monroe and Toledo

THE HISTORICAL GEOGRAPHY
OF DETROIT

CHAPTER I

THE GEOGRAPHIC SETTING OF DETROIT

DETROIT is situated in the heart of the Great
Lakes region, near the eastern edge of the Great
Central Plain of North America. Its development,
therefore, is associated closely with the geographic
conditions and development of the Great Central Plain
and more especially with the immediate portions of
that plain about the Great Lakes.

The plains of the world always have been important
in the economy of nations. In the early periods, the
river plains of the Nile, the Tigris and Euphrates, and
the Ganges supported the developing civilizations. In
the modern period the humid temperate plains have
come to be recognized as the great producing areas for
the world's population. The geographic conditions of
these plains favor the development of a high stage of
civilization; and where social, religious, or political
factors do not control, such plains are the homes of
the most progressive and the most influential of the

nations. Among the many geographic factors that
seem to make these plains the most suitable for the
homes of men, the more important are—

(1) Abundance of well-watered fertile land, and a
stimulating climate,

(2) Rich deposits of useful minerals,

(3) Low relief, ensuring easy communication between all parts,

(4) Accessibility to the ocean.

All these requirements are met in a large degree in
the Great Central Plain of North America.

The Great Central Plain extends 2500 miles northward from the Gulf of Mexico, and 1,500 miles eastward from the Rocky Mountains to the highlands of
New York. A large portion of the northern third of
this great area is covered by snow and ice many
months in the year and a broad strip along the western
border is too dry for diversified cultivation, yet there
remain fully 1,250,000 square miles of land capable
of the highest agricultural development. Man in
North America is only in the early stages of his ad-
justment to the soil. For many decades certain sections of the Central Plain have contributed largely to
the world's cereal crop; the ultimate agricultural possibilities of the region, however, are far from being
attained.

The resources of the Central Plain lie not alone in
its agricultural possibilities, for there are rich deposits
of iron, salt, coal, copper, gypsum, and various sorts
of building materials. The great stretches of valuable
forests which once covered much of the region have
played an important part in the development of the

region about the Great Lakes; and furs, the pioneer product of the forests for which the eastern section of the Central Plain was coveted by both the French and the British, have long since been depleted.

The Central Plain is in general of low relief. Minor elevations here and there break its monotony, but these offer little obstruction to intercourse between the various parts. Although the Great Central Plain does not border an ocean, its low relief, its many navigable rivers, bays, and gulfs, and the low passes through the highlands to the east, all permit freedom of intercourse with the Atlantic, the most important ocean in world commerce. To the north there is easy access to Hudson Bay. Though ice-bound for seven or eight months each year, this exit to the Atlantic was an important one for the fur trade of the regions to the north and northwest of the Great Lakes for over two hundred years, and in the future it may prove of great value to the developing regions in the northern part of the arable portions of the interior plain. On the south for 1500 miles the Great Central Plain borders the Gulf of Mexico. Along this coast there are ports with easy communication to the interior that may serve as logical doorways to the trade of Central and South America. Along the eastern border are the highlands of Canada and the Appalachian Mountains. These are the only barriers between the plain and the Atlantic. Around the northern end of the Appalachian ridges, along the southern border of the "old land of Canada," extends the St. Lawrence Valley, the lowlands of which, as far west as the escarpment at Niagara, are less than five hundred feet above tide. To the south of this great valley, across the State of New York from the plains about Lake Ontario to the Hudson River, is the Oneida-Mohawk depression, also with low altitudes. These two valleys constitute the notches in the barrier to the east. These have ever been among the chief, if not the chief, lines of communication and traffic, the "gateways" between the Great Central Plain and the Atlantic Ocean.

The Great Lakes region includes that irregular and somewhat indefinite area, on the eastern side of the Great Central Plain, that borders and includes the five Great Lakes of North America. It is not separated from the other parts of the Great Central Plain by any marked topographic feature. It is not in any way an isolated geographic unit; yet it is a unit. Its abundant resources make it one of the most important areas of the interior plain. Its chief importance perhaps lies in its position at the west entrances of the "gateways" to the Atlantic. Since the great markets for agricultural products are in eastern United States and Europe, this position makes a large part of the Great Central Plain naturally tributary to the Lakes region[1] During the long period that the merchants of Montreal and Quebec controlled the economic activities of the great interior of North America, the area tributary to the Great Lakes included most of the territory to the north of the Ohio and the Missouri rivers, and west to the Rocky Mountains. Today the Great Lakes region has for its sphere of commercial influence more than two-thirds of the Great Central Plain.

1. *Hunt's Merchants' Mag.*, LVIII, 109.

Great as are the resources of the mines, the forests, and the fields, the Great Lakes region owes much of its importance to the Great Lakes themselves. There are few other regions of like area that can furnish such opportunities for inland transportation. From the lower end of Lake Michigan to the eastern terminus of Lake Erie there are nearly a thousand miles of unobstructed deep waterways. With the overcoming of the barrier at the rapids of the St. Mary's River and the falls at Niagara, six hundred miles more have been added. But transportation advantages on lakes are not to be reckoned by the lengths of the lakes. Innumerable cross routes multiply the above mileage many times. Besides the many hundred miles of deep waterway, there are many minor waterways suitable for smaller craft. These minor water courses were very important in the days when canoes were the chief carrying agent.

In the northeastern part of North America, there is a great area of crystalline rocks, granites, gneisses, and schists. This is the so-called North American "shield," the "old land" of Canada. The southern portion of this area is called the Laurentian Highlands. Lake Superior lies partly within and partly on the border of the Highlands. The southern border of the "old land" skirts the northern shores of Lake Huron and Georgian Bay. From the southern part of Georgian Bay eastward the southern limit extends in an irregular line near the cities of Kingston, Ottawa, and Quebec; from Quebec eastward it makes the northern bluffs along the St. Lawrence River.

To the south of this crystalline area, poor in agricultural possibilities because of its long winters and thin soils but rich in mineral deposits and waterpower, are younger sedimentary rocks. The younger rocks are chiefly sandstones, limestones, and shales. These sedimentary rocks in general are eroded much more easily than the crystallines, so that the region in which these formations dominate is nearly everywhere marked either by lake basins or lowlands. For example, a portion of the estuary of the St. Lawrence, the lower St. Lawrence Valley, the Mohawk depression, Lake Ontario, the Ontario lowlands, Georgian Bay, North Channel, and Green Bay (as well as Lake Winnipeg) have all been carved in Ordovician limestones and shales. Lake Erie, Lake Huron, and Lake Michigan owe their shape, position, and connections in large extent to the erosian of Silurian and Devonian limestones, shales, and dolomite.

Many other topographic and geographic features about the Great Lakes and the St. Lawrence seem to be related closely to the resistance some of the strata offer to erosion. The many islands in the lakes and rivers of the St. Lawrence system as well as the numerous falls and rapids are largely due to the more resistant formations. The Ottawa River with its numerous rapids and falls that made the canoe voyages along its course so tedious, difficult, and costly, runs for the larger part of its course over crystalline rocks. The waters at most of the rapids of the St. Lawrence from Lake Ontario to Montreal flow over gneisses and schists and Cambrian sandstones. The La Chine, just above Montreal, the rapids that barred (before the building of canals) any further passage of ocean vessels to the interior, are in Cambrian sandstones; so, too, are the rapids of St. Mary's River. The falls at Niagara, which so effectively separate Lake Ontario from the other Great Lakes, and the Niagara Escarpment, over which most of the traffic of the Upper Lakes had to pass until the middle of the nineteenth century, are due to a thick layer of limestone (Niagara) overlying softer shales. The same Niagara limestone encircles the north shore of lakes Huron and Michigan. It forms the backbone of the Saugeen (or Bruce) Peninsula, that separates Lake Huron from Georgian Bay. It no doubt is largely responsible for the line of islands along the north shore of Lake Huron, and to the west it forms the enclosing arms of Green Bay.[2] These topographic and geographic features have had their historic consequences. The Saugeen Peninsula lengthened the canoe voyage from the mouth of the French River to Detroit by nearly one hundred miles. The numerous islands in northern Lake Huron made canoe voyages fairly safe across the deep waters of Lake Huron between the French River and the mouth of St. Mary's River. The many islands in the western part of Lake Erie are composed almost entirely of Niagara limestone. These islands made possible a trans-lake canoe route and shortened the distance for canoe voyages between the mouth of the Detroit River and Sandusky Bay. This trans-lake route was much used by the British and Indians in their raids against the whites on the Ohio. Some of these islands

---

2. *Guide Book* No. 5; Can. Geol. Survey, 1913, 75; *Atlas*, Vol II, Wis. Geol. Survey, 1877, Plate IV; Prof. Pope, 71, U. S. Geol. Survey, Plate I.

offered harbors of refuge to the vessels of the lakes in the early days of lake navigation when the vessels were small.

Though the bed rock offers the conditions for differential erosion, it was mainly the waters and the ice of the Glacial Period that gave much of the land in northeastern North America its present topographical expression. In some sections erosion took place, in others deposition.

The story of the work of the ice and water in the Glacial Period is a story so well known that it needs no lengthy discussion here. The "old land" was swept bare of its residual soil, the accumulation of ages. At places in the "old land," where conditions were suitable, lake basins were gouged out. These lakes are numbered by the thousands in the Laurentian Highlands. Many are connected by rivers, making many nearly continuous water routes, suitable for canoes from the St. Lawrence Basin to Hudson Bay.

In the region of the younger, sedimentary rocks, the work of the glacial ice was much more pronounced. The basins of most of the Great Lakes are partially, if not largely, the result of the erosive action of the ice upon the limestones and shales. The material eroded from the sedimentary rocks, combined with that from the "old land," was strewn here and there in a more or less systematic fashion, forming moraines, outwash plains, till plains, valley trains, and other features over the region to the south of the "old land," as far south, in general, as the Ohio and Missouri rivers.

The most important of the moraines, the ones that

have had the greatest geographic and historic significance, are the ones that make up the divide between the St. Lawrence and Mississippi river-systems. As the ice during the retreat of the ice sheet withdrew to the north of this divide, the water resulting from the melting of the ice was ponded between the divide and the ice front, and temporary lakes were produced. The existence of such lakes explains the presence of most of the many sandy and gravelly lake ridges and lacustrine plains about the present lakes. At low places in the divide, outlets were found by the water and broad channels were carved. In these channels the headwaters of the tributaries of the St. Lawrence and Mississippi river-systems lie so near to each other that only a short portage is necessary for canoes and small boats in going from one system to the other. In flood periods it is possible to pass from one system to the other without portaging. The most important of these portages are the Fox-Wisconsin Portage, from the Fox River to the Wisconsin; the Chicago Portage, from the Chicago to the Des Plaines; the Fort Wayne Portage, between the headwaters of the Maumee and the Wabash; and the Oneida-Mohawk Portage, from Lake Oneida to the Mohawk River. Between Georgian Bay and the lower St. Lawrence and between Georgian Bay and Lake Ontario there are similar channels, due mostly to glacial action or erosion of the waters of the Glacial Period. The former is the Ottawa Channel occupied by the French River, Lake Nippising, and Ottawa River, the latter is the Trent River or Toronto Channel occupied in part by Trent River.

One cannot overestimate the importance of these lakes, rivers, and channels in the history of the nations, savage and civilized, that have operated in and about these two great river systems. These channels were used by the Indians in their migrations, intertribal trade and wars, long before the white man reached the Great Lakes. They influenced the courses of the early French explorers in their search for the Western Sea. For over two hundred years they were traversed by French, English, and American traders. Forts were built in them. The early settlers on their way to settle in the Middle West followed them. They later built their wagon roads in them. Canals were dug along them. Today the railroads find along these water courses their easiest grades.

During the French occupation of the Great Lakes region, the English fully recognized the advantage the French had in controlling these outlet channels. Colden in his *Memoir on the Fur-Trade* in 1724, said, "This (after speaking of the Great Lakes and the St. Lawrence River), however, but half furnishes the view the French have as to their commercial command in North America. Many of the Branches of the River Mississippi come so near to the Branches of the rivers that flow into the Great Lakes that, in several places, there is but a short land carriage from one to the other. As soon as they get into the branches of the Mississippi, they open to themselves a large field for traffic in the southern part of North America. . . . . . If one considers the length of this river and its numerous branches he must say that by means of the St. Lawrence River and the lakes there is opened to his view such a scene of inland navigation as cannot be paralleled in any other part of the world."[3]

Detroit, situated within the basin of the St. Lawrence, on one of the connecting waterways between two of the Great Lakes and not far from the eastern entrance to the Maumee-Wabash outlet channel, has been influenced profoundly during its development by these waterways. Its very existence during the first hundred years of its history was directly dependent upon these lakes, rivers, and portages.

The French and English explorers found the basin of the St. Lawrence, and a part of the basin of the Mississippi, covered with a rich forest. With the exception of a few clearings about the various settlements in the basin of the St. Lawrence, these forests remained almost untouched until the coming of the American farmers. Though dense in places, these forests were in general open enough to allow free passage of man or beast. Paths through them, however, were few. In traveling from one part of the region to another the waterways generally were followed. Dawson says, "In the summer the voyageur's canoe and in winter the habitant's sleigh made the mesh of waterways available long before the settlers had time to build roads and bridges."[4]

These forests had little direct influence on the development and history of the region up to the early part of the last century. They furnished timber for building purposes, but there were few people and

3. *Docs. Rel. to Col. Hist. of State of New York*, V, 727. For this reference the abbreviated form, *N. Y. Col. Docs.*, will be used hereafter.
4. S. E. Dawson, *North America*, I, 49 (Stanford's *Compendium*).

hence few buildings. Vessels were built upon Lake
Ontario and Lake Erie and the Upper Lakes, but they
were small and few in number. Along the shores of
the St. Lawrence, as along the New England coast,
some timber was shipped to Europe, but the industry
was small when compared to the development in later
periods. Their chief importance during both French
and English occupation of the Lakes region was indirect—they harbored a great variety of wild game.
Sheltered in the depth of these great forests there were
many fur-bearing animals, such as the beaver, the
otter, the mink, the fox, the raccoon, the bear, and
others, that made the Great Lakes region desired by
French, British, and American traders. The control
of the rich harvests of furs of the Lakes region was
undoubtedly the chief prize fought for by both French
and British nations in the long struggle for supremacy
in America.

The fur trade was easily over-exploited, and as the
animals became scarcer and scarcer, the hunters were
obliged to go farther and farther into the depths of
the forest in search of them. Yet for more than one
hundred and fifty years Detroit was one of the chief
centers of the fur trade in the Lakes region. Situated
in the heart of this region, the many lakes, rivers, and
portages gave it access to a large area from which to
draw furs.[5]

The Indians of the Great Lakes region were members
of two great families, the Iroquoian and Algonquian,[6]

5.   The influence of the forests and the fur trade in the develop-
      ment of the Lakes region and Detroit will be discussed
      in greater detail in subsequent chapters.
6.   *Handbook Amer. Inds.*, I, 38, 601, *Bull.* 30, Bur. Amer. Eth.

with the Siouan family figuring in the history only in a minor way. Though the many tribes were migratory in their habits, each tribe or band kept to fairly definite hunting grounds.

The Iroquoian family, as determined by linguistic studies, was composed of the Hurons, the Neutrals, the Iroquois (or Five Nations of New York), and the Tuscarora. These tribes occupied at one time or another the lower valley of the St. Lawrence, New York State, part of Pennsylvania, and the shores of Lakes Ontario and Erie, and the east shore of Lake Huron.[7]

The most important tribes of this family were the Iroquois of New York. They had a strong confederacy, formed about 1570,[8] which, up to 1722, was made up of the following tribes: Mokawk, Oneida, Onondaga, Cayuga, and Seneca. In 1722 the Tuscarora of the upper Susquehanna Valley joined their confederacy, and henceforth the Iroquois were known as the Six Nations.[9] The leaders of the Five Nations were crafty diplomats and even the French and English statesmen found them their equal on many an occasion. Colden in 1765 complained to Johnson, "The Iroquois assume too much to themselves in directing the affairs of all other (Indian) nations and something should be done to check their ambition of having the lead everywhere."[10] Champlain's expedition against them in 1609 made them from the very first the enemies of the French and the firm allies of the English. From

---

7. *Ibid.*, 615.
8. *Ibid.*, 618; *Jes. Rel.*, LI, 295.
9. *Handbook Amer. Ind.*, I, 615.
10. *New York Hist. Coll.* of 1877, 19.

their central position in New York they were able to make quick attacks in any direction upon the surrounding tribes. The Susquehanna, the Delaware, and the Allegheny rivers led southward from their country. The Mohawk depression and the Hudson-Champlain depression with their waterways gave them access to the north and to the southeast. Lake Ontario and the St. Lawrence gave them easy passage to the north and northeast. The Trent River route, the Ottawa route, Lake Erie and the Maumee-Wabash route offered easy approach to a vast region to the west.[11]

Due to their proximity to the coast and the trading posts on the Hudson, the Iroquois were the first to obtain firearms from the Dutch.[12] With white man's weapons, the Iroquois were able to wage relentless and successful wars against the neighboring tribes, and even storm the very gates of the French forts at Montreal and Quebec. For many years the Jesuit reports (*Jesuit Relations*) contained numerous complaints of their depredations. In the *Relations* for 1642, it is written, "The Iroquois have as usual acted like fiends; they have been in the field winter, spring, and summer. They have massacred many Hurons and Algonquians, they have captured Frenchmen and killed some. There is only one conclusion, peace must be made or the Iroquois exterminated."[13] At times they threatened seriously the trade of Montreal with the western Indian tribes. The *Relations* for 1645, commenting on the fear the Indians of the West had of

11. Schoolcraft, *Hist. of Ind. Tribes of N. A.*, VI, 34.
12. *Jesuit Relations*, XXXIV, 123.
13. *Ibid.*, XXII, 43.

the Iroquois, say, "Were it not for the latter [the Iroquois] they would come and enrich this country with their furs and we should visit them to enrich Heaven with the glorious spoils that we should wrest from the powers of Hell."[14]   And again the Jesuit Fathers write, "Truly, our hearts bleed when we see ourselves at the gate of so fair a harvest and unable to enter; when we see so many fall into Hell, when they are so near the Kingdom of Heaven.   And what is the cause of all of this?   A little handful of Iroquois who all together would not equal a thousandth part of those whose salvation they prevent."[15]   This powerful tribe held the balance of power in America for one hundred and fifty years.   Their alliance with the British gave the latter a great advantage in the struggle for supremacy in America.   One reason for the founding of Detroit was to curb the power of the Iroquois in the Upper Lakes region.

The Hurons occupied a portion of the Ontario lowlands between Lake Ontario and Georgian Bay   Many of their villages were about the shores of Lake Simcoe. These Indians constructed bark cabins and lived within palisaded walls.   They lived a semi-sedentary life, cultivating corn, beans, pumpkins, and tobacco.   They were keen traders and served as middlemen between the French and the Neutral Nation, the latter not having ready access to the waterways that led to Montreal.[16]   In 1648-50 the Iroquois fell upon the Hurons and drove them beyond the Straits of Mackinac, even to the woods of northern Wisconsin.   The

14.   *Ibid.*, XLV, 185.
15.   *Ibid.*, 189.
16.   *Ibid.*, XXXVIII, 235; I, 21.

Huron tribes were scattered never to be united firmly again.   Henceforth they cast their lot with the Algonquian tribes about the Lakes.[17]   A few bands of Huron Indians established themselves at the Detroit Mission about 1736.

The Algonquian family occupied a vast area in Canada and the United States, extending as far south as the Carolinas.   It was composed of many tribes. About Lake Superior and the Ottawa River lived the Ottawa, Chippewa, and other tribes.   Because of thinness of soil in this region many of these tribes practiced little agriculture, and wandered about . in search of fish and game.   The Chippewa lived most of the year at the falls of the St. Mary's River where fish were plentiful.   The Ottawa, living on one of the great canoe routes, were skilful traders and made long voyages to the west and east.   They were for many years middlemen between the tribes of the prairies, who had no canoes, and the French at Montreal and Quebec.[18]

Farther to the west in the Wild-Rice region about Green Bay, the Fox River and the many lakes of Wisconsin, were the Sauk, Fox, the Menominee and others.   The Wild-Rice region probably sustained a population equal to that of all the rest of the Northwest Territory.[19]   The sustaining power of the region was due not only to the great abundance of vegetable and animal food, but also to furs, after the whites furnished a market.   Great quantities of furs were

17.   *Ibid.*, XXXIV, 123; I, 26; Upham, *Minnesota in Three Centuries*, I, 95; *Handbook Amer. Indians*, I, 588.
18.   *Handbook Amer. Indians*, I, 38-40.
19.   Jenks, *Nineteenth Ann. Rept.*, Bur. Amer. Eth., Pt. 2, 1106.

taken in this region as late as the middle of the nineteenth century.

The Sauk and Fox Indians from an early date (about
1685) were hostile to French interests. For a time
they closed the Fox-Wisconsin route to French traders, [20] and in 1712 bands from these and other tribes
attempted to destroy the post at Detroit.[21] At a much
later date they allied themselves with the English in
the endeavor to keep the American traders and settlers out of the Lakes region.

The Potawatomi, another powerful Algonquian tribe,
lived about the shores of Lake Michigan. A French
traveler describes a portion of their country about the
mouth of the St. Joseph River in southwest Michigan
as he saw it in 1718 as follows: " 'Tis a spot the best
adapted of [for] living, as regards the soil. There are
Pheasants as in France, quail and perroquets [?]; the
finest vines in the world, which produce a vast quantity of very excellent grapes, both white and black,
the berries very long. It is the richest district of all
that country."[22] The Indians of the Wabash-Maumee
Valley lived in a region fully as rich in game and in
agricultural possibilities as did the Potawatomi. The
Potawatomi were numbered among the Indian population of Detroit during part of the French and most of
the English period of occupancy.[23]

20. *Jes. Rel.*, IV, 187.
21. Campbell, *Pol. Hist. of Mich.*, 81. See also discussion in
     Chapter III.
22. *N. Y. Col. Docs.*, IX, 90.
23. Many of the Algonquian tribes took so active a part in the
     early development of the region down to their expulsion
     and migration in the early part of the nineteenth cen-
     tury, that the details of their connection with the affairs
     of the region will be left for later consideration.

The Algonquian tribes lacked the ability possessed by the Iroquois to form strong and lasting confederacies. This lack of union may have been the result of a lack of unity in their geographic environment. It was largely the cause of their downfall. Occupying such a vast territory, living under such varied conditions, in valleys, along lakes, and separated by great bodies of water, the bands and tribes were unable to become united even under the stress of a common cause. Under Pontiac in 1763, they formed an alliance to resist the occupation of the Lakes region by the English, but this alliance was only temporary. One by one the chiefs were won over to the British cause, and Pontiac found himself without support. Later, under the powerful leader Tecumseh, the tribes again made an attempt but showed their failure to cooperate.

Detroit was founded to check the western advance of the English and Iroquois.[24] Though Cadillac had personal motives, he also had the good of France at heart. He wished to draw about him many Indian tribes and form them into a local army,[25] develop the agricultural possibilities of the region, and make Detroit a strong outpost of French power in the Lakes region. Could this have been accomplished and Cadillac allowed to work out his ideals, the history of the Lakes region would have been far different from what is written. He succeeded in drawing about him only a few Indian tribes. A few Ottawa, Hurons, and Potawatomi came and made their villages near the

24.   *Mich. Hist. Colls.*, XXXIII, 132, Cadillac Papers.
25.   *N. Y. Col. Docs.*, IX, 812.

French Fort.[26]   The Hurons came from Michillimackinac, whither they had returned from northern Wisconsin.   The Ottawa came from the shores and islands
of Georgian Bay.   They, too, had felt the powerful
hand of the Iroquois and had fled to the forests of
northern Wisconsin, but had returned about 1666,
after a treaty had been made between the French
and Iroquois.[27]

All these Indians about Detroit figured largely in
the development of the region.   As with many primitive people, to trade with them was to win their friendship.   They were a power in warfare.   Both the English and French sought to control them.   Because of
their barbarity and ferocity, their employment in war
meant an intensification of the hatred between the
contending parties.   During the English regime in the
Lakes region the Indians about Detroit and Lake Erie
were a serious menace to the incoming American settlers along the Ohio and in the Northwest.   It took
many costly expeditions to break their power.   They
retarded the development of the Northwest for many
years.

---

26.   *Mag. of Western History*, III, 158; *N. Y. Coll. Docs.*, IX, 888.
27.   *N. Y. Col. Docs.*, V, 75.

CHAPTER II

Events Leading to Founding of Detroit

THE founding of Detroit was one of the events in the long struggle between the French and English for the mastery of the region about the Great Lakes. Through the discoveries of Cartier, the French had entered the estuary of the St. Lawrence River, and following the waterways that led to the westward had extended their possessions along a strip of territory two thousand miles in length, from the Gulf of St. Lawrence to the Gulf of Mexico. The English, basing their rights of possession on the discoveries of the Cabots,[1] had planted their settlements on or near the coast farther to the south—between the 35th and 43d parallels— and laid claim to all the land westward to the Western Sea. That these two nations should cross each other's paths, and clash, was predetermined by the position of their coastal settlements and the direction of their lines of advance into the interior.

The events leading to the founding of Detroit arrange themselves logically as follows:

1. The search for the passage to the Western Sea. Some of these voyages furnished the bases for claims to land.

2. The planting of settlements on these lands discovered.

1. *N. Y. Col. Docs.*, IV, 475.

3. The movement inland from these settlements.

4. The clash of interests, the beginning of the struggle for the mastery of the Lakes region, and the founding of Detroit.

The voyages of Verrazano, Cartier, and the Cabots were only a few of the many expeditions undertaken in the fifteenth, sixteenth and seventeenth centuries in pursuit of the "Quest of the Age," an all-sea route to the Orient. Early in the history of discoveries in the New World, it was realized that the land that had been reached was not Cathay, the land of jewels, gold, and spices, and that America was a barrier through which a passage must be sought. In this search, English, French, Dutch, Portuguese, and Spanish navigators explored every inlet on the eastern coast of North America that seemed to promise a passage to the West. Of chief interest here are the voyages that led to the planting of settlements on the St. Lawrence and Hudson rivers.

After the discovery of the cod fisheries of the Grand Banks by Cabot in 1498, Norman and Breton fishermen, as early as 1504, began to visit the coast of Newfoundland and the mainland to the west.[2] In 1523 Jean Verrazano under a commission from Francis I, landed at various points along the eastern coast of North America, and traded with the Indians.[3]

The Paris Documents state[4] that subsequent to this expedition, the French king "sent Jacques Cartier of the town of St. Malo to discover new continents, who

2. *N. Y. Col. Docs.*, IX, 266, 378.
3. *Ibid.*
4. *Ibid.*

made two voyages, one in 1534 and the other in 1535;
he was the first European who with two large King's
ships, each eight hundred tons burthen, entered the
river St. Lawrence and ascended it 120 leagues as
far as the island of Orleans."

The broad estuary of the St. Lawrence, the entire
absence of a current, the deep water, and the saltiness
of the water, all, probably, led Cartier to believe that
the St. Lawrence was a strait and that the Western
Sea lay just beyond.   Cartier undoubtedly had seen
the map, then recently drawn by Mazzilo (1527),
which showed a great interior sea, the Mare Indicum,
in the heart of North America, and separated from
the Atlantic by only a narrow strip of land.[5] Although
Cartier failed to find a passage to the Western Sea,
his voyages resulted in a discovery of great importance in the history of eastern North America, the
discovery of a broad opening to a vast interior.   With
the discoveries of Cartier began the history of Canada,
and began also "the most determined and long continued efforts to discover a route to the Pacific.   To
follow these waterways until they should lead to the
Mer de l'Ouest (Western Sea) was one of the guiding
motives of many of the explorers of New France from
Cartier to La Verendrye."[6]

In 1609 Henry Hudson, in the employ of the Dutch
East India Company, set sail from Holland to find a
shorter route to China and Cathay.   Failing to find
a northeast passage, he turned the prow of his vessel
toward America, and coasting along the New England

5.   Douglas, *Old France in the New World*, 20.
6.   Burpee, *Search for the Western Sea*, 234.

shores, finally reached the mouth of the Hudson River. The deep soundings and tidal movements of the waters induced him to explore this river beyond the site of Albany.[7] Here he found a down current, fresh and clear, and the channel narrowing and shoaling; yet unwilling to abandon his long-cherished hope, he dispatched a small boat to examine the river further up stream. The return of this party and the announcement that they "found it to be at an end for shipping to go in," blasted his hopes of reaching the Western Sea by this route.[8] The bay and the river of the Delaware were also explored during this voyage. The Hudson River later came to be known as the "Great North River" and the Delaware, the "South River."[9]

The land between these two rivers the Dutch called New Netherlands, and from the first they meant to occupy and hold it to the exclusion of all other European nations, although it was included within the territory which James of England had granted to the Virginia Company in 1606.[10] The attitude of the Dutch in this matter was similar to that of all the other colonizing nations at that time, for the "sole market" doctrine, the doctrine that "the commercial prosperity of a country depended upon the creation, maintenance and extension of a sole market for its products and for its supplies," was particularly pre-

7. Brodhead, *Hist. of State of New York*, I, 31.
8. *N. Y. Col. Docs.*, I, 94, 275; *N. Y. Hist. Soc. Colls*, I, 20; *Annals of Albany*, I, 11, report written by Robt. Ivet, a member of the expedition.
9. Brodhead, *Hist. of State of New York*, I, 26; Wilson, *Hist. of U. S.*, I, 73.
10. Brodhead, *Hist. of State of New York*, I, 35.

valent in Europe.[11]   It was the spur of this doctrine
that brought about the rivalry between the maritime
powers of Europe in the fifteenth and sixteenth centuries in the search for the Western Passage to the
Orient.

The British made only half-hearted attempts to
explore the many tidal estuaries of Chesapeake Bay,
but in the examination of the shores of Hudson Bay
they were at their best.   Here Gilbert, Davis, Hudson,
Baffin, and James battled with ice and cold.   Though
these hardy explorers left little to commemorate their
attempts beyond the names they gave to straits, bays,
and rivers, it was upon the basis of their discoveries
that the British laid claim to the region about Hudson
Bay; and it was on this claim that the Hudson Bay
Fur Company was granted, in 1670, commercial privileges over a large part of what is now the Dominion
of Canada, north of the Great Lakes.[12]   How this company came into the affairs of Detroit in connection
with the fur trade, will be discussed in a later connection.

Although by degrees the European nations came to
recognize the uselessness of further search for a water
passage through the barrier of North America, the
French continued the search well on into the middle
of the eighteenth century.   Even after Cartier had
told the story of the winter's suffering of 1540 at the
head of a contracting gulf which received the clear
fresh waters of the St. Lawrence River, the hope still

11.   Rogers, *Econ. Interpretation of History*, 323.
12.   Bryce, *Hist. of Hudson Bay Co.*, 63; Burpee, *Search for the
      Western Sea*, 5, 22, 24.

was cherished that the mighty river might lead the explorer to the treasures of Asia. The name La Chine, applied to the rapids in the St. Lawrence near Montreal, is a memorial of the hope that the Western Sea lay along this route.[13]   Indian descriptions, painted with the colors of a powerful imagination, led the French explorers to the Gulf of Mexico and the foot-hills of the Rocky Mountains.

In 1608 Champlain founded Quebec.   In the seventy-three years intervening between the visit of Cartier and the planting of this settlement the French had not been idle in their attempts to colonize their posses-sions.   Between 1541 and 1544, both Cartier and Roberval made vain attempts to found a colony at the head of the St. Lawrence estuary[14] and from 1544 to 1608, though nothing definite was done, the fre-quent visits of the fishermen and traders to the Banks of Newfoundland kept the idea of colonization ever in mind.   Between 1543 and 1545 two vessels are said to have sailed daily during January and Febru-ary for America from the ports of northwestern France.[15]

In 1608 De Monts, who held a concession from the French crown to trade in the New World, having failed in 1605 to plant a permanent colony on St. Croix Island in the Bay of Fundy, fitted out two vessels for a new venture.   For a leader he selected Champlain.   The latter had taken part in three pre-

13.   Bryce, *Hist. Hudson Bay Co.*, 78; Douglas, *Old France in the New World*, 9.
14.   Douglas, *Old France in the New World*, 44-51.
15.   *Ibid.*, 69.

vious enterprises and knew every feature of the gulf and river, and was thoroughly acquainted with the habits and nature of the Indians. The aim of the expedition was to colonize as well as to trade, but "money making was more important than empire building," and Quebec remained for many decades a mere trading post. This, however, did not detract from its importance as a center of French power in America, for it became the political center of New France, and until the founding of Montreal in 1642 was the only important base from which explorations, trade, and settlement were carried along the waterways far to the west and southwest.

There are many favorable elements in the position of Quebec that were of value in making it a permanent colony of New France. It is at the head of a great estuary fully 800 miles from the Ocean. It therefore had all-sea communication with the mother country. Being situated so far from the ocean, it was not likely to be subjected to frequent attacks from maritime marauders. It is at the mouth of a great river, having thus access to a vast area from which, during more than two centuries, enormous quantities of furs were obtained. This gave it a product for export from which large profits were drawn. It is at the eastern end of the plains of the St. Lawrence, the most fertile part of Lower Canada. The area for agriculture is small, the growing season short, yet a few of the settlers tilled the soil and supplied some of the food of the colony in spite of the greater opportunities offered by the fur trade for gain.

Although France took the lead in the earlier decades

as a colonizer in northeastern North America, neither the English nor the Dutch escaped the epidemic of colonial expansion. It was the profitable fur trade with the Indians on the great North River that first led a few adventurous Dutch to build a small fort, or trading post, far up the river some four years before any systematic attempts were made toward colonization.[16] In 1615 the New Netherland Company was granted an exclusive right to trade for three years in the region called New Netherlands,[17] and the same year they built a small fort on North River on Manhattan Island.[18] The New Netherlands Company grew into the West India Company, and in 1623 the latter made two settlements on the Hudson River, one at Fort Amsterdam (New York) and the other at Fort Orange (Albany).[19] These colonies were planted exclusively for trade. Agricultural colonization was not the purpose of the Dutch. In the *Holland Documents* for 1638 it is written,[20] "nothing comes from New Netherlands but beaver skins, minks, and other furs." Of these two posts Fort Orange was the best situated for the trade in furs, being farther inland and nearer the fur-producing region. It was built on the west bank of the Hudson, near the head of deep-water navigation, on the edge of the fertile territory of the Iroquois, and only about fifteen miles south of the mouth of the Mohawk River. Like Quebec, it thus

16. Wilson, *Hist. of Amer. People*, I, 73.
17. Brodhead, *Hist. of State of New York*, I, 66.
18. *N. Y. Col. Docs.*, I, 564.
19. *N. Y. Col. Docs.*, I, 564; *Jesuit Relations*, XXXIV, 311; Weise [*Hist. of Albany*, 21] says Ft. Orange was built in May, 1624.
20. *N. Y. Col. Docs.*, I, 107; *Holland Docs.*, II.

had access to a large area rich in furs, and an all-sea communication with Europe. The advantages of the position of Fort Orange were seen by the French, who as early as 1540 attempted to build a fortified trading post near the site of Albany. In 1614 the Dutch built Fort Nassau on Castle Island, but later abandoned the post.[21] Many early writers commented on the favorable position of Fort Orange.[22]

As previously stated, the Dutch territory lay within the boundaries claimed by the English, and the latter lost no time, when opportunity and a sufficient force permitted, to enforce their claim to all the coastal lands. This opportunity came in 1664, and Fort Amsterdam became Fort James; Fort Orange, Fort Albany; and New Netherlands, New York.[23] Thus the English were at the entrance of one of the gateways into the interior, fifty-six years after the French had planted their permanent settlement at the entrance to the gateway of the St. Lawrence.

To the French must be given much of the credit for the exploration of interior North America.[24] From the founding of Quebec almost to the close of the eighteenth century the tide of French traders, missionaries, and soldiers rolled westward up the great valley and traversed all the main waterways from Montreal west-

21. Weise, *Hist. of Albany*, 4.
22. See *Colden Papers*, 1751, in *N. Y. Hist. Colls.* for 1876, p. 67; Long, *Travels*, II, 49, Thwaites Ed.
23. Brodhead, *Hist. of State of N. Y.*, I, 743, 744.
24. Recent research has demonstrated that the Virginians made several expeditions across the Appalachian Ridges to the basin of the Mississippi River between 1650 and 1674. See Alvord and Bidgood, *Trans-Allegheny Explorations* (1912).

ward nearly to the base of the Rocky Mountains, and from the Gulf of Mexico northward far into Canada.[25]

In 1615 Champlain ascended the Ottawa and went thence by Lake Nipissing to Georgian Bay and Lake Huron. On his return he traveled along the north shore of Lake Ontario. Nicolet was sent by Champlain in 1634 to find a passage way to the Sea of China, make the acquaintance of the Indian tribes near Lake Huron, and establish a trade in peltries. He visited the rapids of the St. Mary's River, and later, reaching Green Bay, passed up the Fox River a short distance.[26] In 1666 Father Allouez paddled along the south shore of Lake Superior, saw copper at Keweenaw Point, and farther west near the site of Ashland founded the mission of La Point de Saint Esprit.[27] Father Albanel was sent overland from Quebec, along the network of rivers and lakes to Hudson Bay.[28] In 1673 Joliet and Marquette set out for the South Sea. They went by way of the Fox-Wisconsin route to the Mississippi, down this to the mouth of the Arkansas, and brought back the first official report of the discovery of the "Father of Waters."[29] Nine

25. Burpee, *Search for Western Sea*, 193; *Mich. Hist. Colls.*, VIII, 418 (Walker).
26. Utley and Cutcheon, *Mich. as a Prov., Terr. and State*, I, 46.
27. *Jesuit Relations*, LVIII, 93, reported by Dablon.
28. *Ibid*, LVII, 149, 185, 217.
29. *Ibid.*, LIV, 189. Marquette announced his plan in 1672. He had been told that the Great River emptied into the ocean at Virginia. He could not believe this and was determined to see whether it emptied into the Western Sea or the South Sea. It is claimed that Radisson and Grosseilliers had been on the Mississippi River at an earlier date. See *Thwaites, France in America*, 55; *N. Y. Col. Docs.*, IX, 268, 305, 797.

years later La Salle, following the Chicago-Illinois route to the Mississippi, reached the mouth of the great river and saw the South Sea, but not the sea that washes the shores of Cathay.

On the basis of these and other discoveries the French laid claim to the interior of North America. In 1671, though Marquette and Joliet had not yet seen the Mississippi, and La Salle had not reached the Gulf, under impressive ceremonies at Sault Ste. Marie they took formal possession of the great interior. They based their rights upon priority of discovery, for at that time "it was an established custom and rightly recognized by all Christian nations that the first discoverer in an unknown country not inhabited by Europeans [acquired] property in that country for the prince in whose name he [had] taken possession of it."[30]

The Dutch and English with their trading posts at the very entrance to the Mohawk Gateway had gone scarcely beyond sight of their stockade. One historian states that up to 1685 Greenhalgh had been the only Christian under the New York government who had gone as far as the Seneca Country in western New York[31] and Dongan, Governor of New York, in his report of February 22, 1687, writes, "Before my coming hither no man of our government ever went beyond the Senicaes [Senecas] country. Last year some of our people went a trading among the far Indians called the Ottowais [Ottawas at Mackinac] inhabiting

30. *N. Y. Col. Docs.*, IX, 203, 266, 268, 303, 378, 701, 702; *Ibid.*, I, 688-Denonville on French limits in America; Winsor, *Narr. and Crit. Hist.*, IV, 178.
31. Brodhead, *Hist. of the State of New York*, II, 429.

about three month's journey to the west and northwest of Albany, from whence they brought a good
many bever [beaver]."[32]   Four years before, it will be
remembered, La Salle had reached the mouth of the
Mississippi.

The chief reason for such inactivity is to be found
in the presence of the Iroquois in central New York,
who, besides furnishing the posts at Albany and New
York with furs from their own hunting grounds, acted
as middlemen for some of the tribes to the west.   By
1649 the beaver country of New York had become
nearly depleted of its fur-bearing animals, and the
Iroquois found it necessary to extend their hunting
grounds.   The most logical direction for expansion,
because of suitable waterways and better hunting
grounds, was to the westward; and so in 1649 and 1650
they fell upon the Huron and Ottawa Indians in the
Ontario Lowlands and drove them far to the north.[33]
In this attack there was a double purpose—avenging
old wrongs with the Hurons, and increasing their
hunting grounds.[34]   On the basis of this conquest the
Iroquois claimed the right to hunting grounds as far
west as Lake Michigan, and thus a large tract of
beaver country was made tributary to the post at
Fort Orange.[35]   The quiet Dutch trader, therefore, had
but to remain at his post on the Hudson and reap his
profits, and had no incentive to traverse the unknown

32. *N. Y. Col. Docs.*, I, 100.
33. *Jesuit Relations*, XXXIV, 123; *Wis. Hist. Colls.*, III, 127
        (Shea).
34. *Handbook of Amer. Indians*, I, 587, 588; *American Anti-
        quarian*, I, 229 (Baldwin).
35. *N. Y. Col. Docs.*, IV, 908.

lands to the west.   As for the aggressive Englishman in
the northern colonies, for many decades he was too
busy exploiting the New England region of its furs and
enforcing his claim to coastal lands against the Swedes
and Dutch to examine the lands in the Interior or
search actively for the Western Sea.   It was not until
the British had become supreme on the Atlantic Coast,
and had entered actively into the trade in furs in the
New York region, that they became at all interested in
lands about the Great Lakes.

The trade in furs began with the first arrival of
European explorers on the eastern coast of America.
The Norsemen, as well as Verrazano, Cartier, Roberval, and others, carried furs back to Europe.[36]   Hudson
in his voyage up the "Great North River" traded in
furs, and in 1610 in his expedition to Hudson Bay he
began the trading that has continued to be the chief
occupation of white men on the shores of that great
bay down to the present.   The trade in furs played
no less a part in interior exploration.   One writer has
said, in effect, that the waterways permitted exploration, while the furs of the region promoted exploration.[37]   The trade in furs was a feature of nearly every
expedition, and many of the expeditions into new
regions were undertaken in the interest of the trade.
Nicolet was sent in part to develop a trade in peltries.
The chief reason for the expedition of La Salle down
the Mississippi River was to extend his trading terri-

---

36. Thwaites, *France in Amer.*, 3; *Johns Hopkins Univ. Studies*,
        Series IX, Nos. 11 and 12, p. 11 (Turner); *N. Y. Col. Docs.*,
        IX, 266, 378.
37. *Johns Hopkins Univ. Studies*, Series Nos. 11 and 12, p. 22.

tory.[38] De Vaudreuil recommended, as a preliminary step in the search beyond the Great Lakes for the Western Sea, that three posts be established to the west of Lake Superior, at which points furs could be collected to pay the expenses of the expedition. Colden remarks in this connection,[39] "The French have been indefatigable in making discoveries and carrying on their commerce with nations whom the English know nothing about, but what they see in French maps and books. The barreness of soil and the coldness of the climate of Canada oblige a greater part to seek their living by traveling among the Indians or trading with those who do travel."

The trade in furs will ever be associated chiefly with French exploration and occupation of the region about the Great Lakes and along the St. Lawrence. Purchase, in his *Pilgrimages* (London, 1614), says,[40] "The great river Canada [St. Lawrence] hath like an insatiable merchant engrossed all those commodities so that other streams are in a manner but mere peddlars."

As previously stated, it was the desire on the part of the English to participate in the profits of the trade in furs in the Lakes region that induced Dongan to send the first English party to the Ottawa country. Though this expedition marked the beginning of the struggle in the trade in furs in the Detroit region, the clash of the rival French and English interests had begun already on Lake Ontario.

38. *N. Y. Col. Docs.*, IX, 127.
39. *Ibid.*, V, 727.
40. Winsor, *Narr. and Crit. History*, IV, 163.

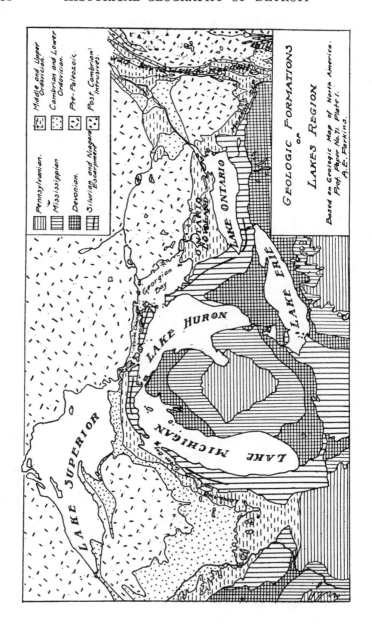

While the English were active along the Atlantic
seaboard, spreading their settlements and exploiting
the resources of sea and land, the French, aided by
the numerous waterways of the St. Lawrence System,
had visited, preached to, ministered to, and traded
with most of the Indian tribes about the Great Lakes.
Though the French traders never hesitated to drive a
sharp bargain, their fraternal feeling toward the savages and the self-sacrificing devotion of their missionaries, won them many an Indian friend. Their success in this was so great that at the ceremonies at
Sault Ste. Marie in 1671, some ' fourteen different
savage nations were represented.[41] These victories of
the French gave them no little satisfaction. Talon in
1671, writing to Louis XIV, commented on the seeming advantage of the French as follows:[42] "The foreign
colonies [the English] so long settled on the seaboard already tremble with fright in view of what
His Majesty has accomplished here in the Interior
within 7 (seven) years. . . . They are already
aware that the King's name is spread so far abroad
among the savages throughout all those countries that
he alone is there regarded by them as the arbitrator
of peace and war."

The French, however, were not to be left long in
the undisputed commercial control of the western
Indians. Tonty, writing in 1670, complained that the

41. This was a timely and masterful move on the part of the
     French in their attempts to control the traffic in furs in
     the Upper Lakes region. Brodhead, *Hist. of State of
     New York*, II, 179.
42. Brodhead, *Hist. of State of N. Y.*, II, 179; *N. Y. Col. Docs.*,
     IX, 72, 73.

English at Boston and the Dutch at New York were drawing to themselves yearly more than twelve thousand livres of beaver, trapped by the Indians in the country claimed by the French,[43] and the very year that Talon wrote the above to his king, the Lakes Indians were sending their peltries, by means of the Iroquois, to the post at Albany. This expansion of the trading area of Albany into the territory both nations considered as belonging to the French was due largely to the cheaper and better goods of the English. The post at Albany sold goods to the Indians at prices much lower than did the French at Montreal and paid more for furs. The cheaper goods of the English were a vital factor in the struggle for possession of the Lakes region and Canada. A trade war preceded and accompanied the appeal to arms, and the English trader won frequent victories by spreading among the Indians the desire for English goods. As the struggle progressed, many if not most of the French officials came to realize the uselessness of the numerous posts that had been built to bar the English traders. Twenty years after the post at Detroit was founded, Charlevoix wrote,[44] "There is not a man in all Canada, who does not agree, that we can never succeed in hindering the Indians from carrying them [the English] their commodities, let them be settled where they will and all the precautions we can possibly take, except by causing them [the Indians] to find the same advantage in trading with us as in the province of New York."

43. Brodhead, *Hist. of State of N. Y.*, II, 170.
44. Charlevoix, *Journal*, II, 6—Quoted in *North Amer. Rev.*, XLVI, 423.

There were several reasons why the English at Albany could sell goods to the Indians cheaper than could the French at Montreal and pay more for furs. These are stated well by Colden in his Memoir on the Fur Trade. In brief they are as follows:

The vessels that plied between New York and London could make two voyages a year, and vessels from Bristol (the port from which most of the goods for the Indian trade were exported), could complete a round trip in about four months. On the other hand, French vessels, plying between the St. Lawrence estuary and France could make only one voyage a year, because the season of navigation in the St. Lawrence is so short. The harbor at New York is open the year round.

The English goods were transported across the ocean at much less expense and at much less risk than were the French commodities, as the lower premium for insurance showed. As for the cost and risks of transportation inland from the ocean, Albany had a great advantage, as the Hudson River is nearly straight, and free from sandbanks and rocks so that a vessel could always sail as well by night as by day and had the advantage of the tide upward as well as downward. The St. Lawrence, on the other hand, had numerous hidden rocks, the winds usually opposed incoming vessels, and a strong current between Montreal and Quebec made up-stream navigation difficult. Vessels almost never sailed at night.[45]

Albany was almost as near as Montreal to the Indian country; but these comparative distances had

45. *N. Y. Col. Docs.*, V, 728, 729; *Ibid.*, VII, 343.

little consequence for the English traders, who, as did the Dutch before them, purchased their furs from the Iroquois Indians at Albany and thus avoided the trip inland. The French traders, on the other hand, went into the Indian country with their goods to make their purchases of furs, and thus were put to a double expense: the expense of transporting the goods to the place of disposal, and the expense of carrying the furs to Montreal or Quebec. Furthermore, they could buy only the better grades of furs which could stand the heavy cost of transportation. The English could handle all grades.[46]

The differences in prices at Albany and Montreal are shown in the following table:[47]

The Indian paid for	at Albany	at Montreal
8 pounds powder	1 beaver,	4 beaver;
40 pounds lead	1 beaver,	3 beaver;
A blanket of red cloth	1 beaver,	2 beaver;
4 shirts	1 beaver,	2 beaver;
6 pairs stockings	1 beaver,	2 beaver;
1 gun	2 beaver,	5 beaver;

The French were at a further disadvantage in the matter of procuring suitable goods for the Indian trade. Strouds were much prized by the Indians. They seem to have been made only in England, and could be procured only from the English, either in Europe or America. Many French at Montreal were forced to purchase strouds at Albany. The English, seeing the advantage they had, passed laws prohibiting the sale

---

46. *Ibid.*, IX, 408.
47. *Ibid.* Determined by a French investigator of the period.

of these goods to the French.   This was a severe blow
to the Montreal merchants.[48]   Rum was another article
in great demand by the Indians.   Because the French
had no commodity which they could exchange for rum
in the West Indies, they had to supply the Indians
with brandy.   This cost much more than rum, yet was
of no greater value in the Indian trade.[49]

Besides all these difficulties, the French trader had
to buy his goods from a monoploy and was restricted
from selling his furs to any but a monopoly agent.
For permission to trade he had to purchase a license
at a cost of six hundred to seven hundred livres for one
canoe.[50]

In two particulars the French were at an advantage
over the English.   They were better situated to enjoy
the benefits of the waterways of the St. Lawrence
region, and their boatmen (voyageurs or batteaux men)
cost them much less, both in salary and provisions.

The first move in the struggle for the mastery of the
trade of the Great Lakes was the building of Fort
Frontenac on Lake Ontario in 1672.[51]   Frontenac
reached Canada the preceding summer.   A great congress was held at Montreal, and five hundred savages
in one hundred and fifty canoes came down the St.
Lawrence to meet the new Governor.   At this meet-
ing a new treaty of peace was agreed upon by the
Iroquois.   To confirm this treaty the Governor in-
vited the Iroquois chiefs to meet him on the north

48.   *Ibid.*, VII, 954; VI, 577, 607, 682, 287, 709, 741.
49.   *Ibid.*, V, 728.
50.   *Ibid.*   The livre is an old French coin—about twenty cents in
          U. S. money.
51.   *Ibid.*, IX, 12.

shore of Lake Ontario at Cataracouy (Kingston). There the French flattered the Iroquois with presents and got their consent to build a fort, where, as the French said, the Iroquois might come and trade.[52] Father Hennepin says,[53] "They [the French] found it necessary to build this fort for a bulwark against the incursions of the Iroquois and to interrupt the trade in skins that these savages maintained with the inhabitants of New York, . . . for [the latter] furnish[ed] the savages with commodities at a cheaper rate than the French of Canada." To aid in the collection of furs, two vessels were built to ply upon Lake Ontario.[54] By these means the French hoped to capture all the traffic of the Lakes.

The English took no retaliatory measures until after 1682, when Dongan became Governor of New York. His first move was to send traders to the Upper Lakes to seek the trade of the western Indians.[55] In 1685 he licensed La Fontaine and Roseboom to hunt beaver in the woods among the western savages. They were received cordially by the Indians and brought back many beaver skins.[56] This advance of the English into territory the French had taken possession of fifteen years before, and which since had remained uncontested as a part of New France, caused consternation at Quebec and Montreal.

To guard the French trading territory against

52. Brodhead, *Hist. of State of N. Y.*, II, 193.
53. *N. Y. Col. Docs.*, VI, 893.
54. *Ibid.*, VI, 894.
55. Winsor, *Narr. and Crit. Hist.*, IV, 192; Brodhead, *Hist. of State of N. Y.*, II, 429.
56. *Doc. Hist. N. Y.*, I, 100. (Not the same series of documents as *N. Y. Col. Docs.*)

further English encroachment by way of the "Straits,"
Du Luth was sent in June, 1686, to establish a post
somewhere on the rivers between Lake Huron and
Lake St. Clair. He located it at the foot of Lake
Huron, and named it Fort St. Joseph.[57] Dongan,
hearing this, decided to make a more determined effort
to win the trade of the Upper Lakes, and sent word
to Denonville at Quebec that he intended sending two
parties to the Upper Lakes the following spring.[58]

Denonville looked upon such action with great apprehension, and in one of his reports in 1686 wrote,[59]
"If that detachment attacks that fort [St. Joseph]
. . . no more terms are to be observed with the
English. Please send me orders on this point for I
am disposed to go straight to Orange, storm their
fort, and burn the whole concern." He saw nothing
but ruin to the colony of New France if such expeditions were to continue, for, as he pointed out, the
cheaper bargains the English gave, drew not only the
Indians to their side, but attracted many of the French
of the colony who were in the habit of resorting to
the woods.

The next spring (1687) the first party of English
was arrested on Lake Huron, and in June the second
party was met on St. Clair River and captured. The
French saw a commercial motive behind this encroachment and declared that the whole was "an in-
trigue of the Orange merchants who [made] presents
to the Colonel" [Dongan].[60]

57. Winsor, *Narr. and Crit. Hist.*, IV, 192.
58. *N. Y. Col. Docs.*, IX, 309.
59. *Ibid.*, 287, 309.
60. *Ibid.*

Denonville now saw that a post at Niagara would accomplish quite as much as, if not more, than the post on the connecting waters of Lake Huron and Erie. He therefore asked (1686) for two good battalions and the funds necessary to build a post at Niagara; for, he writes,[61] "Such a post would absolutely close the road to the Outaoua [Ottawas] . . . and the English and place us [the French] in a position to prevent the Iroquois carrying their peltry to the latter."

The English likewise saw the need of a post at Niagara. In his report, February 22, 1687, Dongan states his plans as follows:[62] "To preserve the beaver and peltry trade for Albany, and to be an encouragement for our beaver hunters, I desire I may have an order to erect a company fort upon the Delaware River, . . . another upon the Susquehanna, . . . and another at Oneigra [Niagara] near the Great Lakes in the way where our people go a beaver hunting or a trading, or anywhere else where I shall think convenient. It being necessary for the support of trade, maintaining [the maintenance of] a correspondence with further Indians, and in securing [the security of] our rights in the country." It was the policy of the English Government to make the colonies self-supporting as far as possible, and Dongan found it hard to secure money for any of his undertakings. In February 1688, he tried again to stir the English Government to action. He states that the Iroquois must be kept fast to the English, "for they are able

61. *Ibid.*, 278; VI, 893.
62. *Doc. Hist. N. Y.*, I, 99.

to ruin all the King's colonies in these parts of America." Then he adds,[63] "We must build forts in the
country upon the Great Lakes as the French do,
otherwise, we lose the country, the beaver trade, and
our Indians."

In July 1687, the French established a post at
Niagara.[64] This was six months before Dongan made
his second appeal to the British Government. When
he heard of the erection of a post, he raised such a
storm of opposition that the matter was carried to
London and Paris. The result was, the French were
requested to evacuate, which they did in September
1688.[65] The two nations were supposed to be at
peace and such a move on the part of the French
seemed to the English a violation of international law.
The building of the fort was clearly an encroachment
on the territory of the Iroquois, over which the English exercised a sort of protectorate.

During King William's War (1689-1697) France and
England were in open hostilities; and although the
appeal to arms ceased with the treaty of peace in
1697, the commercial struggle did not, and the British
continued to plan to get complete control of the trade
of the western Indians. The St. Lawrence and Mo-
hawk-Oneida routes both lead to Lake Ontario. Rival
parties advancing up these waterways logically would
meet at that Lake; here is where one might expect the
first clash, but the Lake is large and there were few
people near it. Real contact came only where the

63.   Brodhead, *Hist. of State of N. Y.*, II, 495.
64.   *N. Y. Col. Docs.*, IX, 335.
65.   *Doc. Hist. N. Y.*, I, 147; Brodhead, *Hist. of State of N. Y.*,
       II, 506-509.

waterways narrowed down to a river,—in the Niagara River. Here, as the French rightly thought, was the best place for a fort to cut off the westward advance of the English from Albany, and here a post was built; only to be later abandoned. The next logical region of contact to the west is the waterway connecting Lakes Erie and Huron. Here Fort St. Joseph was built; it accomplished its purpose by checking the advance of the English for a time, and then was abandoned. The strife becoming more heated, a new post was needed, and that the new post should be located on the lower part of the "Straits" between lakes Huron and Erie was evident to both parties; and both conceived the idea at about the same time.

Livingston in 1699 laid a project before Lord Belmont for establishing a post on the "Detroit." Nearly all the great trade of Albany had been destroyed during the late war. The French, he claimed, had instigated the "Far Indians" to make war on the Five Nations. The former, therefore, ceased to sell their furs to the Iroquois, and moreover were afraid to carry the furs themselves through Iroquois territory to Albany; it was therefore necessary to build a post to the west of the Iroquois country and near the lands of the "Far Indians." He was sure that when the western tribes saw the plenty and cheapness of the goods of the English, they would bring all their furs to the new post and by that means augment the English trade tenfold.[66] The same year in which Livingston laid his project before Lord Belmont, Cadillac was in France presenting his proposals to the Crown.

66. *N. Y. Col. Docs.*, IV, 500.

The next year (1700) Livingston again presented his projects, this time more earnestly; he pointed out the need of sending traders to the Indians. He said, "We shall never be able to rancounter the French except we have a nursery of Bushlopers as well as they;" to effect which, he considered that a post at "Wawyachtenok, called by the French De Troett," near the best hunting grounds, was necessary. He describes the Detroit region as "the most pleasant and plentiful inland place in America by all relations. Where there are arable lands for thousands of people, the only place of bever [beaver] hunting . . . Here you have millions of elk, deer, swans, geese and all sorts of fowl." As to the strategic importance of such a post, he says,[67] "Neither would it be necessary to settle farther up the country than Wawyachtenok, for all the Indians would resort thither, where they can come in ten days by land if they might be safe, and then no great difficulty would appear in making a firme [firm] peace between them and the Five Nations in spite of the French." To make their claim to the Detroit region secure, the English, on July 14, 1701, induced the Iroquois to deed to them all the land east and west of Detroit from Lake Ontario to Lake Michigan.[68] Seven days later Cadillac with his followers landed at the site of Detroit and soon began the building of a fort.[69]

67. *Ibid.*, IV, 650, 651 (April, 1700).
68. *Ibid.*, IV, 908.
69. Kingsford, *Hist. of Canada*, II, 408.

CHAPTER III

Detroit Under Cadillac (1701–1710)

THE first authentic description of a visit to the
Detroit region by white men is by Father Hennepin, who in 1679 accompanied La Salle on his way to
Green Bay in the "Griffin," the first vessel on the
Upper Lakes. Few Indians lived on the banks of the
river before 1701, and consequently the region attracted neither trader nor missionary, both of whom
sought the Indians around their camp fires. Moreover, the Detroit region lay on the warpath of the
Iroquois, who made frequent excursions to the west,
even to the prairies of Illinois.[1]

Father Hennepin describes the Detroit region as follows:[2] "The country between the two lakes is well
situated and the soil is fertile. The banks of the
Streight [Strait] are vast meadows and the prospect is
terminated with some hills covered with vineyards.
Trees bear good fruit. Groves and forests are so well
disposed that one would think Nature alone could not
make, without the help of art, so charming a prospect.
That country is stocked with stags, wild goats [?],
and bear, which are good for food and not so fierce
as in other countries. Turkey-cocks and swans are
also common. . . . The forests are chiefly made up

1. *Mich. Hist. Colls.*, VIII, 419 (Walker).
2. Thwaites, Hennepin's *A New Discovery*, I, 109.

of walnut trees, chestnut trees, plum trees and pear trees [?] loaded with their own fruits and vines.   There is also abundant timber fit for building; so those that shall be so happy as to inhabit that noble country, cannot but remember with gratitude those who have discovered the way by venturing to sail upon an unknown lake for 100 (one hundred) leagues."

On a map[3] of unknown authorship, published about 1690, is printed the following, concerning the Detroit region: "All this country which is in the region of Lake Terocharronting [Lake Erie] is discovered and explored.   The winters are moderate and short. Grapes are in abundance.   Savage oxen [buffalo], fowls, and all sorts of game are found in abundance and there is still much beaver."

To the explorer accustomed to the thin soils and rigorous climate of the lower St. Lawrence, Detroit must have seemed a fruitful region, especially when visited in the summer.   Hennepin's description doubtless is overdrawn, but the locality had a strong attraction for the French trader, voyager, and settler apart from its strategic importance.   Hennepin writes that he tried to persuade La Salle to make a settlement on the "charming streight."[4]

Cadillac was in command at Michillimackinac from 1694 to 1697.   It was while stationed there that he witnessed the ready access of the Iroquois traders to the Upper Lakes along the connecting waterways, and conceived the idea of building a post on the Straits which should be a stronghold of French power, a check

3.   Winsor, *Narr. and Crit. Hist.*, IV, 216.
4.   Thwaites, Hennepin's *A New Discovery*, I, 109.

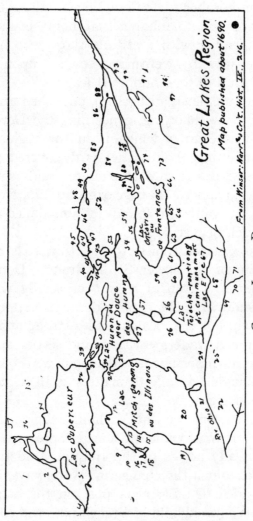

GREAT LAKES REGION

(From Winsor's Narr. and Crit. Hist., IV, 216)

Map published about 1690. The Detroit region is designated by number 26, the description of which is as follows: "Tout ces pays est celuy qui est aus Environs du lac Teiochariontiong est decouvert. L'hivers y est modere et court; les fruits y viennent en abondance; les boefs savages, poules dinde et tout sorte de gibier s'y trouvent en quantite et il y a encore force castor."

to the westward advance of British commercial interests, and a barrier to the Iroquois on their western raids. Trading in furs without a license was prohibited in New France, but the English had no such restrictions, and drew many of the French traders to them. A post on the Straits would also check these *coureurs de bois* from carrying their furs to Albany. His final conception was that it should be a colony, a settlement with a garrison, traders, and farmers, all working together for the advancement of the glory of France. About it he would collect the Indian tribes, and teach them the ways of civilized man. There should be schools for the Indian and white youths, in which methods of agriculture could be taught. A regiment of Indian soldiers might be organized.[5]

Many of the French officials both in Canada and France opposed the building of a post so far inland. The king pointed out that with the establishment of so remote a post, traffic would be drawn from the settled portions of the colony and those engaged in the trade would move to the newly established center. This would tend to weaken the colony on the lower St. Lawrence. He thought the expense for the upkeep of the fort and the pay of the soldiers would be great.[6] Cadillac had anticipated such an objection by stating in his plea that it would not be necessary "to grant any concessions at that place for fear of weakening the colony by extending it too much," and he hoped to

5. Hubbard, *Memorials of a Half Century*, 113; *Mich. Hist. Colls.*, VIII, 425; XXXIII, 42, 198 (*Cadillac Papers*); Burton, *A Sketch of Life of De La Motte Cadillac*, 13; *N. Y. Col. Docs.*, IX, 812.
6. Kingsford, *Hist. of Canada*, III, 408.

conduct affairs such that the post would not be an expense to the Crown.[7]

The project was much debated at the French court. The real question to be answered was, whether the Indians then and ultimately were to be made subjects of the English or the French monarch. The extension of the fur trade constantly was bringing new tribes of Indians into trade relations. Whether the French or the English would find friends among these new tribes depended on which party was the more accessible.[8] This fact decided the issue. A post at Detroit would facilitate the trade with the western Indians and lay the foundations for a friendship that would make them the allies of the French.

The effectiveness of the cheaper goods of the English in winning the friendship of the Indians must have been discussed, for Cadillac and the Company of the Colony of Canada, which for a time held the monopoly of trade at Detroit, asked His Majesty to supply them "with powder, lead and arms for trading with the savages, at the same price as he got them from the contractor, so that by supplying them to the savages cheaper than the English, they [the French] might take away from them [the savages] all incentive to take their furs to that nation."[9]

At length after much discussion, Cadillac was given power to establish his post. On October 16, 1700, Callières, then Governor of Canada, wrote to Pontchar-

---

7. *Mich. Hist. Colls.*, XXXIII, 42 (*Cadillac Papers*); *Wis. Hist. Colls.*, XVI, 218.
8. Winsor, *Narr. and Crit. Hist.*, I, 303.
9. *Mich. Hist. Colls.*, XXXIII, 44 (*Cadillac Papers*).

train as follows:[10] "I shall send Sieur de la Mott [Cadillac] and Sieur de Tonty in the spring to construct a fort at Detroit. My design is that they shall go by the Outaouacs River [Ottawa River] in order to take possession of that post from the Lake Huron side, by that means avoid the Niagara passage, so as not to give umbrage to the Iroquois through fear of disturbing the peace, until I can speak to them to prevent any alarm that they might feel at such proceedings, and until I adopt some measure to facilitate the communication and conveyance of necessaries from this to that, through Lake Ontario."

Peace having been made with the Iroquois on September 8, 1700,[11] the French were careful not to do anything that would give them offense. The Iroquois heard of the intentions of the French to establish a post at Detroit, and complained grievously to the Governor of New France and also to the Governor of New York.[12] Later they insisted that His Britannic Majesty apply to the French king for redress.[13] In August, 1701, about one month after the arrival of Cadillac and his party at Detroit, De Callières met the assembled tribes of Abenaks, Algonquians, Hurons, Ottawas, Illinois, Miamis, and Iroquois. He pleaded for peace, explained the establishment of the fort at Detroit, and stated that it was his policy to exclude the English from proceeding thither.[14]

The party of Cadillac arrived in the Detroit River

---

10. N. Y. Col. Docs., IX, 713.
11. Kingsford, Hist. of Canada, II, 398.
12. N. Y. Col. Docs., IV, 891.
13. Ibid., V, 633, 736.
14. Kingsford, Hist. of Canada, II, 402.

on July 24, and after examining the river up and down for a suitable spot on which to erect the fort, they chose a site on the first terrace. Though the ground behind was higher, it was too far from the river; the location selected gave the fort a commanding position. Palisades were constructed enclosing about three acres of land. On July 26 the foundation of a church was laid, and log houses soon were constructed.

In the *Paris Documents*, it is claimed that the party considered the building of the fort and settlement on Grosse Isle, some fifteen miles down the river. "Grand Island," they say,[15] "is very fine and fertile and extensive. It is estimated from six to seven leagues in circumference. There is an extraordinary quantity of apple trees on the island. . . . Abundance of excellent mill-stones are found. . . . All around are found fine prairies. It was for a long time doubtful whether Detroit should not be founded there. The cause of the hesitation was the apprehension that timber might some day fail."

Cadillac brought with him provisions for only three months. Having arrived too late for the planting of corn and the sowing of wheat, the party had to depend on the Indians and the chase for food. They got land ready for sowing fall wheat, which was grown with great success. Next spring soldiers and civilians were urged to plant and cultivate as much land as possible. Supplies for the Indian trade were brought from Montreal, and the little settlement was fairly established by the second winter. Burton says, [16] "What on July 23,

15. *N. Y. Col. Docs.*, IX, 887 (*Paris Docs.*, VII, 1718).
16. Burton, *Cadillac's Village*, 10.

1701, was a wilderness, on the next day was a houseless
city of a hundred souls, and in eight month's time
was a rival of Montreal and Quebec in trade."

Cadillac did his best to gather many Indian tribes
about him. His experience with Indian life at Michillimackinac[17] had taught him how to win the confidence
of the savages, and many came. Burton says that
during the winter of 1701 and 1702 about six thousand
Indians wintered at Detroit.[18]

On one of his early trips to Montreal and Quebec,

17. There is much confusion in history literature of the Lakes
region concerning the spelling and use of the words Michillimackinac, Mackinac, and Mackinaw, and even of the
location of the post which so long bore one or another of
these names. The island now known as Mackinac was
during the French and English periods called Michillimackinac Island. The term Michillimackinac has also
been used for the region in the neighborhood of the island,
on both sides of the Straits. Father Marquette in 1671
removed his mission from La Pointe on Lake Superior to
St. Ignace, at which point a year before a mission had
been established. (Thwaites, *Father Marquette*, 93, 116).
A mission was maintained at St. Ignace until about 1706,
when many of the French and Indians withdrew to Detroit. (Bain, *Alexander Henry's Travels and Adventures*,
40; Williams, *Early Mackinac*, 24, 26). About 1712 or
1714 De Louvigny was sent by the French to reestablish
a post at Michillimackinac. He erected the palisades on
the south side of the Straits at the site of the present
Mackinaw City (also called "old Mackinaw"). This
post was taken by the British in 1764. In 1780 Major
Sinclair was sent to rebuild the fort at Michillimackinac.
He selected a site on Michillimackinac Island. (Bain,
Alex. Henry's Travels and Adventures, 39; Williams, *Early
Mackinac*, 36, 41; Kelton, *Annals*, 133; Schoolcraft, *Hist.
of Indian Tribes of N. A.*, I, 243). The Americans have
maintained a fort on the island since except for the short
period of British occupation in the War of 1812, until
recently.
18. *Mich. Hist. Colls.*, XXIX, 237.

Cadillac brought back two canoe-loads of wheat (five to ten tons) to be used as seed, together with many other kinds of grain, and the materials for a mill.[19] The difficulties of getting horses and cattle to Detroit were great. They could not be brought in the small boats commonly used, and to bring them by land along the shores of the Lakes through the pathless forest and underbrush, across rivers too deep to be forded, was an almost superhuman task. However, Cadillac brought three horses at an early date, two of which soon died; for many years the survivor was the only horse in the settlement. From the Paris Archives it is learned that in 1707 "Sieur de la Motte had horses and cattle taken overland." "There are," the report says,[20] "already a small number of pigs there and a quantity of poultry. Still larger numbers are to be taken this year together with some sheep."

The first large migration of people took place in the summer of 1706. Cadillac the year before had taken steps to have more complete control of the settlement. To encourage thrift, make the settlers more contented, and insure the permanence of the settlement, Cadillac granted land to actual settlers.[21] The first grant was made March 10, 1707, to Jean Fofard, an interpreter[22]; others followed. Such grants, however, were not in fee simple; they remained in possession of the owner only as long as the land granted was cultivated. In reality all the land belonged to the

---

19.   *N. Y. Col. Docs.*, IX, 806; Campbell, *Pol. Hist. of Mich.*, 74.
20.   *Mich. Hist. Colls.*, XXIX, 228 (Quoted by Burton).
21.   *N. Y. Col. Docs.*, IX, 827; *Wis. Hist. Colls.*, III, 168 (Cass MS.).
22.   Mitchell, *Detroit in Hist. and Commerce*, 6.

Crown or to the seignorage. The feudal system was in vogue in New France and Cadillac was virtually a feudal lord. He owned the fort, the church, the grist-mill, the brewery, the warehouse, the barn, and the very fruit trees brought from France. He was the court of last resort in all civil matters. After 1707 he controlled the privileges of fur trading and the grant-ing of licenses at the post.[23]

In 1707 it was reported that there were two hun-dred seventy persons in the settlement, including twenty-five families, and it was expected that fully one hundred more families would come the following summer.[24] More than one hundred and fifty persons came in the three years 1707, 1708, and 1709; and by 1710 the cultivated farms extended for six miles along the river.[25] But the growth of the settlement was rela-tively slow, largely because there were few people in New France with which a settlement could be built. It is estimated that all New France had less than fifteen thousand settlers in 1700.[26] Detroit was in many respects a premature settlement. It was not the logical outgrowth of a migrating people as were all later American settlements of the interior. It was settled chiefly to aid the French to control the trade in furs. When this trade declined in importance, the settlement naturally would decline. The oncoming tide of American settlers reached it before the fur trade ceased to sustain it. Its real significant growth

23. *American State Papers, Public Lands*, I, 247.
24. *Mich. Hist. Colls.*, XXIX, 229 (Burton).
25. *Ibid.*, 273.
26. *Canadian Yearbook*, 1906, 128; Thwaites, *France in America*, 26; *De Bow's Review*, XIII, 119.

came when the American settlers gave it a surer basis
for existence.

The early growth of the settlement was retarded by
other factors. Ecclesiastical, civil, and military officials for many years opposed it in various ways. The
establishment of a post at Detroit meant the abandon-
ment of Michillimackinac, as the Indians near the
latter post were to be brought to Detroit, and the
trade which had developed there would be centered
at Detroit. Many of the officials were interested in
the trade at Michillimackinac and, therefore, opposed
the post at Detroit.[27] The Jesuits who had the mission at Michillimackinac opposed the founding of
Detroit because it involved the loss of their Indian
converts and friends, and also because they were
debarred by Cadillac from settling there.[28]

When the post was first proposed it was understood
that Cadillac would have the monopoly of the trade;
that, undoubtedly, was one of the motives that actu-

27. *Mich. Hist. Colls.*, VIII, 428 (Walker).
28. If one were to judge of the attitude of the Jesuits at Michil-
       limackinac from their correspondence to Cadillac, it
       would seem that they were heartily in favor of the settle-
       ment at Detroit. Father Carheil, on July 25, 1701,
       writes, "I would deem it a pleasure to proceed at once to
       render you all the service in my power, did the state of
       this mission permit it." On July 28, 1701, Father Joseph
       Marest writes, "You do me the justice of believing that
       I will contribute as far as lies in my power to the settle-
       ment of Detroit; and that if I cannot do it otherwise, I
       will do so at least by the feeble aid of my prayer to the
       Lord." Cadillac wrote on the latter of these two letters
       (only a portion given above), "Those two missionaries,
       very far from conforming to the intention of that letter,
       are employing every means to prevent the Savages com-
       ing here." (*Wis. Hist. Colls.*, XVI, 205.)

ated him in proposing a post. But in 1700 some of the merchants at Montreal asked for the exclusive privilege of trade at Detroit. Cadillac, singularly enough, was one of the applicants. The petition was granted, and a corporation called the company of the Colony of Canada was formed.[29] Within five years the company became insolvent and in 1705 or 1706 surrendered the monopoly of trade to Cadillac.

To the Company of the Colony a fort was not objectionable, for that would aid in collecting furs, but no revenue could be derived from the farms. Farming in the Detroit region, until cheap transportation to the seaboard was provided, was unprofitable. The company therefore opposed the latter in every way. They placed restrictions upon the number of beaver and other fur bearing animals to be killed about Detroit. This "materially affected every hunter and trapper in the settlement and necessarily disturbed trade and made the maintenance of a comfortable life uncertain and precarious."[30] Cadillac says of their attitude,[31] "You may believe that the Company has no other object but to make money at this post and not at all to contribute to its settlement. It has no other aim but to have a warehouse and clerks with no officers, troops, nor settlers, caring little for what concerns the King's glory and his service." In order to deter families from wishing to go to Detroit, the report was spread in Lower Canada that the post would be abandoned at an early date.[32]

---

29. *Mich. Hist. Colls.*, XXIX, 270 (Burton).
30. *Ibid.*, XXIX, 226 (Burton).
31. *Ibid.*, XXXIII, 178 (Cadillac Papers).
32. Burton, *Early Detroit*, 230 (Data from Paris Archives).

The idea of forming agricultural settlements in the interior was often discouraged by the clergy, the civil authorities, and the fur traders. The clergy discouraged agricultural settlements because such settlements might drive the savages away from the missions. Moreover, they knew that the savages probably would learn the vices but not the virtues of civilization. Their teaching, thereby, would come to naught.[33] The civil authorities desired compact settlements in the St. Lawrence region. They wished to concentrate the people about the forts and posts, in order the better to defend themselves. Stringent laws were passed to keep the traders from the woods and to make the settlements compact. The trader, and all interested in the trade in furs, discouraged agricultural development, for that meant the destruction of the forests and the dispersion of the fur-bearing animals. Partly because of these things most of New France was kept a great game preserve.

Enemies outside New France were even more active in their endeavors to defeat the purpose of the French at Detroit. English envoys tried to induce the Indians to remove from Detroit, telling them that they would "furnish them goods at a cheaper rate [than the French] and do them every sort of kindness." They requested them to remove their villages to the shores of Lake Erie and offered "physical aid in case the French showed any opposition."[34]

Vaudreuil, now the Governor of New France, had

33. See letter of Father De Carheil to the Intendant of Canada, *Wis. Hist. Colls.*, XVI, 214, on conditions at Michillimackinac.
34. *N. Y. Col. Docs.*, IX, 751, 752.

formed a strong prejudice against the post at Detroit, and wrote to Pontchartrain that the general consensus of opinion, even of the Indians, was that the post was untenable.[35]   In 1704 he pointed out that it had not prevented the Lakes Indians from trading with the English at Albany; "for five canoes belonging to Detroit," he writes,[36] "have this year been trading at Albany."

The opposition became so strong and the statements regarding the settlement so conflicting, that Cadillac was asked to come to Quebec (1704) to answer certain charges against him, and an investigation of the post was ordered by the King.   Pontchartrain reviewed both sides of the controversy somewhat as follows:[37] "Sieur de la Motte continues to be persuaded that . . . this establishment will have all the effect expected from it.   Others pretend that the land there is good for nothing.   That it will never produce anything there to feed its inhabitants; that the only thing there is very poor fishing; and that the hunting is between thirty and fourty leagues off; and finally it is to be feared that the Iroquois will attack that post without its being in our power to assist it and war will recommence in consequence.   The Company of the Colony complain likewise that it involves them in an exorbitant expense which is out of their power to sustain, if it continually requires them to convey to that post the supplies necessary for the support of the people there."   It was contended also that the route by way

35.   *Ibid.*, IX, 744.
36.   *Ibid.*, 763.
37.   *Ibid.*, 742.

of Lakes Ontario and Erie, which now was used more
or less, could not be kept open.[38]   De Aigremont was
sent to make the investigation in July 1708.[39]   He
strongly advised the discontinuance of the post, as
being prejudicial to Canada.   He reported that the soil
was not productive—this of course was untrue.   He
also reported that even if the land were productive,
there was no market for the produce raised, and the
trade would never be useful to France; that therefore
the post was a burden on the colony and the kingdom.[40]

Detroit was experiencing the troubles common to
most Canadian undertakings; for greed, jealousy, and
prejudice were rampant throughout all New France.
Pontchartrain, always a firm friend of Cadillac, considered the report strongly prejudicial to the latter.
He censured the author severely, but at the same
time accused Cadillac of having sordid motives.   He
wrote to De Aigremont as follows: "It seems to me
that your sojourn there was not long enough to obtain
a thorough understanding of it.   Besides Sieur de la
Motte complains that you did not confer a sufficient
length of time with him to appreciate the reasons
why he acted. . . .   In a country like that, new
maxims are sometimes necessary which may appear
censurable on their face, and be intrinsically good.
Nevertheless I find too great cupidity in Sieur de la
Motte, and that his private interests in establishing
that post may have engaged him to prefer his special
advantage to the general good of the Colony. . . .

---

38.   *Ibid.*, 826.
39.   *Wis. Hist. Colls.*, XVI, 242.
40.   *Mich. Hist. Colls.*, VIII, 437 (Walker); *Wis. Hist. Colls.*
        XVI, 251–257.

His Majesty has thought best to withdraw his troops
from that place, and to leave it to de la Motte to do
what he pleases with it, without any other privilege
over the other inhabitants of Canada." The reasons
he gave for withdrawing the troops were, (1) the great
expense incurred in the support of the garrison, (2) the
difficulty of assisting the post, should it be attacked
by the Iroquois, (3) the bad quality of the soil, (4) the
disappearance of the game-hunting, and (5) the dispersion of the people of Canada.[41]

The troops were not withdrawn, however, and Bonnecamp, with less rancor and pessimism than De
Aigremont, says of the settlement in 1710,[42] "Its situation appears to me to be charming. The beautiful
river runs at the foot of the fort; vast plains which
only ask to be cultivated extend beyond the sight.
There is nothing milder than the climate, which
scarcely counts two months of winter. The products
of Europe and especially the grains grow much better
than in any of the Cantons of France. . . . We
should regard Detroit as one of the most important
outposts of the colony. It is conveniently situated for
furnishing aid to Michillimackinac, to the St. Joseph,
to the Bay [Green Bay], to the Miamis, Ouitanen, and
to the Beautiful River, supposing a settlement be
made thereon. Accordingly we cannot send too many
there; but where shall we find men therefor, certainly
not in Canada."

In 1710 Cadillac was ordered to proceed to Louisiana

41. *N. Y. Col. Docs.*, IX, 826 (*Paris Docs.*, IV); *Wis. Hist. Colls.*,
       XVI, 260.
42. *Jesuit Relations*, LXIX, 191 (Bonnecamp's *Relations*).

as governor of that province.   After ten years the little
colony was still a mere outpost, far in advance of the
civilization it proclaimed, in spite of the aspirations
and hard work of Cadillac.   The fur trade nominally
had its headquarters here, but was not important
enough to make the colony grow.   Cadillac had done
everything he could to advance agriculture, but the
chief occupations of the people were fishing and hunting, tendencies handed down to the French *habitant*
far into the nineteenth century.   The farmer had only
a local market, and so there was little object in raising
products much beyond his own needs.[43]   In 1714,
however, Detroit was furnishing the Indians at Michillimackinac with corn, because the soil at the latter place
was too thin to raise this staple of the frontier.   Between the opening of navigation and October, eight
hundred minots (2400 bushels) had been sent up.[44]

Burton describes the settlement of 1710 substan-
tially as follows.   The land within the palisade was
two city blocks in length, and one block deep.   This
area was divided into lots and garden plots.   The
streets were not more than ten or fifteen feet wide,
except St. Anne's, which was about twenty-five feet
in width for most of its length.   The houses were built
of logs eight or ten inches in diameter, driven into the
ground, and cut off six or seven feet above the earth.
The roofs were made of small logs flattened by an adz.
Brick and mortar also were used in building.   Some
houses had brick floors, and these were considered so
valuable that they were inventoried in the household

43.   *Mag. West. Hist.*, III, 158.
44.   *N. Y. Col. Docs.*, IX, 869; *Wis. Hist. Colls.*, XVI, 308.

effects of their owners. For windows, skins scraped as thin as possible were used. No mention is made of glass. About the fort only a short distance away were the villages of the Indians.

Hunting was a pastime as well as a means of getting a living. Fishing also must have been a pastime, for the river was rich in fish; this could not have been an industry because everyone had both time and the disposition to catch his own fish.

At an early date a mill was built to grind corn and wheat,[45] and probably it was propelled by wind. A brewery was built a short time after the founding of the settlement, and a brewer was brought to the colony. The people lived within the palisades and went out daily to work their farms, some of which were three miles from the fort. Farming was a precarious occupation, for the farmer did not dare live on his property, and at nightfall when he returned to the fort he left his fields, garden, and orchard to the ravages of beasts and savages.[46] About 1710 the village that had grown up around the fort began to be called Detroit.[47]

---

45. *Wis. Hist. Colls.*, XVI, 252.
46. *Mich. Hist. Colls.*, XXIX, 225, 239 (Burton).
47. *Mag. West. Hist.*, III, 158. For a list of early settlers at Detroit, see *Jesuit Relations*, LXVII, 334; LXIX, 245, 277, 306, 310; LXX, 21, 77, 305, 309.

CHAPTER IV

The Detroit Settlement After Cadillac
(1710–1760)

IN 1710 De la Forest was appointed to succeed Cadillac as commander of the fort at Detroit, but on account of business affairs at Quebec he was unable to take charge of his post until 1712. Dubuisson was placed in temporary command, and was in charge when the Fox Indians attacked Detroit in 1712.

Unfortunately for the early growth of the Detroit settlement, there were open hostilities between the French and English from 1702 to 1713 (Queen Anne's War). Though the strife was confined mainly to the eastern provinces, the Lakes region was kept in turmoil. Through Iroquois emissaries the English made very uncertain the hold of the French on many of the tribes about the Lakes, especially the Fox Indians. For many years the latter had been enemies of the French, and their position along the Fox-Wisconsin trade route was a serious menace to French commerce in the region to the west of Lake Michigan. The *Jesuit Relations* represent these Indians as maltreating the French "in deed and word, pillaging and robbing them of their goods in spite of their resistance and subjecting them to unbearable insolence and indignity."[1] Through the Iroquois the Fox Indians had learned of

---

1. *Jesuit Relations*, LV, 187.

the cheaper goods of the English at Albany and they desired to see the English trader enter their country. To make this possible the fort at Detroit first must be destroyed.[2]

Early in the summer of 1712 one thousand Fox, Sauk, and Missauka Indians, three hundred warriors with their women and children, appeared at Detroit and built a stockade a few rods from the post. In preparation for the Indian attack, Dubuisson ordered all the live stock, grain, and other stores taken into the fort. Near-by buildings were destroyed lest they should give shelter to the enemy, or endanger the post if fired. The little garrison of thirty men determined to make the best defense possible. Fortunately the Indian allies of the French arrived before an attack was made and the besiegers became the besieged. After a siege of nineteen days, the Fox, Sauk and Missauka Indians made overtures to surrender, and on the refusal of the French to treat with them, fled to Grosse Point. The French and their allies followed, and after a siege of four days the Green Bay Indians surrendered.[3]

Ever since the founding of the post at Detroit, the size of the garrison had been decreasing. For the privilege of exclusive trade the commandant was charged with the expense of provisions, the pay of officers, privates, and others associated with the garrison, and with the up-keep of the mission. This obligation Cadillac had assumed in 1707, and it was borne

2. Kingsford, *Hist. of Canada*, II, 454.
3. *Wis. Hist. Colls.*, XVI, 267–287 (Dubuisson's *Report*, June 15, 1712); *Ibid.*, V, 78; *Mich. Hist. Colls.*, VIII, 440, 441.
9

by his successors for many years.[4]   Residents within
the palisades were required to pay a rent, and also a
small tax on the lands they tilled.   The various artisans were allowed to ply their trade only providing
they held a license from the commandant.   These
were sold for about two hundred fifty livres per year.[5]

The larger part of the revenues of the commandant
was derived from licenses sold to voyageurs, and
traders resident at the settlement, amounting in all
to more than five thousand livres per year.   The King
also gave the powder for the post each year, and the
commandant sold much of this to the French and
Indians.   The revenue from this latter source amounted
to about fifteen hundred livres per year. . The commandant, it seems, also had a well-stocked "Bureau,"
from which he sold wines and brandy required by the
Frenchmen.   This brought him about two thousand
livres yearly, and in addition to these sources of income, which in all amounted to about 8500 livres, he
engaged in trade with the residents about the post
and with the Indians.   His profits in this trade were
greater than those of others at the settlement, for
each trader's canoe brought free of freight-charges one
hundred pounds of provisions, implements, and tools.[6]
The profits of the commandants were never large, however, and it is probable that these officials were obliged
to keep a small garrison because of their small income.
At any rate, De la Forest in 1714 sent a memorial to
the Government in which he asked that the forces be

4.   *Wis. Hist. Colls.*, III, 167 (Cass MS.).
5.   *Ibid.*, 294.   The livre was an old French coin worth about 20
       cents.
6.   *Ibid.*, XVII, 293–297.

increased; and to enable the commandant to meet the added expense, he suggested that the sale of trading licenses to the settlers be abolished and a complete monopoly given to the commandant.[7] At a much later date, 1736, Governor Beauharnois doubted whether any officer would be willing to take the command of the post if the garrison exceeded thirty men, because of the great expense.[8]

In the memorial referred to in the preceding paragraph, De la Forest expressed the opinion that the plan of Cadillac to make Detroit a place for settlers as well as traders was impracticable, and asked that any further increase to the settlement be prohibited, and the whole converted into a military and trading post. With the garrison as small as it was the settlement could not increase, for settlers would not be able to improve land far from the fort because of the prowling Iroquois. Should any houses be built outside the stockade walls "they would be exposed to be burnt and their occupants killed." Even the Potawatomi, who had no palisade "often [had] alarms which oblige[d] them to put their wives and children into the French fort."[9] Nevertheless, he considered that it was to the "King's glory and the interest of the colony to preserve the post," because of its strategic importance. If it were abandoned, the English soon would render themselves masters, and would carry on the whole trade with all the Indian allies of France. The post was necessary to prevent the Iroquois from

7. *N. Y. Col. Docs.*, IX, 866.
8. *Ibid.*, XVII, 242.
9. *Ibid.*, IX, 868; Campbell, *Pol. Hist. of Mich.*, 85.

making attacks on the western tribes, for such attacks meant the disturbance of the trade in furs. It was also necessary to preserve Detroit as a source of food supply for the post at Michillimackinac. To provide such food, the Indians should be prevailed on to remain at Detroit to cultivate the soil. Besides providing food for Michillimackinac, the post was also an advantageous point at which troops and provisions could be assembled in a war on the Iroquois.[10] Throughout the memorial the strong influence of the commercial spirit that permeated New France is shown. No changes in the management of the fort and no changes in the original plan of Cadillac were made.

In 1717 Tonty was sent to Detroit as successor to De la Forest. Tonty also was an able officer but "avaricious and unscrupulous in trade matters."[11] In 1726 he granted the exclusive right of traffic in furs to four of his associates. This was a violation of the rights of the settlers; for, since the founding of the post, they had been allowed to buy licenses to trade in furs. Accordingly, they drew up articles of remonstrance, which were sent to the Intendant.[12] They stated that they had been done a great wrong because they were "deprived of the douceurs [comforts] and articles [they] were in the habit of receiving from the savages for the subsistance of [their] families." Being at such a distance from the base of supplies at Montreal and Quebec, they could not as individuals make the long journey to supply the needs of their families, and they could not attempt to purchase goods of those who had

10. *Ibid.*
11. Campbell, *Pol. Hist. of Mich.*, 84.
12. *Ibid.*, 88.

the exclusive trade because of the "extreme dearness and high prices put upon the goods when they arrived."[13]

In reply Gatineau, one of the associates, accused the settlers of being idle and lazy and to this alone could they "impute the want of grain and provisions." The lands were able to produce abundantly, yet grain was scarce. Wheat was sold at twenty to twenty-five livres the minot, and corn at fifteen to eighteen livres. Eggs brought twenty to twenty-five sous per dozen, and a cow was worth one hundred livres. These should be considered good prices, and were the people inclined to cultivate their lands they would be in a condition to give provisions to the voyageurs and Indians at a more reasonable rate than they had done and yet make money.[14] As for the right to trade with the Indians, he suggested that if the settlers had the trade they asked for, they would neglect the soil, and the Crown, then, would be obliged to abandon the post and all would leave for want of provisions.[15]

The remonstrance of the settlers seems to have had no effect on Tonty. The accusations of Tonty's associate in regard to the character of the settlers undoubtedly had some basis of truth, at any rate they agree in part with the characterization of the French settler made by later writers for a later date.

In 1728 Tonty was relieved of his command, and Boishèbert was put in charge of the post and settlement. A new era now seemed to be dawning for

---

13. *Wis. Hist. Colls.*, III, 169 (Cass MS.).
14. *Ibid.*, 171.
15   *Ibid.*, XVI, 471.   Intendant's letter to Minister, 1727, regarding petition.

Detroit. Beauharnois, the Governor General, wrote in 1730 that the new commandant "had nothing more at heart than to induce the French to till the soil."[16] In the report of the commandant in 1730, it was stated that the settlers had "sown much more than usual" and it was expected "the harvest would be at least double what it had been in former years." In many respects he found the "establishment but little advanced considering that it was commenced over [nearly] thirty years ago." The soil and climate were good. Anything that grew in France could be produced there. Clearly, Nature was not at fault. The Crown should send more settlers. He thought that if soldiers were sent, and farms granted them, they might be induced to stay and become good settlers.[17]

About 1734 Beauharnois obtained permission from the Crown to make concessions to farmers, in addition to those granted in 1722, as "an Inducement to the Habitants to till the land better than they had hitherto done."[18] These grants were so hedged about by requirements and specifications, however, that when compared to the system under which the American Government later disposed of its lands, they seem foreign indeed. In some of the grants "the grantee was bound to pay to the crown forever a rent of fifteen livres per year in peltries; to assist in planting a Maypole on each May-day before the door of the mansion-house. He was forbidden to buy or sell merchandise carried to or from Montreal through servants, clerks,

16. *Wis. Hist. Colls.*, XVII, 141.
17. *Ibid.*
18. *Ibid.*, 264.

or foreigners, to work at the business of blacksmith, to sell brandy to the Indians, or to mortgage the land without the consent of the government. The Crown reserved all the rights of minerals and timber. . . . All the grain raised was to be ground at the manor windmill where toll was to be given in the same way as in France." All grants had to be confirmed by the king.[19] Under so many restrictions it is not surprising that few took up land. Only six of these concessions were sent to France for confirmation.[20]

In 1736, however, Beauharnois was able to report that the "concessions granted to various inhabitants for several years past have induced them to work more assiduously than they had hitherto done in cultivating the soil," and that "in 1735 thirteen to fourteen hundred minots of wheat were harvested," which, it was expected, would be worth three livres a minot."[21] The post and settlement in 1736 consisted of seventeen soldiers, forty families, and eighty men capable of bearing arms. Sixteen more concessions had been granted to inhabitants who had made requests.[22]

In the report for 1737 an appeal again was made for more troops, "for the Crown," it states, "could expect no marked progress until the garrison was made stronger." The fort needed sixty men and officers, for that was the only way to make the French and the fort "respected by the Indians [who were] turned away by the cheap goods of the English and by brandy."

19. *Amer. State Papers, Pub. Lands*, I, 247; *Mag. West. Hist.*, IV, 374 (Campbell).
20. Campbell, *Pol. Hist. of Mich.*, 92.
21. *Wis. Hist. Colls.*, XVII, 240, 241.
22. *Ibid.*

The writer thought the soldiers would be more likely to remain permanently than the voyageurs, because, he says,[23] "the voyageurs are too busy and too fond of trading to allow us to hope of their settling there and devoting themselves to the cultivation of the soil."

The efforts of Governor Beauharnois and the able commandants at Detroit resulted in enlarging the settlement and increasing trade. De Noyan, the commandant in charge in 1740, reported that one hundred families could be counted in both town and country,[24] "i. e., to say, about as many traders as farmers." Agriculture was not well developed, for the small market the farmers found for their produce compelled them "to be content with harvesting what suffic[ed] for their needs."

About this time the Detroit trade amounted to from one hundred and fifty thousand to two hundred thousand livres of fur per year.[25] In most years ten or twelve licenses were issued to traders, though in some years fourteen or fifteen canoes came.[26] The cost of a license was five hundred livres.[27] There were many free licenses. The missionaries, chaplains, interpreters, surgeons, and sub-delegates were given free permits for one and one-half canoes.[28] It appears that there were too many traders and competition was so severe that the traders sold much of their goods too cheap

23. Ibid., 265.
24. Ibid., 357.
25. Ibid.
26. Each canoe could carry about five thousand pounds.
27. Ibid., 293, 294.
28. Ibid., 298.

and many were not able to pay the Montreal merchants. The report states,[29] "the latter have more mortgages in Detroit than Detroit is worth."

The account books kept at the Jesuit Mission by Father de la Richardie throw much light on the business transactions at the Detroit settlement during the late decades of the French regime.[30] In 1735 La Richardie collected near Detroit some of the dispersed Hurons, to the number of six hundred, "all of whome he converted," and founded the Huron mission on the site of Sandwich, then called Point de Montreal.[31] He "chose that side to avoid conflict of ecclesiastical jurisdiction with the Récollets in charge of Detroit."[32]

Here, according to Hubbard, he built a missionhouse and a church, which stood until about 1850. About 1736 he built a store and warehouse. The account books of La Richardie show the business dealings the mission had with the French *habitants* of Detroit and vicinity, and with the Indians.[33]

29. *Ibid.*, 326.
30. See Daybooks and Ledgers of Detroit Merchants.
31. *Jesuit Relations*, LXIX, 283.
32. *Ibid.*, LXIX, 305.
33. *Ibid.* The following quotations from the account books of the mission illustrate some of the business transactions, and the quaint methods of bookkeeping employed:
   "I borrowed from sieur parent of les miamas The equivalent of 135 boards 10 feet long; those that he lent me are 15 and 12 feet. I am to return them as soon as I can." (*Jesuit Relations*, LXX, 37.)
   "I owe gambille's wife for 200 tacks at 10 sols a hundred: also the same for a pipe with its tongs; she owe me 10 sols for the collection of the blessed bread." (*Ibid.*, 41.)
   "I have received from Madam La Duc 5 partridges of which she owed me 3 less 5 sols." (*Ibid.*, 43.)

These dealings seem to support the statement made
by Cadillac that "the priests while occupied in saving
souls were most thrifty withall."[34]

The mission soon came to own a well-stocked farm,
a store, a sawmill (probably a "hand" mill), a gristmill,
and a blacksmith's shop.   The mission farm furnished
poultry, eggs, butter, beef, and corn to the *habitants.*
To the mission store the small trader brought his
peltry and venison and took in return beads, vermillion, lead, awls, and other goods that he could use in
the Indian trade.   Most of the trade was by barter.
At this store also were kept kettles, tacks, files, steels,
window-glass, knives, awls, lead, pig lead, bullets,
porcelain beads, blankets, vermillion, brandy and Portuguese wine, mitasses, leggings, shirts, hats, porton
thread, Renes thread, cotton, cheese, salt, pork, veni-

"I have lent to Sieur Chapotom, sergeon of this fort,
the sum of 100 livres in raccoon and lynx skins, which he
is to pay me in the month of May, 1743, in similar peltries."   "Taechiaten borrowed from me about 15 castor's [beaver] worth of porcelain beads, both black and
white; he is to repay me in kind or in peltries."   (*Ibid.,*
LXIX, 249).

"I let Chas. Courtois have 40 livres worth of pork and
40 livres worth of brandy.   The same owes me THE
MONEY for 4 livres of hide which Caron delivered to
him for me; also the MONEY for two masses which
Francois Campau asked me to say."   (*Ibid.,* 259.)

Iron was very scarce; nails were sold not by the pound
but by the hundred.   One record in the old account book
illustrates some of the transactions in this useful commodity as follows: "I owe Francois Campau 500 large
nails, at 45 sols a hundred.   I owe the same 800 shingle
nails at ten sols a hundred, also 200 shingle nails at 20
sols;   .   .   .   .   and 300 large and medium sized
nails."   (*Ibid.,* 249.)

34.   Moore, *Northwest Under Three Flags,* 58.

son, beef, cow hides, boards, sawn plank, and other articles.[35]

Goods came from Montreal by way of Lake Ontario and Lake Erie in batteaux and canoes, escorted by one hundred or more soldiers. One trip a year was made. The arrival of the convoy was a great occasion, and served to close one fiscal year and start the next.

The rate of wage for the ordinary laborer seems to have been about one hundred and fifty to one hundred and sixty livres per year.[36] In comparison with the present, few occupations were carried on at the Detroit settlement in the middle of the eighteenth century. Father la Richardie had transactions with Parent, the joiner; Sieur Delatti, the interpreter; Campau, the farmer; Cauvin, the blacksmith; Meloche, the mill operator; Sieur Varte, the armorer; Sieur Roy, the voyageur; and others.[37]

In 1744 the third of the Colonial Wars (King George's) began, and for four years Britain and France

35. *Jesuit Relations*, LXX, passim.
36. The following quotations indicate the rate of wage: "Prisque has reengaged to serve for one year more,—that is to say, until the convoy of 1741 comes,—for the sum of 160 livres in peltries, a shirt, and a pair of matasses [leggings]" "Advanced to Roy for clearing the land, at 20 livres an arpent, 2 minots of grain,—one of French wheat and the same of Indian corn; also a minot and a half of Indian corn; also 7 livres of tallow, at 10 sols a livre [a French pound of twelve ounces], finally 50 livres of flour; also half a minot of wheat, 5 livres." (*Jesuit Relations*, LXIX, 245.)
  "To-day, august the 8, 1741, Pierre Rencontre, a native of La Prairie de la Magdaline, has engaged himself to me to serve for a year, in consideration of the sum of 150 livres, which I am to pay him in peltries at Detroit prices." (*Ibid.*, 247.)
37. *Ibid.*, passim.

were engaged in open hostilities. The fort built at Niagara by the French in 1726, the second at this place, had much to do, perhaps, in checking the advance of the English to the west.[38]

But now the English traders appeared in the Ohio Valley in greater numbers and began to compete more actively for the Indian trade in the territory immediately south of the Great Lakes. It is reported that in 1740 over three hundred crossed the mountains of Pennsylvania with pack-horses loaded with goods for the Indian trade. For several years their center of trade was Pickawillany (Pichtown, Piqua) on the Great Miami River.[39] Here they carried on their trade with the Ohio and Wabash Indians until about 1750, when the post was destroyed by a body of French and Indians from Detroit. Nevertheless they continued to bring their pack-horses over the mountains. A few went as far west as the country of the Miamis.[40] They so undermined French influence that at times the latter nation had hardly a tribe in which it could place confidence.[41] The English were particularly friendly with Nicholas, a Huron chief, who lived near the marshes of Sandusky Bay. The Sandusky Indians were especially insolent to the French and unceasing in their efforts to gain allies for the English.[42]

In 1747 five Frenchmen who were on their way

38. *Doc. Hist., N. Y.*, I, 446 (*Paris Docs.*, VII.)
39. Benton, *J. H. U. Studies*, Series 21, *The Wabash Trade Route*, 28; Winsor, *Narr. and Crit. Hist.*, V, 571; Moore, *Northwest Under Three Flags*, 83.
40. *N. Y. Col. Docs.*, VII, 953.
41. *Ibid.*, X, 247.
42. *Ibid.*, 138.

from White River to Detroit were killed by some of the bands of Nicholas. Shortly afterward a plot to destroy the French at Detroit was discovered.[43] The arrival of the Montreal convoy on September 22, 1747, escorted by about one hundred fifty men, including the merchants and their servants, gave the little colony much peace of mind.[44] The long distance from Montreal, the possibility of delays in the frequent handling of the goods en route, the danger of shipwreck, or of capture by English or Iroquois gave the commandant at Detroit much worry. By good management the Indians were kept in ignorance of the real state of affairs, and by diplomacy and show of force they were kept from making their attack.

In 1748 the Ohio Company was formed, to settle a tract of 500,000 acres on the south side of the Ohio River. One hundred families were to be sent within seven years, and a fort was to be built.[45] The westward advance of the English settlers stirred the officials of New France to promote emigration to Detroit. About 1748 the Government began to offer financial aid to settlers. Any settler was offered gratuitously one spade, one axe, one plough, one large and one small wagon. Advances were to be made for other tools, to be paid for within two years. Seed would be given, to be returned at a third harvest. The settlers would be given a cow and a pig. Women and children were to be supported one year. It was to be understood, however, that any who would "give

43. *Ibid.*, 83, 84, 114.
44. *Ibid.*, 140.
45. Winsor, *Narr. and Crit. Hist.*, V, 10.

themselves up to trade instead of agriculture" should be "deprived of the liberality of the King."[46] These efforts of the Government greatly promoted emigration; but it was complained that some "contented themselves with eating the rations that the King provided. Some of them even by their natural levity have left the country and gone to seek their fortunes elsewhere."[47] About 1749 many emigrants from France came, and the settlement was extended rapidly. The farms of the newcomers soon began to show appearances of neatness and comfort. Orchards were set out, the trees having been brought from France. Currant, apple, pear, cherry, and plum orchards extended for miles along the river front, and the settlement became noted for its excellent fruit.[48]

Governor la Galissonnière in 1750, in his *Memoir on the French Colonies in North America*, again called the attention of the king to the importance of the post and settlement at Detroit. He writes,[49] "This last mentioned place now demands the greatest attention. Did it once contain a farming population of a thousand, 'twould feed and defend all the rest. Throughout the whole interior of Canada it is the best adapted locality for a town where all the trade of the lakes would concentrate; were it provided with a good garrison and surrounded by a goodly number of settlers it would be able to overawe all the Indians of the continent.

---

46. *New Eng. Mag.*, XXIX, 199 (Keep, quoted from Farmer, *Hist. of Detroit*).
47. *Jesuit Relations*, LXIX, 193.
48. *Mag. West. Hist.*, IV, 375 (Campbell).
49. *N. Y. Col. Docs.*, X, 230.

It is sufficient to see its position on the map to under-
stand its utility."

As a result of the endeavors of Governor Galissonnière more settlers came in 1750 and 1751, advances
having been made them by the Government. They
seem presently to have prospered, for in 1759 Bigot,
the Intendant, reported that the settlers of 1750 and
1751 had taken care of themselves and had been selling
wheat since 1754, from which time they had entailed
no expense on the Crown.[50] During the French and
Indian War much of the supplies of the French forces
operating along the Ohio and in Pennsylvania came
from Detroit.[51]

Between 1749 and 1755 the Detroit settlement grew
so rapidly under the Government bounty act that it
was thought necessary to enlarge and strengthen the
fort.[52] This was done especially to prepare Detroit
for defense against the British and their Indian allies
in the struggle that seemed certain soon to come.

The French and Indian War began with the seizure
of the Ohio Company's post at the forks of the Ohio
by a French force in the spring of 1754. This war
was the last of the Colonial Wars and the last armed
struggle between the English and French for the control of the Lakes region and supremacy in North
America. The English won, and Major Rogers was
sent in November, 1760, to receive the surrender of
Detroit.[53] Major Rogers estimated that there were in
Detroit at that time from eighty to one hundred

50. *Ibid.*, 1048.
51. Campbell, *Pol. Hist. Mich.*, 108.
52. *Ibid.*, 107.
53. *Ibid.*, 109.

families, that six hundred persons lived within the palisades, and that the population of the settlement on both sides of the river was two thousand five hundred. Croghan estimated that there were three hundred families in the settlement in 1764, and that within the stockade there were eighty houses.[54]   After a century and a half of occupation, all New France could boast of less than eighty thousand whites, and these were scattered over a vast territory.[55]   Kingsford says that the settled territory ended near the island of Montreal, and that with the exception of a few small hamlets about Fort Frontenac and Fort Niagara, the country was a wilderness to Detroit.   There was not a French Canadian in what constitutes the province of Ontario. From Montreal, a wearisome journey of nearly six hundred miles along the St. Lawrence and through Lakes Ontario and Erie was necessary to reach the next center of civilization at Detroit.   During four or five months of the winter, travel was possible only on snow-shoes.   Some settlers were gathered at the Wabash Portage (later Fort Wayne), Ouiatanon, Vincennes, Kaskaskia, Fort Chartres, Cahokia, Michillimackinac, and Sault Ste. Marie.   These, however, were separated from Detroit by scores and in some cases by hundreds of miles.   "A few thousand souls were gathered (in these places) without schools, removed from the world, nursing their prejudices, forming their convictions with their hopes and their material wants."[56]

54. Hinsdale, *The Old Northwest*, 48.
55. Thwaites, *France in America*, 128.
56. Kingsford, *Hist. of Canada*, V, 1.

A half century of occupation at Detroit had made little impression on the wide-spreading forests. Clearings were confined to lands bordering the streams. Here, for eight miles along the Detroit River, the colonists had erected their little whitewashed cottages so close together as to give the appearance of a nearly continuous village.[57] The east side of the river presented a similar appearance.

Near the center of the settlement stood Fort Frontenac. It formed a parallelogram, with a river frontage of about half a mile, enclosed by a picket fence about twenty-five feet high, with a bastion of light artillery at each corner and a block-house over the main gateway. It contained a barricade, quarters for officers, a council house, and a church, and also enclosed about one hundred small houses.[58]

A single road led along the river following all the windings of the shore, avoiding the marshes and usurping the higher lands. This highway met all the needs of the times for land communication between the parts of the settlement. Only a few Indian trails led into the wilderness, one to the Indian villages on the Saginaw River near its mouth, another westward across the Rouge and Huron rivers beyond the site of Ypsilanti. These were the more important trails.

The river formed the main highway of travel—in summer for the canoe, in winter for the sleigh. Roads could not be built in a heavily wooded country except at great expense and labor, and when built they were

57. Hubbard, *Mem. of a Half Century*, 12; *Am. St. Papers, Pub. Lands*, I, 264.
58. Kingsford, *Hist. of Canada*, 3.

11

out of use for several months each year. Most of the farmers had birch-bark canoes or dugouts. All the houses were built near the river bank in order to be near the main line of communication. The farms were long and narrow, in most cases extending two miles back from the river, but only twenty or twenty-five rods along its course. The need of mutual protection, together with the desire of all settlers to be near the river highways, determined the shape of the farms. With the houses close together, alarms could be sent easily from house to house. The houses were of hewn logs. Nails were hand-made and expensive, consequently few were used. Many parts of the house were held together by wooden pins. For lath, small poles were used.

The house in most cases was surrounded by a garden, enclosed by a whitewashed picket fence. In most yards, near the house was an oven in which the family baking was done. It resembled a large bee-hive, and like the chimney to the house, was made of sticks plastered with clay. The household utensils were simple. Wooden churns, wooden buckets, a few copper kettles and earthen jars made up the larger part of the list. Water was brought from the river in buckets hung from a wooden yoke. In the summer, drinking water was kept cool by pouring it into jars partly buried in the ground. The washing was done in the river. The clothes were dipped in the water, rubbed with soap (probably soft soap), and pounded with a small paddle called a "battois."

Like the houses, the barns were built of logs, but they were constructed much more roughly. Much of

the livestock was unsheltered in winter.   Hubbard says
the ponies "roamed at large beyond the enclosure,
picking up an independent living by browsing.   Even
in the winter they seldom received aid, except what
was stolen from the barns or stacks of their masters."[59]

Behind the barns stretched the fields of corn, wheat,
beans, barley, oats, potatoes, and buckwheat.   A small
part of the farm was devoted to a well-kept orchard,
and the back part commonly was given over to pas-
tures or a wood lot.   Since grain could not be exported profitably, only enough was produced to meet
local needs.[60]

Ferris, speaking of the French farmers at Detroit,
says,[61] "They were extremely ignorant and most miserable cultivators of the soil.   The French Canadian
seemed to have no idea of improvement in agriculture.   They continued to plow, sow, and reap just as
their fathers had done time out of mind.   Whenever
a field had become exhausted it was abandoned.   Instead of striving to enrich the land the people trusted
to the efficacy of prayer and threw the manure into
the river."

Industries were mainly in the "household stage" of
development.   As the settlement increased in size,
however, skilled artisans came.   Before 1749 the quarry
on Stoney Island was worked.   The settlers probably
burned lime.   The waters of the Savoyard River furnished power for gristmills.   One ingenious French-

---

59.   Hubbard, *Mem. of a Half Century*, 124.
60.   *Wis. Hist. Colls.*, VIII, 294; *Mag. West. Hist.*, IV, 376; Hub-
        bard, *Mem. of a Half Century*, 125; *Am. St. Papers, Pub.
        Lands*, I, 264.
61.   Ferris, *States and Terr. of Great West*, 76.

man devised a mill to be run by the current of the Detroit River, but it is said not to have been a success. There were windmills on every point and headland.

An English official says of the educational attainments of the settlers of this time,[62] "They were wholly illiterate, and if we except five or six Canadian farmers . . . there will not be found twenty persons, nor perhaps one-half that number, who have the least pretensions to education or can even write their name or know the letters of a book."

The easy conditions of existence, isolation from the markets of the world, lack of schools, a paternal government, and devotion to the Church helped to develop distinctive characteristics among the people. In many ways the French at the Illinois settlements had the same traits, for their heredity and environment were very similar. Many of the French at Detroit and in the Illinois region were of a different class from most of those at Montreal and Quebec. Many peasants from Normandy and Picardy had come to the inland settlements. At Montreal and Quebec many were of the "*noblesse*;" they were in general dissolute, lazy, and shiftless, and had come to New France to retrieve their fortunes or to win glory that should place them in the court's favor.[63]

---

62. *Mich. Hist. Colls.*, XI, 642 (Robertson).
63. Utley and Cutcheon, *Mich. as Prov., Terr. and State*, I, 313.

CHAPTER V

Detroit Under the British

(1760–1796)

ON September 8, 1760, M. de Vaudreuil, Governor General of Canada, surrendered Montreal to General Amherst. This was the last stronghold of the French. Early in September, 1760, Rogers was sent from Montreal with a force of two hundred men in whale-boats to take possession of Detroit and Michilli-mackinac and to administer the oath of allegiance to the inhabitants.[1] He reached Detroit, November 29, having been nearly three months on the journey. The French commandant, perceiving that resistance would be futile, surrendered the post. Four detachments from Detroit were sent to take Miami on the Maumee River, and Ouiatanon. The next year Michillimack-inac, Sault Ste. Marie, and St. Joseph were occupied by the British.

Many Indian tribes in the Lakes region had assisted the French in the late war, and continued to look on them as their friends. They would have been glad to see the country restored to French control, a hope much entertained by many of the French in the Indian country. In 1763 a plan was communicated to the French Government whereby an insurrection was to

1. *N. Y. Col. Docs.*, VII, 959.

recapture New France; but there were no French officers in America to carry out the plans.[2]

There were several reasons why the Indian friends of the French came to oppose the English. Many things had occurred to spread the belief among the Indians that the English had intended to deprive them of their lands. People from the colony of Connecticut had attempted to force the Indians to grant lands to them on the Susquehanna River. The New Englanders moved there and declared they would maintain possession, and there they remained until the beginning of the French and Indian War.[3] In western Pennsylvania and Virginia the British-American settlers were encroaching on the Indian lands. The Ohio Company of 1748 had made settlements on the Monongahela. Immediately after the French and Indian War, many traders sought leases of land about "the carrying places," whereby they might reap a profit from the traffic in furs which must necessarily pass that way. For years some of the Indian tribes had controlled the transfer of goods at these carrying places, and as Johnson says "this fell severely upon those natives."[4] Public advertisements, the news of which soon circulated among the Indian tribes, appeared concerning a colony which was to settle a large tract of land along the Ohio River. The colony was to march there in two divisions and take and hold the territory by force.[5] The Indians had been quite willing to receive the British when their intercourse was

2. *Ibid.*, X, 1157.
3. *Ibid.*, VII, 962 (Johnson).
4. *Ibid.*, 959.
5. *Ibid.*

merely for trade, but now that the British were coming to take their lands many of the tribes turned against them.

The French had been very liberal in their presents to the Indians, and the Indians had come to expect this as an indication of good will towards them. The British officials when they took over the Indian affairs were ordered to discontinue, or reduce to the smallest amount possible, this costly practice.[6] Many presents sent to the Indians were appropriated by the dishonest officials and sold to the Indians at prices suitable to the officials. This policy, so unlike that of the French, was not at all conducive to the development of friendly relations with the Indians.

Following the acquisition of the Lakes region by the British, many traders entered the district. Johnson reported that "Sundry persons from his Majesty's dominion, induced by favorable accounts and agreeable prospects of advantage" came to engage in Indian trade.[7] These were mostly Dutch, but some English traders also came, to whom Johnson refers with much bitterness in his review of 1767. He cites many instances of the mischief done by these greedy and unscrupulous adventurers, who cheated and deceived the Indians, and made all Englishmen obnoxious to the savages. So detrimental to British interests were these traders that Johnson was sent to Detroit in 1761 and given power to take any measures he saw fit to correct the abuses.[8]

---

6. *Ibid.*, VIII, 56.
7. *Ibid.*, VII, 961.
8. *Ibid.*, 727.

The English were weak in the Lakes region in 1763. No time had elapsed since the Territory had come into British possession, for the settlements to receive any acquisition of people from the colonies on the seaboard. The long time necessary for an expeditionary force to traverse the distance from Montreal to the Lakes region, as shown by the slow movement of Rogers' party, made the position of the British perilous in the extreme.[9]

The pent-up feelings of hostility among the Indians needed little to stir them to action. Their hostility became open when, in 1763, they heard that England and Spain were at war, that a French fleet was waiting at the mouth of the St. Lawrence to assist Spain, and that the French in the Illinois region would send them aid.[10] In all this opposition to the British, the leader was Pontiac, chief of the Ottawas. He was at the head of a loose confederacy of Ottawas, Chippewas, Potawatomis, and other tribes. He had come to the conclusion that, with the extension of English power in the interior, the security of his people was threatened, and, unless the English were checked, he and his people must ultimately be driven from their forest homes. The time to strike, therefore, was before the English became numerous in the Lakes region. The British posts on the frontier were to be attacked secretly and simultaneously in early May 1763. The attempt against Detroit, the most important and most commanding, was to be undertaken by Pontiac himself. Sandusky, St. Joseph, Miami, Ouiatanon, Pres-

9. See Lees, *Journal of John Lees of Quebec, Merchant.*
10. Kingsford, *Hist. of Canada,* V, 11.

que Isle, LeBoeuf, Venango, and Mackinac, all fell to
the savages.   The frontiers were depopulated, the outposts with most of the garrisons destroyed, and the
trade ruined.   All the traders at the captured posts
and much the greater part of those who were on their
way with cargoes were plundered, and many were
murdered.[11]

Detroit alone held out.   But for the communication
with Niagara, kept open by vessels and large fleets of
batteaux on Lake Erie and Detroit River, the garrison
probably would have been obliged to surrender.   Even
with water transportation the line of communication
was kept intact only with difficulty.   On the open lake
the vessels and batteaux were rarely molested, and
escape was easy; in the Detroit River, however, with
its numerous marshy or wooded islands, behind which
the Indians lurked ready for sudden attacks, and its
strong current, against which the oarsmen of the
batteaux must pull and the large vessels be pushed
by the wind, the Indians made their attacks.   At one
time an attempt was made to burn the vessels at
anchor off Detroit by sending fire rafts downstream
by aid of the current.   On one of its trips the Gladwin
was becalmed in the lower Detroit River and escaped
capture only by the strategy of one of the officers.[12]

On May 20, 1763, a convoy with ten batteaux of
provisions and ammunition was attacked within sight
of the fort at Detroit, and eight of the batteaux captured.   About one month later, June 30, the Gladwin
landed fifty men with provisions and ammunition, and

11.   *N. Y. Col, Docs.*, VII, 962 (Johnson).
12.   Moore, *The Northwest Under Three Flags*, 135.

on the 29th of July Captain Dalyell, with two hundred and sixty men in batteaux, reached Detroit and raised the siege.[13]

The lack of success in taking the most important of the posts of the Great Lakes discouraged some of the tribes, and, by October, Pontiac saw the futility of holding out any longer and sued for peace. The ammunition of the Indians was becoming exhausted. If they should continue they would not have enough for their hunting, "which at that season became necessary for their sustenance." That they sued for peace was very fortunate for the garrison at Detroit, for by "reason of many misfortunes in their supplies they would soon have been reduced to the necessity of abandoning the fort."[14] To bring the Indians to complete submission it was suggested that all trade between the British and Indians be prohibited for the summer. By so doing it was believed the Indians would "more effectually feel the necessity" of British friendship for subsistence.[15]

That the French were the real instigators of the hostility of the Indians was believed by all the British officials. Colden states that the Vicar General and St. Luke le Corn were the leading spirits; and that the Indians said they had secured a large supply of ammunition from Lower Canada by way of the Ottawa River in order to avoid all the British posts.[16] Gladwin in a letter to Amherst wrote that the French were at the bottom of the affair "in order to ruin the British

13.   *Ibid.*
14.   *N. Y. Col. Docs.*, VII, 594 (Colden to Earl of Halifax).
15.   *N. Y. Hist. Col. for 1876*, 274 (Colden).
16.   *Ibid.*, 269.

merchants and engross the Indian trade to themselves."[17] The peripheral position of the Lakes region,
far from the seat of strong military power, was undoubtedly a vital factor in enabling the French to
make these attempts at stirring up disaffection.

Pontiac's war showed the necessity of a better control of the posts, and a change of policy towards the
Indians. Croghan was sent to take possession of Illinois. He called a great conference to meet at Detroit.
Here the Indian confederacy was dissolved and the
discontent of the Indians in regard to many questions
was settled.[18]

To quiet the Indians in regard to the land question,
a Royal proclamation was issued in October, 1763,
decreeing that warrants to land beyond the headwaters of the Atlantic rivers were strictly forbidden.
Settlements could not be made thereon unless such
lands were obtained through the proper crown officials.
According to this policy the whole region west of the
Appalachian ranges would be left a wilderness and a
game preserve. The statesmen of the time thought it
was to the interest of the British at home to make
America a sole market for their goods. They were
shortsighted enough to think that it would be more
advantageous to keep the region drained by the St.
Lawrence a wilderness, in which the trade in furs and
peltries would be developed, than to open it up to the
on-coming settlers by buying the land from the Indians
and regulating its settlement. What would be best for
America was not considered. Colonies should be man-

17. Kingsford, *Hist. of Canada*, V, 322.
18. *N. Y. Col. Docs.*, VII, 765–766.

aged for the benefit of the mother country alone.
They feared that settlements here presently would
manufacture their own goods and that English manufacturers accordingly would lose their market. Many
of the whites, however, considered the land decree as
a mere subterfuge. It had little effect in holding back
the frontier along the Ohio, though it did check for a
time the coming of settlers to Detroit and the Lakes
region.

The proclamation noted above had little effect on
the Indians, the sentiment of all the nations with
regard to the British remaining much the same.
Johnston wrote in 1767,[19] "They entertain a very
slender opinion of our faith and security, they are to
the last degree jealous of our designs."

After the siege of Detroit, the British Government
saw that the post there and at Michillimackinac should
be continued and properly supported in order to keep
its hold on the Indian trade. And in 1768 when
orders came from Great Britain to reduce the forces
at all posts in the interior, except at those absolutely
necessary "for public safety in general and for giving
protection and facility to the commerce of [British]
subjects," the posts at Detroit, Michillimackinac, and
Niagara were retained.[20] The post at Detroit, in the
center of Indian commerce, was considered to be "by
far the most important object, not being confined
merely to the commerce of any particular colony, but
embracing every advantage upon which the safety and
extension of Indian commerce depended."[21]

---

19. *Ibid.*, VII, 966.
20. *Ibid.*, VIII, 56.
21. *Ibid.*, VI, 26.

For many years after the British assumed control of the Lakes region the population of Detroit was less than before their conquest. St. Louis was founded as a trading post in the early spring of 1764, by Maxent, LaClede and Company of New Orleans. The Spanish governor at St. Louis made special inducements to the French of Detroit and the Illinois settlements to come to the west side of the river into the territory of the newly founded government. A large number of French accepted the offer, and it was from St. Louis and the near-by settlements that many of the attempts were made to alienate the Indians from the British by offering the red men free commerce and hunting grounds. These attempts were branded by British officials as "pernicious to British [commercial] interests and the safety of the colonies."[22] Many French, however, remained at Detroit, and so the settlement, though controlled by the English, remained for many years essentially French. Accustomed to a paternalistic government, without political and almost without civil rights, most of the French did not find the military government of the British irksome. Detroit was really under the jurisdiction of the Governor General of Canada, but because of the great distance from the seat of government and the complete isolation of the place, the military officers in command exercised civil and political, as well as military supervision.[23]

Until the Quebec Act was passed in 1774, the common law of England was the recognized law of all Canada.[24] But the peaceful French Canadians knew

22. *N. Y. Hist. Col. for 1876*, 274.
23. *Mich. Hist. Colls.*, III, 15 (Walker).
24. Campbell, *Pol. Hist. Mich.*, 132.

little of this and cared less. Under the Quebec Act, the French in America were given many advantages not bestowed on British subjects. The entire country north of the Ohio and east of the Mississippi was incorporated into the Province of Quebec. The laws of Canada as they had been enforced before the conquest were made the rule in civil affairs, while the English law was to be used in criminal cases. Many English interested in the welfare of Detroit objected to this Act, claiming that it "was contrived and really intended to retard settlement in the colony [at Detroit] and discourage Englishmen from going there, by depriving them of the benefits of English law."[25]

The British, in the Lakes region, were interested in little more than securing military defence and the control of the fur trade. There was a general lack of geographic knowledge of the Lakes region on the part of various officers in charge of the province, and they had little idea of the needs and possibilities of the settlement. Sir Guy Carleton, Governor of Canada, was asked before the House of Commons in 1774 if Detroit and Michigan were under his government. He replied, "Detroit is not but Michigan is."[26] Mr. Lymbruner, agent of the Province of Canada, in 1763 said that the obstacles to the growth of Detroit were such that they "must greatly impede the progress of the settlement for years to come."[27]

Turning from these gloomy aspects of the situation, we find that some officials were interested in the settle-

25. *Ibid.*, 154.
26. Cooley, *Michigan*, 76.
27. *Mich. Hist. Colls.*, XXXVIII, 550 (Fuller).

ment, and that some attempts were made to induce British settlers to migrate to the "Straits." It was suggested by Colden in his report of 1764 that Indian lands be purchased at the various posts sufficient for a few farmers to raise provisions for the garrison. Trade under British supervision had been made open and free to all. Licenses were required, but were issued to any one who gave security.[28] Under such freedom, fur-trading became profitable, and many farms were neglected. This made it necessary to carry provisions to the post at Detroit from the settlements in the East, making the support of the garrison a great expense to the Crown. "At present," Colden stated,[30] "there are a sufficient number of new subjects, about four hundred men, at Detroit who have cultivated farms and raise wheat. In order to make them more industrious in farming, they should be prohibited to trade with the Indians or to keep goods or spirituous liquors in the house for trade."

Not until 1768 did the forming of inland colonies receive serious consideration by the English Government. Before that time Detroit was looked upon merely as a post necessary to hold possession of the country and aid in the fur trade. Propositions in 1768 were made to the Lords of Trade to establish and maintain three English colonies in the Interior, one at Detroit, one at the mouth of the Ohio River, and another in the Illinois country. The Lords of Trade replied,[31] "The proposition of forming inland colonies

28. *N. Y. Col. Docs.*, VII, 837.
30. *N. Y. Hist. Col. for 1876*, 381.
31. *N. Y. Col. Docs.*, VI, 27.

in America, is, we humbly conceive, entirely new; it adopts principles in respect to American settlements different from what has hitherto been the policy of this kingdom, and leads to a system which if pursued through all its consequences, is in the present state of this country of great importance." Although nothing definite was done by the Government to bring many people to the West, there was a slow increase in population. After a time the King's proclamation prohibiting further settlement in the interior received no attention whatever. Since Pontiac's War the settlers had not been disturbed by the Indians. Many farmers who had been living in the fort were now dwelling on their estates. Inventories show that domestic animals were abundant. A census taken in 1773, probably an estimate, showed 1,282 whites (soldiers not included) and eighty-five slaves.[32] This is about half the number ascribed to the settlement by Rogers in 1760.

The British Government at the beginning of the American Revolution was represented at Detroit by Henry Hamilton. Most of the French settlers there were loyal to the British. They had never been on intimate relations with the American colonists, and had never known what the enjoyment of civil rights was. They had never experienced the longings for political liberty so characteristic of the Anglo-Saxon. They had not felt that British rule was irksome during the short time they had lived under the jurisdiction of the English King. The Quebec Act, as previously stated,

32. *Mag. West. Hist.*, III, 272.

had given them more liberty than was possessed by the British in the same region.

Next to Quebec and Montreal, Detroit was the most important settlement in all Canada. It commanded all the Upper Lakes. It was visited by most Indians of the Lakes region, and had means of communication with the various Indian tribes not possessed by any other post. It had comparatively easy connection with Quebec and Montreal, and was on the line of communication between the Upper Lakes and these bases of trade; and as long as the Iroquois and the Indians of Ohio remained loyal to the British cause, it was safe from attack by the Americans. Detroit, therefore, was the natural and convenient point from which to start parties to harass the American frontier.

Indian troubles in the region between Detroit and the American frontier had begun even before the opening of the Revolutionary War. In 1774 parties of "land lookers" got in trouble with the tribes in Ohio, and war was begun. The killing of Chief Logan and his family was the immediate cause of savage hostilities. This resulted in Dunmore's War, in which the Indians were defeated.[33] Though a treaty was made, the Indians continued their hostilities. The year 1777 was distinguished for the activities of the Indians. Many Kentucky settlements were attacked. In July Hamilton reported he had sent out fifteen parties from Detroit to raid the American frontier.[34] In 1778 an attack was made on Wheeling by two or three hun-

---

33. Winsor, *Narr. and Crit. Hist.*, VI, 799–813.
34. Cooley, *Michigan*, 92.

13

dred Indians, accompanied by a party of Detroit Rangers carrying British colors.[35]

To put a stop to these depredations, an expedition was planned to take the British posts in the West. Clark saw that as long as the British held Detroit, Vincennes, and Kaskaskia, the American border would be in danger of attack. His success in taking the posts in the Illinois country and holding them until the close of the Revolution, won the whole Northwest to the United States. Detroit was saved from falling into the hands of the Americans at this time only through lack of American soldiers. Many attempts were made on the part of Jefferson, then Governor of Virginia, and Washington to organize an expedition against Detroit. December 28, 1780, Washington wrote to Jefferson as follows:[36] "I have ever been of the opinion that the reduction of the post of Detroit would be the only certain means of giving peace and security to the whole western frontier, and I have constantly kept my eye upon that object; but such has been the reduced state of our Continental forces, and such the low ebb of our funds, especially of late, that I have never had it in my power to make the attempt." Detroit was left to the British only, as Clark stated, "for the want of a few men."

Little reliance can be placed on the figures given in the British colonial reports regarding the population of Detroit between 1763 and 1796, because of lack of system in classifying the data given. The population included farmers, trappers, soldiers, slaves, and In-

35.   Roosevelt, *The Winning of the West*, II, 1.
36.   Sparks, *Writings of Washington*, VI, 341.

dians. The trappers resided in the settlement only a part of the year; sometimes they were counted as residents, and sometimes not. In some reports the soldiers were included among the inhabitants. Some reports included the settlers on both sides of the river, others only those within the palisades. James May, a merchant, gives us a picture of the settlement in 1778. He says that at this time there were sixty houses, mostly one story high, made of logs.[37] The population consisted mostly of French Canadians. There were thirty Scotch, fifteen Irish, and a few English. Twenty of the inhabitants kept retail stores. The settlement was confined mostly to the banks of the river; "there were no settlements nor improvements in any other part of the Territory than that in the immediate vicinity of Detroit." This must have included only what is now the American side of the river. The Indian trade was excellent. There was little Government money to be had, the circulating medium consisting chiefly of paper money issued by the merchants. Permission was given "to strike off as much money each month as a person had property to redeem it that month." Such a currency would be adaptable to a small community, provided it was "called-in" frequently. The goods used in the Indian trade were imported from Montreal, being brought to Detroit by the King's ships free of charge.[38]

In a report of the "Survey of the Settlement of

37. Croghan gave eighty as the number of houses within the stockade for 1764. Thwaites, *Early Western Travels*, I, 152 (Croghan's *Journal*).
38. James May's *Notebook*, quoted in Roberts, *Sketches of the City of the Straits*, 6.

Detroit taken in 1779," there appear to have been
2525 whites, 60 male slaves, and 78 female slaves in
the settlement. This probably included the soldiers
of the garrison.[39]   The census of 1780 shows 2028
whites and 79 male slaves.   More than twelve hundred acres of land were under cultivation.[40]   A census
for 1782, taken under the supervision of Major de
Peyster, July 20, 1782, shows[41]

321 heads of families,	
254 married women,	
72 widows,	(Excluding all those em-
336 young and hired men,	ployed in the King's service and all those
526 boys,	employed in the In-
503 girls,	dian country, say 100.)
78 male slaves,	
101 female slaves,	

```
  1112 horses,
   413 oxen,
   807 cows,
   452 yearlings,
   447 sheep,
  1370 hogs,
 29250 cwt. flour,
  1804 bushels wheat,
   355 bushels corn,
  4075 bushels wheat sown,
   521 acres under corn,
  1849 acres under oats,
```

39.   *Mich. Hist. Colls.*, X, 326.
40.   *Ibid.*, XIII, 53.
41.   About 500 militia in the settlement, August 1, 1782.   *Ibid.*,
       X, 613; XIII, 54.

13770 acres under cultivation,
 3000 bushels potatoes (supposed) in ground,
 1000 barrels cider to be made.

In spite of the seemingly healthy condition of agriculture at the settlement, not enough was raised to supply the needs of garrisons and some of the settlers at the posts, for in 1780 Haldimand suggested that British settlers be located at Detroit, and about the various other posts, to till the soil and furnish the posts with food. "The expediency of this measure," he says, "is sufficiently evinced by the injury the service has and must always suffer from a want of sufficient supply of provisions." Such a plan carried out would likewise "diminish the immense expense and labor attending so difficult and distant transportation." Instructions were given Lieutenant Colonel Bolton to carry the suggestions "into execution at Detroit."[42]

In the preliminary treaty of November 30, 1782, and the final treaty of September 20, 1783, the boundary line between the United States and British North America was placed at the center of the Lakes and connecting waters. This gave Otsego, Niagara, Detroit, and Mackinac to the United States; and in the negotiations that led to the provisions of the treaty of 1783, the statesmanship of America scored over that of the British. Bourinot in his volume on Canada says,[43] "Three of the ablest men in the United States, Franklin, John Adams, and John Jay, succeeded by their

42. *Ibid.*, XIX, 543.
43. Bourinot, *Canada*, 296.

astuteness and persistency in extending the country's limits to the eastern banks of the Mississippi, in spite of the insidious efforts of Vergennes on the part of France to hem in the new nation between the Atlantic and the Appalachians." And Anderson says,[44] "In every instance have the Americans been [so much] our superiors at negotiation that the results of all our treaties with them and all our commercial arrangements in which they were concerned have amounted to the robbery of the British provinces of their legitimate rights and privileges or a sacrifice of our shipping interests and indeed in most cases of both."

Some of the British merchants tried to place all the blame for the loss of the posts on the British negotiators. The Montreal merchants, in a memorial, "deplored with the deepest regret the impolicy, want of local information, and lavish unnecessary concessions" which induced the negotiators of the treaty "to lay at the feet of the United States the most valuable trade in the country."[45]

In July, 1783, Washington sent Baron Steuben to take possession of the various Lake ports. He was refused by Governor General Haldimand, on the ground that he had not yet received orders from the home Government to evacuate the posts. In November, 1783, New York was evacuated by the British, but the British officials on the Lakes still refused to vacate. The retention of the Lake posts was excused on the plea that the United States had failed to keep certain terms of the treaty regarding the Royalists

44.   Anderson, *Importance of the British Colonies in America*, 282.
45.   *Mich. Hist. Colls.*, XXIV, 338.

who had migrated to Canada at the opening of the Revolutionary War; that British merchants were prevented from recovering *bona fide* debts by laws in many States; that British subjects were insulted when they came to take possession of property in the United States under terms of the treaty; and that the English who had received payment for debt had been paid in depreciated currency.[46] One of the chief reasons for the retention of the posts was the desire to retain complete control of the fur trade of the Lakes. James McGill, a Montreal merchant, gave it as his opinion that furs to the value of £180,000 were shipped from the posts of the Lakes region annually, and that furs valued at £100,000 were "brought from the country now within the American line as fixed by the late treaty."[47] Robertson in a hearing at Montreal in October, 1788, said, "By relinquishing the posts of Detroit and Michillimackinac, we necessarily relinquish the sovereignty of that immeasurable chain of water communication formed by the river St. Lawrence and the lakes to the west, and the noble streams of the Ohio and the Mississippi. We give up a country enriched by nature with the finest soil and climate, accomodated with innumerable navigable rivers, and fitted to become by the exertion of industry, under the protection of favorable laws, the noblest and most extensive colony in the world; and as a necessary consequence of this sacrifice we give up most assuredly the fur-trade, we abandon those advantages which as a commercial people are the reward of our present

46. *Ibid.*, XXIV, 403, *Memoir of Montreal Merchants.*
47. *Ibid.*, XI, 462.

possessions. That forts may be constructed and settlements formed on the northeast side of the lakes, I readily agree, but that they could protect the trade (I allude to the fur-trade) when the whole country where furs are produced would be without their command, under other governments and in the hands of a rival and commercial people, I cannot possibly believe or foresee."[48]

In regard to the latter point made by Robertson, Long in his *Travels in North America* fully agrees. "Were the English," he says,[49] "to remain in possession of every part of Canada except the posts, numberless doors would be left open for the Americans to smuggle in their goods; and, in process of time, the illicit trade would supersede the necessity of the exportation of British goods from England to Canada, and the commercial benefits which would arise from the consumption of our manufactured goods would be entirely lost. In that case Canada would be of little benefit to England in a commercial point of view. How far it is worth the expense of retaining, politically considered, is not for me to discuss."

This opinion was not shared by all British men of authority, among whom was James McGill. He did not believe that the Americans could offer serious competition. The British had posts and vessels on the Lakes and were likely to interfere with American traders. The Americans were unaccustomed to the canoe and could not expect to take the trade in the north. The Americans had no market except London

48. *Ibid.*, XI, 639.
49. Thwaites, *Long's Travels in N. A.*, II, 52.

and they were not likely to send their furs there. There was no danger that furs obtained within the British lines would be sold to the Americans, for they could not pay more than could be obtained for them in London. Since the British were able to transport goods to Detroit much cheaper than the Americans could hope to, they, therefore, could afford to sell goods cheaper than the Americans, and give better prices for the furs and peltry.[50] It is very probable that the Americans, at the time McGill wrote, were in no condition to offer strong competition, for the British not only controlled the markets but had developed a well organized system of transportation between Montreal and the Lakes region. The Americans, up to this time, had little occasion to develop a transportation route from the middle Atlantic seaboard to the Great Lakes.

The British lost not only a large area rich in furs, and the profits that arise from the traffic in furs, but also many of the natural facilities for the transportation of the furs; for in the matter of harbors and places of shelter for vessels, the American side of the Great Lakes is much better supplied than the Canadian. "The Bay of Saginaw," writes a British official in 1800, "in itself a sort of lake, has nearly the same advantages as a lake." It has many harbors and a large river (Saginaw River) flowing into it, up which the largest boats in use on the Lakes in the eighteenth century could sail for several miles. Behind Presque Isle, Middle Island, and Thunder Bay Island vessels may find refuge in storms. The Clinton River (called

---

50. *Mich. Hist. Colls.*, XI, 482.

the Huron of Lake St. Clair, in the British period), the Rouge, Huron, Raisin, Maumee and several other rivers of the south shore of Lake Erie were deep enough for several miles in their lower courses to accommodate the small vessels, and many of the river harbors admitted the largest of the British and American boats. "To counteract these advantages," the writer comments, "recourse must be had to art and expense on our [the British] part."[51]

Repeated attempts were made by the Americans to get possession of the posts, but without success. In 1784 Haldimand, Governor of Quebec, stated that he had thought it his duty to oppose the delivery of the posts to the Americans until his Majesty's orders for the same were received. He believed commercial motives lay behind the attempts of the Americans; for, he writes,[52] "the uncommon returns of furs this year [1784] from the upper country have increased the anxiety of the Americans to become masters of it."

Perhaps the Americans were most anxious about the prevention of Indian depredations on the frontier. It was agreed by all that as long as the British retained these posts, the Americans could not hope for success against the Indians; for from these posts, and especially Detroit, they obtained their supplies of arms and ammunition. One Congressman, in a speech at Washington, stated that until these posts were in the poses-

---

51. *Ibid.*, XV, 12–14. At that time only one harbor on the north shore of Lake Erie was used, and little was known of the harbor facilities on the eastern shore of Lake Huron.
52. *Ibid.*, XX, 269 (*Haldimand Papers*).

sion of the United States it would be in vain to send armies into the wilderness.[53]

The encouragement given Royalists to migrate to Detroit at the close of the American Revolution suggests that the British had deeper reasons than the question of debts due to British subjects. Could they induce a large body of loyal British subjects to settle in the Lakes region, they might hold it by reason of occupation. In 1783 it was proposed to offer to the Loyalists of Virginia an asylum at Detroit. Governor Haldimand wrote to Lieutenant General Hay concerning the proposition as follows.[54] "In regard to persons from Virginia or Maryland who may propose themselves as settlers in the neighborhood of Detroit, great attention must be paid not to receive any whose political characters will not bear the nicest scrutiny . . . none shall be permitted to settle but those of approved loyalty . . . and they must take the oath of allegiance." In 1794 fifty families from near Niagara and twenty-six families from near Fort Pitt sent in their names in expectation of having lands granted them.[55] A letter from Detroit, dated June 2, 1785, to Sir John Johnson, announces,[56] "Several persons arrived yesterday from the neighborhood of Pittsburg, seeking an asylum from the persecution they are subjected to in the States, on account of their principles during the late war, and they say that many others in the same predicament are about to remove to this place or some other within the protection of

---

53. Benton, *Debates*, I, 342.
54. *Mich. Hist. Colls.*, XI, 410.
55. *Ibid.*, XI, 350, 452.
56. *Ibid.*, XI, 452.

His Majesty's government when encouragement will be given them." Land was provided for many Loyalists in part of what is now Ontario. The encouragement given to Loyalists to settle at Detroit, the stringent measures to keep out the Americans, and the retention of the posts, all points to the conclusion that the British never intended to comply with the articles of the treaty of 1783.

Shortly after the French surrender at Montreal to the English, traders began to take over the fur trade of the Lakes region. Alexander Henry, who later became a leader in the trade, was at Michillimackinac when the Indians by strategy captured that post in 1763. Many traders of "good family but narrow means came to America from the Highlands of Scotland."[57] By the time the Americans took possession of Detroit, the Scotch merchants far outnumbered all others. After the close of Pontiac's war the trade increased greatly. Goods for the Indian trade and furs and peltry constituted the bulk of the commerce of Canada. The collecting grounds for furs gradually became exhausted in the Michigan region, and the center of the business shifted to the region north of Lake Superior, with Grand Portage as a distributing center. Hamilton, in 1780, reported[58] that "one year with another [the trade] produces to Great Britain returns to the amount of £200,000 Sterling in furs, one-half from Michillimackinac and dependencies and one-half from the Lower Provinces, Detroit, [and] Niagara." It took about one hundred canoes, each manned

---

57.   Campbell, *Pol. Hist. of Mich.*, 136.
58.   *Mich. Hist. Colls.*, X, 272; XIX, 508.

by eight men, to handle the goods to and from Montreal. Many families were supported by making the goods into clothing for the savages. Henry says,[59] "From Michillimackinac some of the furs passed into the hands of the English traders at Albany, advantage being taken of ships sailing to Niagara, but the leading spirits at Grand Portage were Canadians and their furs reached Montreal by the Ottawa River. The English of New York were hampered by lack of skilled labor. But the Canadian traders found, ready at hand, the French Canadians, the best canoe and bush man in the world." Many of the canoemen were engaged also in other occupations. The canoes of the Northwest Company were usually the first to leave Montreal in the spring, and the men returned early "to harvest the crops and do other needful service."[60]

For twenty years after the conquest of Canada, until after the close of the American Revolution, the fur trade was mostly in the hands of independent companies. In 1784 the Northwest Company was founded by leading fur merchants of Montreal in order to reduce competition among the traders of Montreal, and the better to compete with the Hudson Bay Company. The success of the Northwest Company soon excited the jealousy of the other merchants at Montreal and Quebec, and shortly three different companies were rivalling each other in the purchase of furs, which, as Liancourt puts it,[61] "could not but prove highly detrimental to themselves and advantageous to the In-

59. Henry, *Travels in Canada*, 20 (Editor's note).
60. *Mich. Hist. Colls.*, XIX, 509.
61. Liancourt, *Travels Through U. S. of N. A.*, I, 326.

dians." The Northwest Company, being more opulent than the rest, used its wealth to crush the others. The leaders at last became sensible of the necessity of uniting, and, in 1787 and again in 1805, combinations were made whereby the different fur-traders operating in and about the valley of the St. Lawrence all united with the Northwest Company.[62] This left two great companies to compete for the fur trade of northeast North America, the Hudson Bay Company and the Northwest Company. The region for collecting furs was northwest of Lake Superior, with Mackinac as the great rendezvous. The Northwest Company, being a powerful monopoly, with the chief offices at the seat of the Canadian Government, secured concession after concession from that government. To facilitate the transportation of furs on Lake Superior, it received permission to build a small vessel at Detroit, which was taken around the rapids at Sault Ste. Marie. On Lakes Huron, Erie, and Ontario, it had the precedence in the use of the Government vessels because of the shortness of the season and the great distance to the collecting grounds.[63]

The activity of the Northwest Company in the region northwest of Lake Superior, which was territory claimed by the Hudson Bay Company, caused the latter to change its time-long methods of collecting furs. Formerly, the Indians carried their furs to the various factories on Hudson Bay, but now the company sent its agents in some cases a thousand miles into the interior after the furs.[64] The treatment of the

62. Bryce, *Hist. of Hudson Bay Co.*, 149, 199.
63. *Ibid.*, 117.
64. Liancourt, *Travels Through U. S. of N. A.*, I, 326.

Indians by the Northwest Company was highly com-
mendable; and such treatment, as Johnson long before
predicted, won their friendship. Anderson says of the
managers of the Northwest Company,[65] "In all their
intercourse with the Indians they have not only
avoided quarrels but have universally commanded the
respect of that uncultivated and war-like people both
for themselves and for the British in general. It is
evident then that it is to their merchantile establishment that we are endebted for the cordial co-operation
of the Indians against the Americans." Their great
success in this direction, their wealth, and the strong
influence of their members in governmental affairs
enabled them to control the policy of the Government
in all matters regarding the trade of the Upper Country. It was chiefly for the preservation of their commercial interests in the fur trade that the British
officials evolved excuse after excuse to delay the fulfill-
ment of the articles of the Definitive Treaty of 1783.

About 1787, when there was some agitation on the
part of the British officials to restore the posts to the
Americans, the Montreal merchants claimed that the
Upper Country owed a balance to the Quebec Province and the town of Montreal—a sum not far short
of three hundred thousand pounds Sterling—and that
the returns for at least two years were necessary to
offset the balance. It therefore was necessary to keep
possession of the posts; for were they to be given up,
"a very large proportion of this sum would be lost, to
the hurt of the nation and the ruin of a number of
individuals." They also declared that every article

65. Anderson, *Importance of the British Colonies in Amer.*, 243.

of merchandise employed in the trade was of British manufacture, and that every increase in trade tended to benefit the parent state, "a circumstance deserving the most careful consideration."[66]   When the insistence of the Americans became so great that the British officials seemed about to yield, and when Jay was sent to negotiate a new treaty, the Northwest Company sent memorial after memorial to the Canadian officials in an endeavor to save to itself the control of the fur trade of the Lakes Region.

In December, 1790, the fur-traders sent a memorial claiming that, "not having since the treaty of 1783 encountered any difficulty from the subjects of the American States, they had been led to extend the Indian trade farther and farther to the west."   By reason of this extension their property in that country had increased greatly, any sudden check to their commercial pursuits would occasion their ruin, "and therefore not less than five years would be sufficient for them fully to collect and withdraw their property." If "at the end of that period it would seem fit to cede the posts," they desired that "the Indian country should be considered neutral ground free and open for purpose of trade."[67]

In December, 1791, the fur-traders made proposals to the Canadian Government as to boundaries between the United States and British America. They suggested several lines for boundaries which might be proposed in turn to the United States. First, they suggested a boundary along the Allegheny

---

66.   *Mich. Hist. Colls.*, XI, 473.
67.   *Ibid.*, XXIV, 163–164.

River to the Ohio River. A second proposal was to
place the boundary from Presque Isle to the French
River and down this to the Ohio.⁶⁸   If this could not
be obtained, then the government should strive to get
a line up the Maumee River from Lake Erie and down
the Wabash to the Ohio.   If a greater sacrifice of territory seemed necessary they said the only other natural
boundary was along the water communication to Lake
Huron, through the Straits of Mackinac, then along
the eastern shore of Lake Michigan and around the
head of the lake to the Chicago River. As a fifth line
they suggested the Fox-Wisconsin trade route, and
"if all must be abandoned and still further concessions made under the idea of the spirit of the late
treaty," then as a last resort the Government should
try to secure "a line from Sault Ste. Marie's river to
the Apostle Islands, then ascending a river which falls
into Lake Superior, across from the headwaters of this
to the Chippewa River, and down this to the Mis-

---

68.   The memorial reads, "A line up Lake Erie to Rayago R, up
this to its source, then crossing to the nearest water course
which falls into the Ohio."   The Rayago R. does not appear on any of the maps nor in any of the descriptions
the writer has seen.   (See Evans' map of 1755, corrected by Pownall to 1776, in Moore, *Northwest Under
Three Flags*, 80; Bonnecamp's map, 1730–1750, in Winsor, *Narr. and Crit. Hist.*, V, 569; British map of 1792, en-
dorsed by Simcoe, in *Mich. Hist. Colls.*, XXIV, 383.   All
large rivers along south shore of Lake Erie are named in
this map; British map, 1793, in *Ibid.*, XXIV, 617; Hulbert, *Historic Highways*, VII, 153, 160; Croghan's *Journal*,
in Thwaites, *Early Western Travels*, I).   After the Cha-
taqua Portage, the Presque Isle Portage was the most
important along the south shore of Lake Erie.   The
writer takes the liberty of considering the second line as
passing from Presque Isle to the French River.
15

issippi." This surely should satisfy the stipulations
of the treaty.[69] All these proposed boundary lines
were along well traveled trade routes, which routes, as
previously shown,[70] are geographically determined.[71]

In April 1792, in their petition to the Canadian
Government, they stated that it was "indispensibly
necessary to the security of the northwest trade that
the Grand Portage be left in British hands, or at any
rate that it be considered an open highway equally
belonging to both parties."[72] They gave it as their
opinion that a communication with the Mississippi
certainly was intended by the treaty. "It is a matter
of immense magnitude," they wrote,[73] "that we should
obtain a practicable communication with the Mississippi not only on account of a participation of the
Indian trade on this side but as an opening to us of
new sources of it on the west side of that river, which
is capable of being explored and greatly extended."

These merchants were so influential that the British
Government, in spite of the enormous expense incident to the civil and military administration of Upper
Canada, was induced to make every possible effort to
retain the posts. The total sum included in civil and
military expenses and in presents given the Indians,
frequently amounted for Upper Canada alone, to one
hundred thousand pounds Sterling yearly. Liancourt
states that nearly two-thirds of this sum was paid to
Indians, Indian agents, under-agents, interpreters, and

69. *Mich. Hist. Colls.*, XXIV, 340.
70. Chapter I.
71. See map.
72. *Mich. Hist. Colls.*, XXIV, 406.
73. *Ibid.*, 405.

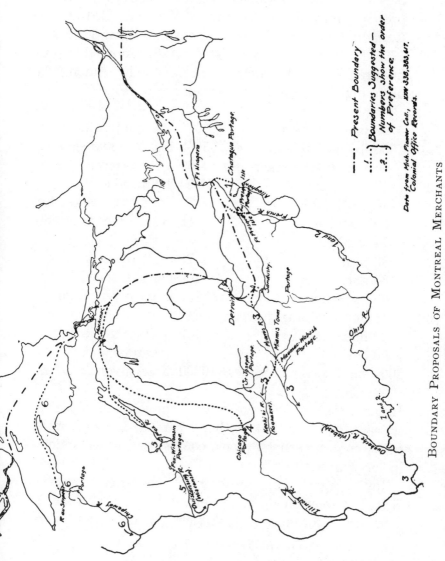

BOUNDARY PROPOSALS OF MONTREAL MERCHANTS

others.[74]   The enormous expense incurred in giving
presents may be judged from the lists filed in the
Canadian Government documents between 1770 and
1796.[75]   In a requisition list for 1782, more than one
hundred kinds of articles were included.   Among the
more important and more expensive were,

4700 pairs blankets,	10000 lbs. gunpowder,
1500 lbs. vermillion,	35000 lbs. ball and shot,
96 doz. silk handker-	10000 lbs. tobacco,
chiefs,	300 lbs. beads,
450 felt hats,	12 nests of brass kettles,
100 castor hats,	15 nests of copper ket-
94 saddles,	tles,
250 bridles,	20 nests of tin kettles,
120 guns,	100 pairs of shoes,
300 tomahawks,	400 large silver gorgets,
45 doz. scalping knives,	440 large silver moons,
300 half axes,	400 large silver arm
1000 ear bobs,	bands, and
5000 small silver broaches,	10000 large silver broaches.

In addition, there were various articles of clothing,
scissors, fish nets, hooks, hoes, thread, buttons, awls,
belts, spurs, feathers, pipes, combs, and other articles
in large quantities.[76]

Jay's negotiations resulted in the order from the
British Government to evacuate the posts, June 2,
1796, in accordance with which general orders were

74.   Liancourt, *Travels Through U. S. of N. A.*, I, 243.
75.   *Mich. Hist. Colls.*, X, 496, 632; XII, 16, 84.
76.   *Ibid.*, X, 632.

sent to Niagara, Detroit, Fort Miami, and Michilli-mackinac.[77] The British flag was lowered, and the American flag for the first time waved over these posts.

Before the final surrender of the posts and after the victory of General Wayne had put an end to private dealings with Indians for lands, British merchants who were largely interested in the fur trade, and thus reluctant to see American control established, made an attempt to get possession of the Southern Peninsula of Michigan by purchase. They endeavored to convince Congress that the Indians really had not been pacified by Wayne, and that nothing but the influence of the Canadian fur merchants ever could bring them to terms and make the fur trade of the Lakes region safe under American rule; their scheme, however, was blocked in Congress. They next tried to gain their point by private dealings with the Indians. A council was held at Detroit, July 1, 1795, with the Michigan Indians, from whom they obtained an area equal to twelve or fourteen counties, for about twenty-five pounds Sterling. Their land claim was not recognized by the United States Government. Had their schemes succeeded, the settlement of the Detroit region would have been delayed for many years.[78]

Throughout the thirteen years that the British held these posts in violation of the treaty of 1783, the frontier of America was subject to repeated ravages from the Indians. In 1790 statistics were collected which showed that since 1783 no less than 1520 men, women, and children in Kentucky alone had been

77. *Ibid.*, XXV, 121 (Colonial Records).
78. *Ibid.*, VIII, 407, 619.

killed by the Indians or carried off into captivity.[79]
Much of the hostility of the Indians was due to the
encroachment of the American settlers into the Ohio
Valley. The Indians insisted that the Ohio River
should be the boundary line between themselves and
the American settlements. In this contention they
were supported by the British officials and the fur
merchants of Montreal, but without success. Treaties
were forced upon them by the Americans in 1784,
1785, and 1786, whereby large areas of land north of
the Ohio were ceded and the Indians slowly forced
westward.[80] "Look back," they said to the United
States commissioners in 1793, "and view the lands
from whence we have been driven to this spot. We
can retreat no farther, because the country behind
hardly affords food for the present inhabitants, and we
have therefore resolved to leave our bones in this
small space to which we are now consigned. We shall
agree that you mean us justice if you agree that the
Ohio shall remain the boundary between us."[81] This,
however, was not possible. The American settlers,
moving westward in an ever swelling tide, could not
be checked; they were land hungry, seeking cheap
lands and new homes. The question of justice to the
Indians was no argument to them. They all had at
heart, if they did not express it, the feeling, so well
put by James Robinson at Nashville in 1781:[82] "These
rich and beautiful lands were not designed to be given

79. Cooley, *Michigan*, 112.
80. Winsor, *Narr. and Crit. Hist.*, VI, 605, 608, 610, 650, 706;
     VII, 446, 453.
81. Stone, *Life of Brant* (quoted by Cooley, *Michigan*, 113).
82. Phelan, *Tennessee*, 130.

up to the savages and wild beasts." Not a few officials of the American Government realized that in
many cases selfish motives, "the roving disposition of
the frontier settlers," and not pressing economic needs,
drove the settlers to the new lands; and that if the
settlements were kept "more nearly connected with
the old settlements, they would be more useful to the
community at large and would not so frequently
involve [the country] in unnecessary and expensive
wars with the Indians." Within the "proper boundaries" of the United States there was sufficient land
where "they might for years to come cultivate the
soil in peace neither invaded nor invading."[83] The
policy of restricting the frontier was not adopted by
the United States Government until many years
later.

The continual encroachment of the settlers kept the
Indians hostile. Finally, in June 1794, General Wayne
was sent with an army over the road along which St.
Clair had led his forces to defeat, and in August 1794
defeated the Indians within sight of the fort that the
British had just constructed on United States territory in direct violation of the treaty of 1783. This
victory completely cowed the Indians, and they were
ready to make peace on any terms.[84]

The Treaty of Greenville (August 3, 1795) gave the
Americans, among various posts and areas of land, the
post of Detroit and all land north, west, and south
between "the river Rosine [Raisin] on the south and

83. Benton, *Debates*, I, 342.
84. Winsor, *Narr. and Crit. Hist.*, VII, 453; Lee, *A Hist. of North
Amer.*, II, 276 (Thomas); VII, 295 (Moran); VIII, 124,
141 (Geer).

Lake St. Clair on the north, and westward to a line
the general course whereof shall be six miles distant
from the west end of Lake Erie and Detroit River."[85]
Wayne's victory gave the United States undisputed
control of the Indians of the Northwest, and the
British now had no excuse to retain the posts. They
made one more attempt, however, to delay the transfer of the posts. Lord Dorchester, April 23, 1796,
thought that the provisions of the treaty made with
the Indians did not agree with the provisions of the
Definitive Treaty of 1783. His Majesty's minister at
Philadelphia accordingly was instructed "to require an
explanation on this subject. . . . Till, therefore,
the same shall be satisfactorily terminated," he wrote,[86]
"I shall delay the surrender of the posts." The matter was speedily adjusted and the posts turned over to
the Americans.

In 1788 it was computed that four thousand people
were dependent on Detroit, including the settlers at
the River Raisin, thirty miles below, where there were
about forty Canadians. Robertson, at a hearing at
Quebec, reported that he did not remember the number of farms in the Detroit region, but they extended
along the west bank of the Detroit River a computed
distance of four miles below and twelve above the
town, and about the same distances on the opposite
bank. There was also a new settlement at the mouth
of the Huron River, near Lake Erie.[87]

Among the public buildings in the Detroit settle-

85. *Amer. State Papers, Indian Affairs*, I, 562; *Mich. Hist. Colls.*,
        XXVI, 279.
86. *Mich. Hist. Colls.*, XXV, 116.
87. *Ibid.*, XI, 636.

ment were two French churches (the English had no church at this time in the Upper Country), a barracks, a Government house, a council house, and a navy dock-yard and necessary buildings.[88]

The lax methods of agriculture, long practiced by the French, had reduced greatly the fertility of the soil, but it still produced good yields of wheat, corn, peas, and oats. Hemp was grown in many places, likewise hops, and it was said that flax also was found to succeed. There was an abundance of timber for the building of houses and ships. Fine red cedar was cut on the islands of Lake Erie and used for the construction of vessels. No attempt was made to export timber.[89]

During the latter part of the period of British occupancy, the population at Detroit became more varied in its composition than heretofore. The committee of Quakers that visited the settlement in 1793 reported that there was a mixed population of French, German, English, Irish, Scotch, Yankee, Indians, and Negro.[90] Their characterization of the French Canadians is much like that of previous travelers and observers. They report that the French in general were poor economists, and lived in miserable houses; yet they "appeared grand abroad." They were told that the French lived much on fish and wild game, and that they were "superstitiously religious, going to mass more than two hundred days in the year." It was expected by many that the English and German farmers would change for the better the manner of

88. *Ibid.*, 638.
89. *Ibid.*, 635.
90. *Ibid.*, XVII, 284.

living and the customs in the places, but they found the old French settlers were influenced but little by contact with the new settlers.[91]   As necessity required, more land was cleared near Detroit.   By 1793 most of the neighboring region was improved, with houses, orchards, and gardens.   The back part of most of the farms was cleared, and abounded in grass on which numerous cattle thrived.   Butter, cheese, beef, and veal were plentiful.[92]

When compared with the American frontier settlements, however, the growth of the Detroit region was slow.   Jacob Lindley, one of the committee, reported that the progress of population was obstructed "not only by the wet, unhealthy state of the country, but also by other circumstances, viz., one-seventh of the country was reserved for the crown; one-seventh for the Episcopal clergy; and, according to an old law of Canada, all real estate was required to be sold at the chapel door at stated time and one-ninth of the proceeds of the land so sold went to the Roman Church."[93] According to McNiff, an early surveyor at Detroit, there were other causes that retarded the taking up of land by settlers.   According to the methods of survey along the navigable lakes and rivers, only two farm lots could be granted in the front, two in the second, and twelve in the third concession.   The people desired to be near the water front, and would not settle on the back concessions because of the expense and labor of making roads.[94]   Still another cause was the almost

91.   *Ibid.*, 594.
92.   *Ibid.*, 593.
93.   *Ibid.*, 609.
94.   *Ibid.*, XXIV, 85.

unlimited claims made to land by various people by virtue of Indian grants.[95] Between 1763 and 1796 about four hundred families settled on grants of land obtained from the Indians. In 1765 Patrick Sinclair purchased four thousand acres lying along the St. Clair River. Between 1771 and 1777 four thousand acres below Detroit were purchased by Canadians. In 1776 Pièrre Combe bought four thousand acres on the La Rivière a l'Ecorse and settled ten families on them. William Macomb in the same year purchased Grosse Isle and Stoney Island, six thousand acres, and established ten tenants on them.[96] A Canadian in 1779 purchased of the Indians eight thousand acres on Otter Creek. In 1780 Joseph Benac secured six thousand acres on La Creque (Sandy Creek), on which he settled in 1792. In the same year thirty-eight small tracts were settled along the River Rouge and at Point au Tremble. In 1782 nineteen families settled on land adjacent to that of Sinclair, and the next year twenty families settled near by. In 1784 one hundred and twenty-one families settled on the River Raisin, and in 1786 Francois Pepin purchased three thousand acres on the La Rivière aux Roches. Other tracts were taken up.[97] McNiff says that "when settlers came from the states, instead of being placed on waste lands of the town they are told that such and such tracts were the property of individuals by virtue of purchase of the Indians, and that there was no land." Many returned to the States or bought land at an enormous price, paying one thousand pounds for one hundred acres.

95. *Ibid.*
96. Stoney Island (see map, Chapter VII).
97. *Amer. State Papers, Public Lands*, I, 265.

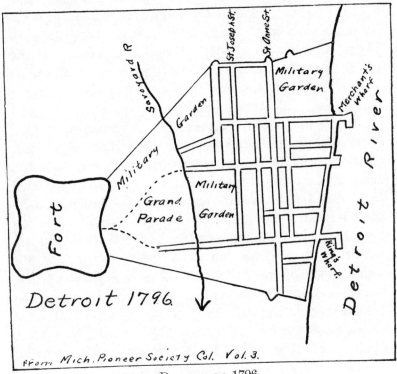

DETROIT IN 1796
(*From Mich. Pioneer Collection, III.*)

Many were kept out by the reports spread at Fort Pitt that there was no free land in Michigan, that all was claimed by a few individuals.[98]

By 1796 much of the land in southeastern Michigan along the rivers and lakes had been taken up from the Indians. The nucleus of this settled region was the palisaded fort at Detroit, with dwellings thickly placed about. Within six or eight miles of the fort to the north and south, the narrow farms of the original French grants made the settlement compact, but beyond this the houses were more and more isolated. Scott's *Gazetteer* describes Detroit in 1797 as being "the largest and best fortified town in the Northwest Territory." "It consists," it says,[99] "of several paralleled streets, which are crossed by others at right angles. The streets are narrow and in the rainy season, dirty. . . . The town is about one thousand feet in length but scarcely that in breadth. It is picketed around, having block houses at each gate. It has four gates, two leading to the wharves, which are erected along the river. . . . There belongs to this place, one brig and twelve schooners. The schooners are larger than those trading between the Atlantic ports and the West Indies. The vessels here are employed in trading between Fort Erie, Michillimackinac, and Detroit." Burnet described Detroit in 1796 as follows.[100] "It had been for many years the depot of the fur-trade of the northwest and the residence of a large number of English and Scotch merchants, who are engaged in it;

98.   *Mich. Hist. Colls.*, XXIV, 85.
99.   Scott's *Gazetteer*, article "Detroit."
100. Ross and Catlin, *Landmarks of Wayne County and Detroit*, 257.

and it was of course a place of great business. The greater part of the merchants engaged in the fur trade both Scotch and English had their domiciles in Detroit."

Isaac Weld, an Irish traveler, visited the Lakes region in his tour of the United States and Canada in 1795 and 1796. He was a keen observer and a truthful writer. He describes the settlement as follows:[101] "Detroit contains three .hundred houses and is the largest town in the western country. It stands contiguous to the river on the top of the banks, which are here about twenty feet high. At the bottom of them there are very extensive wharfs for the accommodation of the shipping, built of wood. The town consists of several streets that run parallel to the river, which are intersected by others at right angles. They are all narrow, and not being paved are dirty in the extreme whenever it happens to rain. . . . About two-thirds of the inhabitants are French and the greater part of the people on the river above and below the town are of the same description. The farmers are mostly engaged in trade and they all appear to be much on an equality. Detroit is a place of very considerable trade; there are no less than twelve trading vessels belonging to it, brigs, sloops, and schooners, of from fifty to one hundred tons burden each. The inland water in this quarter is very extensive, Lake Erie, three hundred miles in length, being open to vessels belonging to the port, on the one side, and lakes Michigan and Huron on the other

101.   Ross and Catlin, *Landmarks of Wayne County and Detroit*, 255–256; Campbell, *Pol. Hist. of Mich.*, 213.

. . . not to speak of Lake St. Clair and Detroit River. . . . The stores and shops of the town are well furnished and you may buy fine cloth, linens, . . . and every article of wearing apparel as good in their kind, and on nearly as reasonable terms, as . . . in New York or Philadelphia."

CHAPTER VI

THE AMERICANS ASSUME CONTROL

(1796–1818)

WHEN it became evident that the American Government was to come into possession of the region so long held by the British, the British subjects at Detroit were brought face to face with the problem of choosing the nation to which they should become attached in the future. "The ties which bind human wards to the Government, laws, and character to which they had been accustomed" were strong enough to induce many to move to Canada and remain British subjects. A large number of the wealthy English and Scotch merchants removed, and purchased land just across the Detroit River. Many British, however, remained at Detroit. In either case their action was guided quite largely by the belief that they would secure liberal treatment in regard to gifts of land from the respective Governments they selected. The British Government was very liberal in granting lands to any who would move to Canada. A gratuitous concession of two hundred acres awaited all who would choose to settle in British territory.[1]

General Simcoe imagined that this would induce all the British to leave Detroit. It seems, however, that

1. *Amer. State Papers, Miscellaneous*, I, 461.

the grants of land made by the British did not include in all cases a right in perpetuity from the first, and the property sooner or later would be given to the persons making the right use of the lands. Under such conditions it seemed certain to some observers that if "the conduct of the American Government towards these families should be such as the interests of America dictate," there would be little probability that any great number would leave "their long cultivated estates merely for the desire of living under the British dominion." Unfortunately for the good of the Detroit settlement at this time, the disposal of lands to settlers about Detroit was much delayed by the complexity of titles to the lands. The United States Government appointed commissions to inquire into titles of lands at Detroit. It was found that there were "nearly thirteen good titles" in the whole of southeastern Michigan, and that the remainder "abounded in defects which must be deemed fatal."[2]

The titles to lands in southeastern Michigan were found to be of six classes:

(1). Grants made by the French governors of Canada and confirmed by the King.

(2). Those made in same way but not confirmed by the King.

(3). Those obtained through occupancy by permission of the French commanding officer. In these there were no confirmations and no grants, but the title rested on long and undisturbed possession.

(4). Those held as the result of occupancy during French regime. No permission to occupy the lands

2. *Ibid.*

17

had been granted but there had been long and undisturbed possession.

(5). A large number obtained in a similar way while the region was under the British.

(6). Those held by virtue of occupancy since the region had been under the control of the United States.

The treatment of such a perplexing problem required considerable foresight on the part of the officials who had it in charge.   The anxiety and confusion of persons interested in the growth of Detroit was especially great.   Sandwich and Amherstburg which had grown up on the eastern side of the Detroit River, struggled hard to attract settlers from American territory.   The critical moment came when fire in 1805 wiped out every house in the American settlement within an hour.   There was great danger that the superiority of the Canadian towns would be established, and when once established it would take years for Detroit to regain its position.[3]

Both Governor Hull and Chief Justice Woodward saw the necessity of quick action, and visited Washington.   They prevailed upon Congress to grant homesteads to the fire sufferers, and an Act was passed giving the Governor and the Chief Justice power to lay out a new town and convey a lot therein to any person over seventeen years of age who at the time of the fire had owned or inhabited a house in the old town.[4] Thus harmony was established and assurance given that the land question at Detroit would be settled to

3.   *Ibid.*, I, 264.
4.   Cooley, *Michigan*, 153.

the satisfaction of all, and the supremacy of Detroit among the settlements on the "Straits" was assured.[5] The question of titles of land outside Detroit was settled shortly afterward, the people securing quit-claim deeds to the land they occupied. They were thus encouraged to make lasting improvements.

American emigration to southeastern Michigan began shortly after 1796. Previous to this time the British had taken special pains to discourage the coming of American settlers; but with the withdrawal of the British forces and the settling of the complex question of land titles, the region was open for settlement, and every year saw a few Americans straggling in. The movement, however, did not reach any great magnitude until after 1818, which marked the beginning of steam navigation on Lake Erie and the opening of a land office in Detroit.[6] In 1802 Detroit was given a certain dignity by being incorporated as a "town," and the same year there was established a regular mail with Washington. These innovations were doubtless the result of the enterprise of the newcomers from the East. Gradually the old methods and prejudices of the French were moulded under the influence of American methods, but the process was slow for American settlers were few in number. In 1805 the population of Detroit numbered only 551.[7] There were still in 1810 so many French in the Territory unable to read English that they petitioned to have the laws of the United States published in the French language.[8]

5. *Amer. State Papers, Miscellaneous*, I, 264.
6. See Chapter VIII.
7. *Mich. Hist. Colls.*, XXXVII, 450.
8. *Amer. State Papers, Miscellaneous*, I, 71.

In 1810 the .total population of Michigan Territory numbered only 4762.[9] About 750 of these were. inhabitants of Detroit.[10] A few families were gathered about the rapids at Sault Ste. Marie and at Mackinac, the remainder were in southeastern Michigan, scattered between Lake St. Clair and the northern boundary of Ohio. During the War of 1812, there were few settlers between the River Raisin and the rapids of the Maumee River, many having fled to Ohio and Detroit.[11]

In Ohio, settlements were confined to the southern and eastern portions of the State. The south shore of Lake Erie in 1810 was settled as far west as Cleveland.[12] To the west, however, between Cleveland and Sandusky there were in 1812 only a few scattered settlers along the lake shore. These were separated from settlers in southeastern Michigan by large areas of forests and swamps. The line of communication between Detroit and these settlements was across Lake Erie or through a roadless wilderness. Moreover, to reach Detroit from these settlements by land, a long detour about the west end of Lake Erie and the Great Black Swamp was necessary.[13] From Fort Malden, at the mouth of the Detroit River, whither the British had withdrawn after the evacuation of Detroit, hostile forces could easily be sent across the river to cut off any weakly guarded supply train on the over-

9. *Twelfth Census*, I, *Population*, Part I, 24, 25.
10. Variously estimated at 150 to 200 houses. *Niles' Weekly Reg.*, IV, 47; Heriot, *Travels Through Canada*, 24.
11. *Niles' Weekly Reg.*, IV, 47 (Mar. 20, 1813).
12. See maps.
13. For description and origin of this swamp see Chapter XI.

land journey from Ohio. A strong force was, therefore, necessary to keep open the line of land communication. At that time little agriculture was practiced
in the settlements about Detroit, and the people and
garrison had to depend on Ohio for most of their supplies. The most logical line of communication between
the settled part of the United States and this outpost
was by the Detroit River and Lake Erie. The nation
that could control Lake Erie could also control Detroit

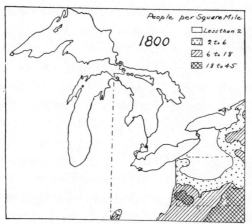

DISTRIBUTION OF POPULATION IN THE
LAKES REGION IN 1800
(*From Statistical Atlas, Ninth Census, XVI.*)

and Michigan. The Americans had few vessels on the
Lakes at this time and Fort Malden at the entrance to
Detroit River completely controlled all water traffic
between Lake Erie and Detroit. The mouth of the
river is about four miles wide, but the only navigable
channel for the larger vessels lay between Bois Blanc

Island and the Canadian mainland.[14]   All large vessels were obliged, therefore, to pass almost under the guns of Fort Malden.

In the one hundred and more years that the Europeans had been interested in the commerce of the Detroit region, little had been done to bring the region into closer communication with the Atlantic. The isolation of the region from the Atlantic seaboard in the first decade of the nineteenth century is well shown by the difficulties met by Governor Hull and family in the journey to Detroit to take up the duties of his office.   From Albany their route was up the Mohawk River, over the Rome Portage to the Otsego River, thence to Lake Ontario.   This Lake they traversed in small boats.   From the site of Lewiston to Buffalo the route was overland.   At Buffalo they found a vessel which carried them, in the course of four or five days, to Detroit.   Before they reached the Lakes, civilization had been left behind; on every hand was the wilderness.[15]   But distance was not the worst factor in the isolation of Detroit.   To the north was a nation not at all friendly to the United States.   In the wilderness all about were bands of Indians still friendly to the British, still trading with Montreal fur companies, still receiving presents annually from the British military authorities at Malden.   The Indians were, in reality, pensioners of the English Government; if war should break out, they were sure to take the part of their old ally.   Hull, in his report to the Secretary of

14. See map, Chapter VII. (Improvements have been made lately).
15. *Amer. State Papers, Ind. Affairs*, I, 746.

War in 1807, wrote that the British had previously had the Indians in conference, and that they informed them that a war would soon take place between the British and the Americans and asked them to take up the hatchet against the Americans.[16] He plainly saw that in the event of war the little settlement on the very frontier of civilization would be encompassed by foes so numerous and bloodthirsty that they might overwhelm it and destroy it before assistance could be rendered, as the British were in full control of Lake Erie. In 1808, in a communication to Congress, Hull again pointed out the exposed condition of the settlement and suggested the building of armed vessels on the Lakes to protect the communication to the Territory. In 1811 for a third time he told the Secretary of War that the Canadian forces in the region numbered twenty to one of the Americans, again pointed out the isolated position of the post, the lack of sufficient communication, and the need of an armed force on Lake Erie. Early in 1812 Governor Hull was given command of a body of soldiers, mainly Ohio militia, which was to be sent to Detroit to strengthen the garrison there. They left Dayton, Ohio, on May 25, and, constructing their road as they went, reached the rapids of the Maumee the latter part of June. As there were no adequate roads between the Maumee River and Detroit, Hull loaded his baggage, hospital stores, and invalids in a small vessel and sent it on from the Rapids towards Detroit. The next day Hull received word that war had been declared between Great Britain and the United States on the 18th of

16. *Ibid.*, I, 746.

the preceding month.   When the vessel reached the
mouth of the Detroit River, it was fired on by the
British and easily taken.   Hull now rushed his army
on to Detroit by forced marches.[17]

On July 16 (1812) the armed brig Caledonia, carrying two hundred and fifty traders and agents of the
Northwest Fur Company, and five hundred Indians,
appeared before Fort Mackinac (Michillimackinac).[18]
The little garrison of fifty-seven men was unprepared
for a siege, and surrendered.   The possession of Mackinac by the British at this time was of the highest
importance to them, as by controlling Mackinac they
controlled the majority of the Lake Indians.   Nothing
but a show of force on the part of the Americans up
to this time had held the Indians neutral; now they,
one and all, joined the British.   The Northwest Company, in participating in the expedition, was actuated
undoubtedly by the desire to control again the fur
trade centered at Mackinac.

The consequences of the isolated position of Detroit
soon began to develop.   A detachment of soldiers,
having been sent to Monroe to guard a company of
Ohio troops which was bringing provisions to the fort
at Detroit, was cut off and routed by a force sent out
from Fort Malden.   A second force, this time of six
hundred men, was sent out to bring in a provision
train.   This likewise was routed.   In a few days a third
was sent; but before this one returned a force of
British appeared before the fort and Hull surrendered.
Obviously, the chief reasons for the fall of Detroit

17. *Niles' Weekly Reg.*, II, 359.
18. Campbell, *Pol. Hist. of Mich.*, 283.

were its isolated position and the failure of the United States Government to provide an adequate force for its preservation.

Malden, likewise, suffered from its isolated position when war was carried to Canadian soil. It, too, was cut off from land communication with the base of supplies to the east, by hundreds of miles of forests. Provisions for the troops had to be brought from the lower St. Lawrence, and much even from far-away England. The natural and only available line of communication was by lake and river. Proctor, therefore, watched with anxiety the result of the battle between the two fleets on Lake Erie. Nearly every pound of his provisions had to be supplied from the East, and could be delivered only under the convoy of a strong naval force. He had with him one thousand men and three thousand five hundred Indians, all of whom had to be fed from British stores. He delayed the attack on Perry, because his vessels were poorly manned and reinforcements from Montreal were expected to arrive at any time, until the British forces were "so perfectly destitute of provisions . . . that there was not a day's flour in store and the crews of the squadron . . . were on half an allowance of many things, and when that was done there was no more."[19] The defeat of the British fleet on Lake Erie was the death knell to the possession of Detroit by the British, for the Americans now controlled the line of communication to the East by way of the Lakes.

The difficulties experienced by both the Americans

19. *Mich. Hist. Colls.*, XXV, 525 (*Colonial Office Papers*).

and the British in fitting out their fleets in preparation for the battle that should decide the control of Lake Erie bespoke the isolation of the Northwest at that time. Proctor wrote to Prevost, August 26, 1813, as follows,[20] "Your excellency speaks of seamen valorous and well disciplined. Except I believe the twenty-five whom Captain Barclay brought with him, there is none of that description on this lake, at least on board his Majesty's vessels. Men are scarce enough and of a miserable description to work the vessels, some of which cannot be used for want of hands." Meanwhile, Perry at Presque Isle was being retarded by the seeming neglect of the Navy Department. People grew weary looking to Lake Erie for the sailing of the flotilla. *Niles' Weekly Register* of July 31, 1813, reports,[21] "The anchors for the sloops of war, it appears, left Philadelphia only last week and an Erie paper of June 16 tells us that Capt. Perry has received information of the seamen being on their way to man his little fleet. The British have launched a new vessel at Malden to carry twenty-four guns and it would seem as if our flotilla was to wait until she is ready."

During the War of 1812, the Northwest Company rendered the British Government valuable service. A fleet of canoes, two vessels, and many men were held in readiness on the Upper Lakes to aid the British forces should the occasion arise. It has already been noted that nearly the entire force that captured Mackinac was composed of Indians and employes of the

---

20.   *Ibid.*, XV, 360.
21.   *Niles' Weekly Reg.*, IV, 354.

Northwest Company. According to the terms of Jay's treaty, the British fur merchants were to be allowed to trade in the Lakes region until 1812. The Northwest Company had extended its operations far to the west of Lake Michigan,[22] collecting furs in the Missouri Territory to the west of St. Louis.[23] Most of the furs from this latter region were carried to Montreal by way of the Straits of Mackinac. The capture of Mackinac, therefore, gave it full control of the fur trade over a vast region, and left it in the enjoyment of it during the War of 1812. Naturally at the close of the war the company was reluctant to see such a prize slip from its grasp. On March 28, 1815, McGillivray, a member of the Northwest Company, wrote General Prevost,[24] "On negotiating a commercial treaty with the United States, as they have much to ask for, it is still in the power of the [British] government to make some stipulations by which British subjects may be permitted to carry on trade from Canada to the Mississippi and Missouri by way of Michillimackinac and for relieving the said trade from at least a part of the present duties which amount to about thirty per cent on all goods imported into the United States and the Indians country, and which of itself if continued would operate as a prohibition." In a memorial sent to the officials on April 20, 1815, two of the leading Montreal fur merchants asked the British official in charge to please "reconsider the question of delivery of the posts of Michillimackinac to the Ameri-

---

22. See Chapter V.
23. *Mich. Hist. Colls.*, XXV, 217.
24. *Ibid.*, XVI, 67 (*Ottawa Papers*).

cans, unless he has instructions from his Majesty's Government positively directing the speedy delivery of the *Post of Michillimackinac by name* and not by general words conveying implications that the said Post is intended." Then they show how two articles in the treaty may be construed so as to retain the post until the commissioners who were to decide the location of the boundary at various places had acted.[25]

This may explain why the British delayed the delivery of the posts in 1815, so that Colonel Butler, June 1, 1815, was compelled to write to the officer at Michillimackinac.[26] "More than three months have elapsed," he wrote, "since the ratification of the treaty of Ghent and altough every disposition on the part of the United States has been manifest for executing that treaty still the delivery has been delayed and avoided on the part of the government of Great Britain."

In 1809 John Jacob Astor and others succeeded in getting the American Fur Company incorporated by the New York Legislature, with a capital of $1,000,000. The growth of the company at first was slow, for there were several fur-trading companies in the field. It was not until after 1815, after the United States Congress had passed an Act (in winter of 1815-16) excluding foreign companies from engaging in the fur trade in the United States, and after John Jacob Astor had by financial deals merged some of the other companies with his own, that the American Fur Company came to be the leading company of the interior of the United States. Michillimackinac was the center of the trade

25.   *Ibid.*, XVI, 77, 78 (*Ottawa Papers*).
26.   *Ibid.*, XVI, 123.

for the Lakes region. Here Astor brought together many clerks and voyageurs from Montreal, long schooled in the services of the British companies. The goods used by the American Fur Company were bought in England and came by way of Montreal. From Montreal they were transported in batteaux to the Lakes region, mostly by way of the Ottawa route.[27] The company continued for a long time to import most of the goods used in the Indian trade from England. Buckingham states that this was the case as late as 1841. "The blankets," he says,[28] "cannot be manufactured to suit the Indian's taste as well anywhere else." The American Fur Company established posts at many points along the shores of the Lakes, one of the more important posts being at Detroit. Many of the towns of Michigan situated at the mouths of rivers and near the Lakes owe their early start to the fur trade of this period.

Detroit, in the early decades of its history as an American town, was unfortunate in being visited by both fire and war. The fire of 1805, as previously stated, destroyed every house in the town. During the war the whole region was pillaged, houses burned, and crops destroyed. The financial resources of the settlers were exhausted. The economic conditions of all frontier towns are of such a nature that such calamities bear particularly hard upon the sufferers. The people of the frontier have always been the debtor class. Money has been borrowed to start various enterprises. The frontiersman is self-reliant, over-con_

27. *Ibid.*, VI, 343 (Lieut. Kelton, U. S. Army).
28. Buckingham, *The Eastern and Western States of America*, III, 356.

fident. He has high aspirations. His outlook upon
the problems and the destiny of the town or the region
with which he happens to be associated is broad.
Guided by such feelings and aspirations he is likely
to build big, often the superstructure is too large for
the foundation to support. Should adversity come,
the results are inevitable. Obligations cannot be met,
banks fail, a financial crisis follows. Over-investment
and land speculation on the frontier have been contributing causes to several financial panics. Money
has generally been a scarce commodity on the frontier.
What is borrowed goes back to the manufacturing
East to pay for tools, machinery, and other equip-
ments. At the close of the War of 1812 most of the
settlers had no money with which to buy the necessities of life. Business and trade were slack. It took
several years to overcome the effect of the war.

The unsettled condition of the country during the
War of 1812 also deterred emigration. Another potent
cause for the slow migration was the spread of information that the Detroit region was unhealthful. Dwight,
ex-President of Yàle University, reported in his travels
in 1804 that the situation of Detroit was unhealthful,
"not from the waters of the lakes but from the marshes
which line its borders."[29] About 1815 the United
States surveyors reported as their deliberate judgment
"that Michigan was unfit for cultivation, an irreclaim-
able marsh and wilderness, which was not worth the
expense of a survey."[30]

It took many years to break down the prejudices

29. Dwight, *Travels in New England and New York*, IV, 78, 79.
30. *Mich. Hist. Colls.*, V, 24, 535. Full discussion in Chapter
     VII.

created by such reports.   The belief was countenanced
by geographers and the writers of the emigrant *Guides*
of the time.   The travelers Blowe, Evans, and Darby,
did much to break down the prejudices by spreading
glowing accounts of the region in New England and
other parts of the East.   John Farmer's maps of 1826
and later, much in demand by people seeking homes
in the Interior, showed more nearly than ever before
the true conditions of the land in Michigan and the
Detroit region.   The Territorial newspapers of these
years also did a wonderful work in directing the migration, the Detroit *Gazette* being one of the more active
of such agents.

The opening of a United States land office in Detroit
in 1818 in response to a petition from the citizens of
the town did much to bring in settlers.[31]   The first
sales took place in September of that year.

In 1818 Evans, who visited the town, reported that
the trade was considerable and was rapidly increasing.
The city had begun to transact business over a wide
area.   Besides the business carried on with the different parts of the Territory and with the Indians of
the neighborhood, it had trade intercourse with the
upper parts of New York, Pennsylvania, Ohio, and
also with the inhabitants of Canada.   "In the summer
season," he says,[32] "there is a considerable concourse of
strangers from the Eastern States by way of Buffalo.
These furnish considerable sums as passage money to
the ship owners.   In the spring of the year the Indians

31.   *Niles' Weekly Reg.*, XIV, 151 (Apr. 25, 1818).
32.   Thwaites, *Early Western Travels*, VII, 222; *Wis. Hist. Colls.*,
         VIII, 211 (Gen. Ellis's Recollections).

resort thither to dispose of their furs and to make their
purchases. Indeed a considerable part of the trade
is in furs, many being brought from Chicago and
Green Bay." Darby says,[33] "Detroit is now a place
of extensive commerce with all the attributes of a
seaport; it forms the uniting link between the vast
interior, inhabited as yet by savages, and the civilized
Atlantic seaboard." Daniel Blowe reported the town
as "a place of considerable trade." Previous to his
visit several wooden piers to accommodate the growing Lake traffic had been built, one of which was one
hundred and forty feet long and could accommodate
a vessel of four hundred tons burden. He was sur-
prised at the size and number of the stores in the
town, and the large stock of goods which they carried.
One could buy cloth, linen, and every article of wearing apparel as good in their kind as in New York
and nearly as cheap.[34] A newspaper had been established, called the Detroit *Gazette*. *Niles' Weekly Register* in 1818 comments on this as follows:[35] "It is
pleasant to observe the progress of improvement. We
have before us a very neat newspaper published at
Detroit, a striking evidence of the business transacted
at that important station, which, no doubt will soon
be a large city." The town contained 770 inhabitants, and the district (Southeast Michigan), 2,227.
Besides the fort there were many public buildings,
including a bank, a council house, a jail, a printing
office, a warehouse, and the Roman Catholic Church.[36]

33.   Darby, *Tour from New York to Detroit*, 190.
34.   Blowe, *Emigrant's Directory*, 696.
35.   *Niles' Weekly Reg.*, XII, 339 (Feb. 28, 1818).
36.   *Worcester's Gazetteer*, article "Detroit."

Detroit was beginning to be a market for the products of the various river settlements. Farmers as far away as the Raïsin River sent their produce to Detroit. The prices current at that time were, flour $12 per barrel, pork $26 per barrel, corn and wheat $2 per bushel, and other things in proportion.[37] These prices were high for the frontier and bespoke an active market and a limited supply. Evans says there was great need of Yankee farmers, for with their knowledge of agriculture and their industry they could in a very short time acquire a handsome estate. The French had no ambition to excel in "this honorable and profitable calling." The region was not yet self-supporting. Large sums were paid for produce which had to be transported across the Lake from New York, Pennsylvania, and Ohio.[38]

There were few roads as yet, and facilities for land transportation were not well developed for many years. The Lakes were not much used, and travelers were obliged to take advantage of the occasional schooner from Buffalo westward. Darby, in his visit to Detroit in 1818, had a tedious voyage of eleven days on a schooner from Buffalo.[39] A writer in *Niles' Weekly Register* in 1833 says, "The few sailboats then [1818] on these waters were supposed to have done well if they made the trip from Detroit to the foot of the lake in the time that is now required for a packet to make the trip to Liverpool.[40]

The separation by both water and land from the

37. *Niles' Weekly Reg.*, XIII, 96 (Oct. 4, 1817).
38. Thwaites, *Early Western Travels*, VIII, 219 (Evans).
39. Darby, *Tour from N. Y. to Detroit*, 172.
40. *Niles' Weekly Reg.*, XLIV, 95.

19

East had an important bearing on the route of trade
and the social, political, and commercial affiliations of
the city. The population of the city at the beginning
of the American period was distinctly foreign, and the
isolation made it difficult to ⌐ ⌐rcome these tendencies.
It was politically and commercially an isolated community with few ties of interest to unite it with "the
sovereignty of which it formed a part." Darby, writing about 1818, says,[41] "Much of the association is
formed with and a great part of the trade is yet towards a foreign state."

The frontier character of Detroit was well reflected
in the primitive conditions of life, in trade, commerce,
and customs. Much of the trade was still by barter.
A merchant "selling out" in 1820 demanded that his
debtors settle in cash, beans, or flour. Prices for produce were high. Small industries were practiced even
by those who were employed in public service and in
the professions. The postmaster cultivated seeds for
sale. There were few or no public utilities. Drinking
water was carried from the river in pails or barrels.
For fire protection barrels with handles were used to
carry water. French conservatism stood in the way
of progress. The French would not sell their property
for lots and they opposed the widening of streets.[42]
The value of real estate was very low. Belle Isle was
bought in 1817 by Mr. Campau for $5000 and "paid
for in bank notes of a broken Ohio bank." This price
was considered large for that time. "Indeed," as one
writer puts it,[43] "to pay seven dollars for a lot by the

41.   Darby, *Tour from N. Y. to Detroit*, 188.
42.   *Mich. Hist. Colls.*, XXXVIII, 553.
43.   *Ibid.*, XVIII, 646.

side of the town hall was considered the act of a luna-
tic." Many Indians still lived in the vicinity of Detroit as late as 1818, and the streets were generally
crowded with Indians of one tribe or another, who
collected there to sell their furs and skins. The town
was still enclosed in a palisaded fence, and at night
all Indians who were not admitted into private houses
and remained there quietly were driven out of town.[44]

As is common in small communities, democracy
reigned supreme, common interests uniting the people
in a big village family. Mrs. Palmer says,[45] "Our
society in those days consisted of army officers, their
wives, the old French families, and the few Americans.
We were all friends, Indians, soldiers, French, and
Americans. All sociable and interested in each other."
Evans remarks,[46] "In Detroit there is much good
society; and hospitality is a characteristic trait in the
character of the people." The few Americans were
gradually changing the aspect of things. A new era
was dawning. Schools were being established. A
lyceum was in existence. The Territorial Legislature
in 1817 passed a bill, framed by Augustus B. Woodward, creating the University of Michigan, and the
buildings were now already nearing completion.[47] The
commercial relations of Detroit began to be with the
East rather than with Montreal and Quebec. Much
was hoped of the Erie Canal, upon which excavation
was begun in 1817. The arrival of the steamboat in
1818, and the completion of the Erie Canal in 1825,

44. Daniel Blowe, *Emigrant's Directory*, 896.
45. *Mich. Hist. Colls.*, XIV, 537.
46. Thwaites, *Early Western Travels*, VIII, 218 (Evans).
47. *Mich. Hist. Colls.*, XXXIX, 131.

ushered in a period of active emigration. Slowly the savage tribes retired, and civilized man felled the forests and established his home over the wide area to the west of Detroit, which scarce a dozen years before was believed an impassable morass. About 1818 serious attempts were made to penetrate the region to the west and northwest of Detroit with a view to settlement. During both the French and English regimes, settlers desiring land for tillage were few, and settlements were confined for the most part to the lands immediately along the streams. Little was known of the interior of the State, except the narrow areas along the few streams, as the Clinton, Rouge, and Huron rivers, or along the Indian trails. The swampy nature of the land in the spring and fall,[48] and the dense vegetation of the summer, served to check travel and exploration in this region. It is stated that many Americans who had gathered at Detroit after the War of 1812, for the purpose of taking up land to the west of the town, became disheartened by the prospects and left to seek homes elsewhere.[49] In the early fall of 1818 a party of Americans at Detroit "resolved to penetrate into the interior and ascertain whether the country was or was not habitable." The party followed the road then being built by the United States soldiers, which had reached a point about four miles from the Detroit River. From there they were led by an Indian guide along a trail to the site of Pontiac. The report which these men brought back "electrified the hearts of the Ameri-

48. See Chapter VII.
49. *Mich. Hist. Colls.*, III, 565.

cans in Detroit and utterly astonished the French."[50]
"The first settlement formed in the interior was by
a few families who had moved into the Territory from
Upper Canada and ascended what was then called the
Upper Huron (now the Clinton) River, some ten or
fifteen miles from its mouth.   They settled on an 'oak
opening' and raised an excellent crop of wheat.   They
had been there a year or more before it was generally
known in Detroit, and the fact was regarded as a
remarkable instance of enterprise and hardihood."[51]
The next settlement made was Pontiac.   From this
time on the tide of immigration steadily increased from
year to year.[52]

About 1818 it was the alleged intention of the Government to reduce the military forces at the fort at
Detroit.   The Americans at Detroit took active measures to prevent such action.   They maintained that
the strategic position of Detroit was too important to
warrant the withdrawal of the troops.   At that time
the sores caused by the late war were not yet healed.
It was still a fundamental belief of the people of Michigan that the Canadians and British in general were
enemies to be treated with suspicion.   A strong force
at Detroit was necessary to protect the town and
shield settlers coming to Michigan from possible British
intervention and Indian hostility.   Such a force would
tend to hold the Indians of Michigan in check in time
of war, for Detroit controlled the route the Indians
took to Amherstburg (Fort Malden) for their presents

50.   *Ibid*. (Thomas Drake).
51.   *Ibid*., II, 38; XV, 12.
52.   *Niles' Weekly Reg*., XLV, 2.

and the disposal of some of their furs. Detroit, with
Fort Gratiot (built in 1814), shared with Fort Malden
the command of the "Straits" from Lake Erie to Lake
Huron. It exercised, therefore, some control of the
Upper Lakes country and the trade of the region to
the west of the Lakes. In the event of war Detroit
was a strategic point from which to invade Canada,
for it could command the roads which led to Sandwich and Amherstburg, and thus could control a large
part of the settled area of western Canada.[53] The
War Department was persuaded fully of the importance of the post, and a garrison was maintained until
1827, when the fort was razed.

---

53. *Amer. State Papers, Miscellaneous*, II, 597.

CHAPTER VII

Local Geography of the Detroit Region

WITH the exploration and settlement of the region to the west of the Detroit River and Lakes St. Clair and Erie, the physiographic features, soil, and mineral resources of Southern Michigan began to be factors in the development of Detroit. For more than one hundred years this region had furnished the people little more than logs for buildings and vessels; fuel; fresh meat, and furs for clothing and for commerce. The French and English, however, used the region in the way their economic needs demanded. With the coming of the American settlers a different economic order was instituted and a different demand was made on the resources. The new demand was for land on which crops could be raised, homes built, and industries developed. To the American settlers, the forests were obstructions to be removed by the easiest and quickest means to get to the soil. Incidentally, however, the forests furnished logs for lumber, rails for fences and fuel for the household and for a time for the industries. It is only in recent decades that the mineral resources are being exploited actively.

Detroit is located on the eastern edge of a till plain on which there are low recessional moraines of clay and sand, boulder belts, beach ridges, sand bars and spits, and low dunes. This plain extends from Lake Huron southwestward about the west end of Lake

Erie into northwestern Ohio, and is really a portion
of the plains that almost everywhere border the Great
Lakes.   In southeastern Michigan this plain is from
sixteen to twenty-five or more miles wide, and has a
very gentle slope to the southeastward.   It is singularly devoid of any marked elevations or depressions.   The western border of the plain (lowest Maumee Beach) lies about 770 feet above sea level and the
eastern border about 590 feet, making an average slope
of about eight or nine feet per mile.[1]   Most of the
eastern portion of the plain has a slope of only three
to five feet per mile.

This till plain is bordered on the west by a pronounced
ridge, the Defiance Moraine, of rough topography, the
knolls of which vary in altitude from 840 to 900 feet,
or from 70 to 120 feet above the western margins of
the plain.   The eastern slope of this morainic ridge is
much steeper than the western.   To avoid the high
knolls and the heavy grades many of the trans-state
railroads, radiating from Detroit, find it advantageous to cross this morainic belt along the larger river
valleys.

To the west of the Defiance Moraine over most of
the southern half of the Southern Peninsula of Michigan, the topography consists of till plains, outwash
plains, kames, eskers, valley trains, and low recessional moraines.

In a strip along the eastern margin of this broad
area, in the Interlobate Morainic region, the knob and
kettle type of topography dominates.   The numerous
depressions are occupied by small lakes.   These lakes

---

1.   Data from Sherzer, *Geology of Wayne Co.*, 75.

regulate the flow of water in the streams that receive their overflow, serve as fishing grounds, and the higher lands on their borders offer excellent sites for summer homes.

The dominant topographic features of the plains are the result of glaciation. During a large part of the glacial period, southeastern Michigan lay beneath hundreds, if not thousands, of feet of ice. Over much of the area a thick deposit of boulder clay accumulated (ground moraine), the upper part of which was leveled to a plain, hence the term till plain. The boulder clay is soft when wet, and has a tendency to flow and creep under its own weight. The Michigan Rock Salt Company was forced to abandon one of its shafts at Ecorse in 1902 because of the flowage of the glacial clay at a depth of eighty feet. The engineers of the Detroit River Tunnel were forced to make the bore of the tunnel more nearly circular than at first planned in order to enable the casing of the tunnel to stand the pressure resulting from the creep of the clay.[2] There are in many places lenticular masses of quick-sand and gravel within the clay, which when charged with water likewise have a tendency to flow, making deep piling for tall buildings necessary. In the construction of the Penobscot Building at Detroit layers of quick-sand were encountered and the company was put to an extra expense of $20,000 to secure a safe foundation. Such lenses of sand and gravel are not in all cases unmitigated evils, for they furnish a copious supply of water, when tapped, for domestic purposes.[3]

2. *Ibid.*, 51, 279.
3. *Ibid.*, 294.

The retreat of the ice front down the slope of the plain was slow, undoubtedly, and lakes, the waters of which came from the melting glacier, were formed between the ice front and the higher lands to the west and northwest. The shore lines of these lakes are characterized by beach ridges, bars, and spits of gravel and sand. The beach ridges have, roughly, a northeast-southwest trend and are much used for roads, sites for farm buildings, churches, and cemeteries, and furnish gravel for metaled and concrete roads. Some of these beach ridges occur within the city limits of Detroit.[4]

These minor topographic features lie on the till plain, the surface of which seems to have been little modified by the waves and currents of the lakes, and on which little lacustrine material was deposited. At a few places lake clay was deposited in shallow depressions on the till plain. This clay is generally free from pebbles and is well suited to the making of brick and tile. It is sticky and tenacious, but when wet is easily

---

4.   It may be interesting to note that these ridges in the immediate vicinity of the settlement were observed as early as 1793 by Jacob Lindley (his visit noted in a previous chapter) and called lake ridges. "This day," he says, "I walked out a mile into the woods where my further excursion was prevented by swamps, bogs, and marshes. In my route I found stones in diverse places such as are found upon borders of lakes. The land is generally almost sunk under water. My mind was strongly impressed with the belief that lakes Erie, St. Clair, Huron, and Michigan were once united and that tens of thousands of acres of low adjacent lands were all overflowed. By the breaking and wearing away of the great falls * * the water has been lowered to the present surface." (*Mich. Hist. Colls.*, XVII, 609). The true explanation of these ridges did not become a part of physiographic science until seventy or more years later.

worked to a soft plastic mass. It is to the lake clay more than to the glacial clay that the wretched condition of the roads leading out of Detroit from the early decades of American occupation down to very recent times is to be ascribed. These poor roads were, no doubt, a factor in suggesting the attempts made in the early thirties to develop a water route between Detroit and Rawsonville and Ypsilanti on the Huron River, and the recent great expenditures in the construction of macadamized and cement roads centering at Detroit. No doubt they have been no small factor in swelling the passenger mileage of the several interurban railroads centering at Detroit.

During the retreat of the ice, little deposition of rock material took place and what moraines were deposited are largely "water-laid," of slight relief and gentle slopes. The most important of these moraines, for this study, is the Detroit Moraine, a broad clay ridge on which Detroit stands. This moraine was deposited by the Lake St. Clair Lobe when the ice front stood at Detroit. Belle Isle and the low clay ridge on which Windsor is built are portions of the same moraine. The highest part of this ridge in Detroit is on Woodward Avenue near the city limits, where the sand-covered surface reaches an altitude of 636 to 638 feet, or about 62 feet above the river level. This ridge slopes rather gradually northeast, southeast, and southwest.[5] Most of the surface of the ground in the business section of Detroit has an elevation of about 600 feet above sea level. The top of the bluff on which Fort Pontchartrain stood, within a

5. Sherzer, *Geol. of Wayne Co.*, 83.

few rods of the present river bank, likewise has an elevation of about 600 feet. This is the highest land to be found anywhere near the west bank of the Detroit River.[6] There are only two other areas near the west bank of the Detroit River that approach this elevation, a sandy ridge on which Fort Wayne is built and another at Wyandotte and Ford, each of which is slightly more than 580 feet in altitude. The need of a post to control the Indian trade of the Upper Lakes and trade and travel along the Maumee-Wabash route determined that Detroit should be located somewhere on the Detroit River, but a recessional moraine determined its particular location on that river.

There are several boulder belts on the plains, but the concentration is not great enough to render the land unsuited for agriculture. The boulders of these belts, unlike the boulders of the ground moraine, are chiefly of crystalline rock and are much used for building purposes.

Although the water-laid moraines, beach ridges, bars, spits, and boulder belts are minor topographic features, they are of sufficient elevation to influence greatly the drainage of the plain. Because of the flatness of the plain, the whole area is poorly drained, and before the forests were cut off, allowing winds and sunshine to increase evaporation, and before the construction of ditches and drains, it was covered with numerous shallow ponds and marshes for four or more months each year. The swamps afforded breeding places for the mosquito which we now know is the cause of the prevalence of the malaria and ague for which this Detroit

6. Note 600′ contour on map.

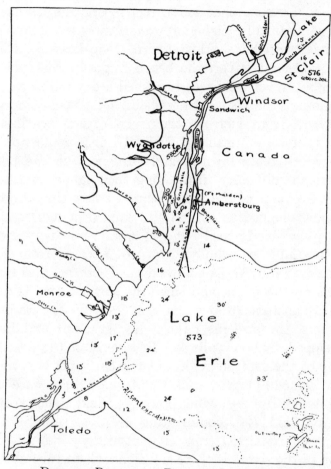

DETROIT RIVER AND PART OF LAKE ERIE

Showing contours and altitudes near the Detroit River, depths of water, and main ship channels in the Detroit River. The channel to the west of Bois Blanc island is the Livingstone Channel.

region was notorious.   It was this poorly drained plain, that had to be crossed in going to the west and north- west of Detroit, that led travelers and surveyors to believe that all Michigan was a morass.   In going northeastward or southwestward along Lake St. Clair or the Detroit River, the beach ridges of the ancient lakes, wherever followed, furnished a dry path or road for most of the year.   In traveling westward or north- westward from Detroit, the trend of the beaches is such that these naturally drained ridges could not be utilized.   Today farmers and gardeners on the plain experience difficulty in draining their lands by tiling, the movement of the water being so slow that the tile becomes clogged with mud and sand in a short time.[7] The plain floods easily and in wet years many crops are partially or wholly drowned.   Losses from this cause are rarely serious however.   There are few large rivers on the plain, and since the surface level is only a slight distance above the base level of the drainage systems, the streams have a low gradient and have developed shallow valleys.   In several of the descrip- tions of the Detroit region in the early periods, men- tion is made of grist mills.[8]   Most of these were un- doubtedly run by wind power.[9]   Weld, who visited Detroit, in 1796, commenting on this, said,[10] "The country around Detroit is uncommonly flat and in none of the rivers is there sufficient fall to turn even a

7.   Sherzer, *Geol. of Wayne Co.*, 129.
8.   *N. Y. Col. Docs.*, IX, 806; Campbell, *Pol. Hist. of Mich.*, 74; *Wis. Hist. Colls.*, XVI, 252.
9.   See Chapter III.
10.   Quoted by Ross and Catlin, *Landmarks of Wayne Co. and Detroit*, 257.

grist-mill." In the western portion of the plain and in the hilly region to the west the gradient of the streams is much greater than near the Detroit River. The Clinton, Rouge, Huron, and Raisin are the principal rivers flowing across the plain in southeastern Michigan. At various points along the upper and middle courses of these streams, dams have been constructed for the conservation of the water power. The Huron River furnishes more power than any of the others, draining as it does a large area to the west of the Defiance Moraine in which are numerous lakes. More than seventy-five glacial lakes have surface drainage into the Huron River and its tributaries. The power developed is used in gristmills or for the generation of electricity consumed in the towns along or near the rivers. There is little possibility that the industries of Detroit will ever be served with power from these streams. In spite of the numerous lakes in the basins of these rivers, the flow is irregular, the floods of early spring not infrequently destroying dams and carrying away bridges. The lower courses of the large rivers of the plains are drowned. During a portion of the Algonquin stage and again in the Nipissing stage of the ancient Great Lakes, much of the drainage of the Upper Lakes was diverted from the St. Clair-Detroit outlet. The surface level of Lake Erie, Detroit River, and Lake St. Clair was, therefore, much lower than at present, and the rivers of southeastern Michigan cut their channels down in accordance with this level. With the restoration of drainage through this outlet, the lower courses of the rivers of southeastern Michigan were drowned. The differential uplift, which the region at present is undergoing, has likewise been a contributing cause for the drowning.[11] The drowning results in a deep mid-channel in the stream, low marshy banks, and dead water (except as moved by the wind) in the lower courses. Government improvements have made the Raisin, Rouge, and Clinton rivers deep enough for most of the lake vessels to navigate for a distance of from one-half to two miles from the mouths. During the British period of control of the Detroit region, most of these rivers were used as harbors. A British official in 1800 wrote that at that time water on the bar at the mouth of the Clinton River was of "sufficient depth for Gunboats and Tow Galleys" to pass. Above the bar, vessels could "lie safely at any place from the river's mouth ten or twelve miles up the country in the midst of a strong settlement," and "on the River Rouge between Detroit and Lake Erie vessels of any size" could be moored; large vessels were being fitted out incessantly. He reported that fourteen vessels were being built and armed by the Americans on the Rouge within a few miles of Detroit. The River Huron was suitable at that time for "small Armed Vessels of any description."[12] For a number of years after 1823, large flat boats were used to carry goods between Detroit and Rawsonville on the Huron, and in 1833 and 1834 several trips were made between Detroit and Ypsilanti by way of the Huron.[13]

The soils in the region commercially tributary to

11.   Leverett, *Surface Geol. and Agric. Conditions of Southern Peninsula of Mich.*, 76; Mich. Acad. Sc., *Outline Hist. of Great Lakes, Rept.*, 1910; Sherzer, *Geol. of Wayne Co.*, 61.
12.   *Mich. Hist. Colls.*, XV, 12–13.
13.   *Hist. of Washtenaw County*, 117.

Detroit in Southern Michigan have resulted from the weathering of mantle rock of glacial or lacustrine origin. Lithologically the soils are composed of material derived by mechanical forces and processes from the crystalline and sedimentary rocks. The soils are new, transported, and therefore mixed. Glacially deposited mantle rock has both physical and lithologic heterogeneity. The lacustrine deposits lack heterogeneity— a separation of the clay, sand and gravel having taken place during the transportation and deposition of these deposits. Owing to the short time the soils have been exposed to chemical weathering and solution, very little leaching has taken place. They are, therefore, relatively rich in soluble mineral plant food. Kedzie found from chemical analysis that the glacial soils of Southern Michigan were rich in phosphorus, containing more than four times the average amount found in the glacial soils of Illinois.[14] The mineral content varies greatly, since the rocks were derived from wide areas. The angularity of the particles aids much in the rapid formation of soil solutions. Angularity, solubility, and lithologic heterogeneity are three dominant properties of the soils of the glaciated region, of which Michigan is a part, that have helped to make it a great cereal area of America.

The water table of the plain is near the surface of the land most of the year, and is kept below the surface only by thorough tiling and ditching. Crops rarely suffer from drought. In the hill regions to the west of the plain, the water table fluctuates greatly with the seasons. In the dry season the water is so

14.   Quoted by Hopkins, *Soil Fert. and Per. Ag.*, 98.

21

far below the surface that crops are not able in many places to secure water through capillary action.

No detailed survey of the soils of the region about Detroit has been made, but surveys of the Pontiac and the Toledo areas give sufficient data to classify most of the soils of Southern Michigan.[15]   Soils derived from clay till are variously classed by the United States Bureau of Soils as clay loam, silt loam, loam, and in some cases fine sandy loam.   Soils from sandy till are classed as stony loam, gravel, gravelly loam, and to some extent sand, fine sand, and sandy loam.[16]

The soil of the till and lacustrine plain (Miami dark clay loam) is identical with that of the Black Swamp area of Ohio.   It is derived from the weathered product of glacial and lacustrine clay that has been mixed with great quantities of organic matter, which because of the moist, cool conditions of the plain grew rapidly and decayed slowly.   The dark clay loam must be thoroughly drained to admit of profitable cultivation. It has been found that when thoroughly drained this soil warms more quickly in the spring than undrained soil, there is a better distribution of moisture at all times, a better yield and quality of product, and a greater certainty of yield.   The dark clay loam is a tractable soil.   It may be worked under a wide range of moisture conditions.   The surface soil consists of granular aggregations of clay, and when dried crumbles into "buckshot" soil, due probably to a high content of lime.   This type of soil is suitable for wheat, corn,

15.   Bureau of Soils, *Fourth Rept.*, 1902, Toledo Area, Field Oper.; *Fifth Rept.*, 1903, Pontiac area, Field Oper.
16.   Leverett, *Surface Geol. and Agric. Cond. in S. Pen. of Mich.*, 80.

and grass and truck gardening. In some portions of the plain the clay content of the soil is great and the organic matter slight in amount. Such soil is much more difficult to manage and is not so productive as the type described above. The particles of clay are small, making the soil compact and almost impervious to water and air. This fineness is of value, for much surface is exposed, so that solution is at a maximum, and capillary, hygroscopic, and ground waters are readily retained. The clay soil shrinks and cracks during the dry season and destroys many of the roots of plants. Under wet conditions the clay becomes plastic, runs together, and thus destroys the tilth; and unless rich in humus and well worked, aeration is poor. With proper handling, however, this soil is durable and will yield abundant crops of cereals. Owing to the flatness of the land, soil erosion on the plain is at a minimum, except along the sides of the valleys. Indeed it is probable that not enough erosion has taken place to remove the worn-out soils fast enough to maintain maximum fertility.[17]

The soil of the glacial clay knolls and ridges (known as Miami clay loam) has a high content of clay and is underlain by a very stiff clay. It contains numerous boulders of crystalline rocks, so numerous that much work is necessary to clear the fields before initial tillage. Because of the steep slopes and the impervious character of the stiff clay, there is much run-off, resulting in soil erosion and in the leaching of lime and other soluble salts from the soil. The low lime content undoubtedly increases the rate of erosion.[18]

17. Hopkins, *Soil Fert. and Per. Agric.*, 61.
18. U. S. Dept. of Agric., *Farmer's Bulletin No. 20*, p. 7.

When wet, this type of soil is sticky, heavy, and almost unworkable. It can be worked readily only within a narrow range of moisture conditions. If very dry it is difficult to turn with the plough, if wet it forms large clods which under the drying action of wind and sun harden so that they are rarely reduced to a granular condition except by repeated freezing and thawing during the fall and winter. The soil of the clay knolls, where leaching and drying are most active, is the most troublesome. The clay soil of the hilly belt is adapted to general farming and grazing, and when well handled will yield good crops yearly.

The sand and gravel soils are found in beach ridges, bars, and spits on the plain and in morainic knolls, outwash plains, valley trains, kames, and eskers in the region to the west. These soils are well drained; in fact, so pervious to water are they, that crops often suffer from drought. They are warm soils, contain little humus, and since the particles are large and its moisture content low, soil solutions do not form readily. These soils are soon exhausted unless handled carefully. Abandoned and dilapidated farm buildings are common on these soils. It is common on the sandy and gravelly soils to allow fields to lie fallow for from one to four years.[19] The crop yield is low. Wheat, corn, truck crops, fruits—as cherries, berries, peaches, apples—and other products are raised. Where there is even a small percentage of clay mixed with the sand or gravel, making a sandy or gravelly loam, the soil is much better. These types are not so hard and sticky as the clay or clay loams and not so light as

19. *Mich. Hist. Colls.*, XIV, 486.

the sand and gravel soil. They are easily managed and combine the good qualities of both the clay and the sand and gravel soils. Sandy loam soil types are widespread in Southern Michigan, in the area commercially tributary to Detroit. The loam soils are adapted to the growing of sugar beets, cereals, and fruits.

Silt occurs mostly in the valley bottoms. Lithologically it resembles somewhat the top-soil of the uplands, through which the rivers flow, but has had additions of humus of local origin. It is mainly the "cream of the uplands," and since the soil in the valley came from glacial soils, it is heterogeneous in mineral composition. Rivers are few, and valleys poorly developed, owing to the youthful stage of erosion, hence the silt soil is not of great extent.

To the early settlers, the soil types were distinguished by the plant growth they carried, and not by their lithologic or genetic differences. The types distinguished were as follows:

(1). Heavily timbered lands, the forests consisting of beech, maple, elm, hickory, and other deciduous species. (Such forests were found on the clay soils of recessional and ground moraines).

(2). "Oak openings," having light soils (sand and gravel in beach ridges, bars, and sandy moraines). The trees on such soils do not grow in dense growths and consequently such lands were easily cleared and the soil easily broken up. The "oak openings" were among the first to be taken by incoming settlers.[20] These lands drain easily. The till plain, on which

20. See Chapter VI.

natural drainage is poor, could not be cultivated until the region was settled well enough for concerted action in drainage problems. The artificial drainage of large areas of lowlands was (and is) often undertaken by townships, and even counties. In the "oak openings" individuals could fit the land for tillage.

(3). Marsh lands, most of which occur in isolated basins (partially filled glacial lakes). Some of these partially filled basins are bordered by tree growths. Some basins are not yet filled, and have open pools of water for most of the year. The marsh lands when drained make the best of truck garden lands.

(4). Barrens, sand dune ridges, along the old lake beaches, where the soil is frequently shifting, and on some of the high sandy morainic hills, where seepage through the soil and evaporation by the strong winds are active.

The mineral resources of the Detroit region are few, and the industries now entirely dependent on local raw products are not as important, from the standpoint of value of products, as many others whose localization is due to factors other than proximity to raw materials. It is only during recent decades that these resources have been exploited to any great extent. They contributed nothing to the spread and growth of population in the region.

Lake clay (previously described), which is in general free from pebbles, has during the late decades been the main factor in the localization of some two dozen plants to the west of Detroit, making drain-tile and building-brick. The glacial clay contains too many pebbles to be used for brick or tile. Some of the pebbles are of limestone. These when heated are burned to lime; later under the influence of moisture the lime slacks and destroys the brick or tile. Some attempts have been made to crush the pebbles or separate the clay from the pebbles by digesting the glacial clay in water and draining off the clay held in suspension. These processes have not proved entirely satisfactory. Pressed brick is not manufactured from the lake clay, the clay having a tendency to laminate and thus weaken the brick.[21]

In southeastern Michigan, in the eastern part of Monroe and Wayne counties near the Detroit River, the drift and lake deposits are so thin that bed rock (limestone and dolomite) is easily reached by quarries. The dip of the formations is toward the northwest, so that bed-rock at Detroit is reached only beneath from 100 to 260 feet of drift and lake deposits. The uppermost of these formations is limestone (Dundee formation, Devonian system) and was "the first to be recognized in the State and utilized for building purposes and in the manufacture of lime." This is a fairly pure limestone containing only small amounts of iron compounds, arenaceous material, and magnesia.[22] A dolomitic limestone (Monroe formation, Silurian system) outcrops on Grosse Isle, Stoney Island, and various other places in the adjacent region. The proximity of the outcrops to the Detroit River and Lake Erie is one reason for their being used for building purposes and lime since the early French period.[23] Burton is authority for the statement that Cadillac,

21. Sherzer, *Geol. of Monroe Co.*, 188.
22. Sherzer, *Geol. of Wayne Co.*, 199.
23. Sherzer, *Geol. of Monroe Co.*, 95–100.

the first year after his arrival at Detroit, knew that limestone could be had a few miles down the river but never made use of the deposits.[24]   A writer about 1788 says,[25] "The only stone quarry in all that country [Detroit region] is on an island granted from the Indians; and the people in the fort and settlement have been obliged for years to buy all stone . . . necessary for their foundations, . . . their cellars, chimneys and other purposes of the proprietor of the quarry."   This island was either Grosse Isle or Stoney Island, for outcrops do not occur on the other islands. It is only in recent decades that the quarrying of stone has become important.   The limestone at present has many uses.   It is shaped into blocks for building, crushed for macadam roads and dustless and weedless ballast for railroads, burned to lime, and used in the manufacture of Portland cement, while the purer limestones are used in the purification of sugar and in various chemical industries.   Several industries in the Detroit region are dependent wholly or in part on the presence of these limestones in southeastern Michigan. A limesand brick is made at one plant, the lime being obtained from the burning of local limestones, and the sand dredged from the bottom of Lake Erie a few miles below the mouth of the Detroit River.

Beneath the limestone and dolomite are deposits of salt.   These have an aggregate thickness of more than six hundred feet, and one bed at the Oakwood salt mine, has a thickness of 369 feet with only minor seams of dolomite.[26]   This thick vein can be reached

24.   Burton, *Fort Pontchartrain du Detroit*, 261.
25.   *Mich. Hist. Colls.*, XI, 647.
26.   Sherzer, *Geol. of Wayne Co.*, 279.

1437 feet below the surface.   Much trouble from heavy
flows of water, flowage of wet clay, and excessive
amounts of hydrogen-sulfid gas, was experienced in
sinking this shaft.   At other plants, salt is obtained
by making and evaporating artificial brines.   The salt
industry along the Detroit River was not developed
in connection with the lumber industry, and consequently did not decline with the decline of the sawmill.   The proximity of the salt blocks to the river has
enabled them to secure cheap coal by boat, and because of competition the freights by rail also are low.[27]
The salt and limestone deposits are utilized in the
preparation of baking soda, sal soda, fused calcium
chloride, caustic soda, and a hygroscopic covering for
driveways.   These industries, dependent on local raw
material, although in general located near and not
within Detroit, are important in the industrial life
of the city and geographically are to be considered
among the industries of the city.

27.   See Chapter XII.

CHAPTER VIII

A Century of Growth at Detroit

ALTHOUGH the growth of Detroit in the last ten decades is in no way remarkable when compared with that of Chicago and other Lake cities, yet it far exceeds the growth of many cities in other parts of the United States which were in its class at the beginning of the century. The following data present the figures for Detroit at the different census years from 1810 to 1910:[1]

Year.	Population.	Increase in Decade.	Percentage Increase.	Rank Among cities of U. S.	Area.
1810...........	750?	....	....	....	.33
1820...........	1,422	672	87	47	1.36
1830...........	2,222	800	56	53	2.56
1840...........	9,102	6,880	309	31	4.17
1850...........	21,019	11,917	130	23	5.85
1860...........	45,619	24,600	117	18	12.75
1870...........	79,577	33,958	74	17	12.75
1880...........	116,340	36,763	46	17	16.09
1890...........	205,876	89,536	77	14	22.19
1900...........	285,704	79,828	39	13	22.19
1910...........	465,766	180,062	63	9	40.79

The absolute growth has increased each decade, but the percentage increase has declined greatly since 1840. Since 1830 Detroit has advanced in rank from the fifty-third to the ninth city in the United States. The figures as given for 1810 are only approximations, for the first census in Michigan was taken in 1820.

1. *Thirteenth Census Rept.*, 1910, *Population*, II, 898; *Ibid.*, I, 79; *Twelfth Census* (1900), I, 430–431; *Mun. Man.*, Detroit, (1912), 186.

In the ten years from 1810 to 1820, assuming that the estimated figures are correct, the increase in population was 672, the city having nearly doubled in size. This growth seems remarkable in view of the factors that tended to retard emigration to the Detroit region in this decade. The fire of 1805, the War of 1812,[2] Indian hostilities, and the unpopularity of the Michigan region, all were deterrent factors. After the War of 1812 the country was impoverished, money was scarce and many settlers could not raise money to buy farms. The movement of settlers towards Michigan did not become rapid until after 1830. During the early decades of the nineteenth century, however, many changes took place which prepared the way for the great waves of migration that occurred between 1830 and 1860.

Soldiers of the War of 1812, on returning to the East, told of the rich, cheap lands to be had in Michigan, and helped to break down the prejudices entertained by many. Travelers like Evans, Blowe and Darby in their writings sought to give the people in the East a true picture of the possibilities in Michigan for the farmer and business man.[3] The Indian titles to lands were extinguished rapidly. The treaties of 1807 at Detroit, and 1821 at Chicago with the Indians threw open large areas in Southern Michigan to settlers.[4] Moreover, a change in the land laws in 1820 made it easier for farmers to take up land. Public

2. McCarthy, *The Governors of the Old Northwest*, 127.
3. Thwaites, *Early Western Travels*, VIII, 218, 220, 222 (Evans); Blowe, *Emigrant's Directory*, 694; Darby, *A Tour from New York to Detroit*, (1818), 190, 199.
4. *Mich. Hist. Colls.*, I, 225.

land now could be obtained for $1.25 per acre in plots
as small as eighty acres.   The States to the east and
south of Michigan were settled rapidly between 1800
and 1820.   The Genesee region was filling by 1800,
"no less than three thousand persons [having] settled
in Ontario and Steuben counties, New York, in six
weeks in the winter of 1798.[5]   A few New Englanders
had already found their way into Ohio.[6]   The larger
number of settlers in Ohio, Indiana, and Illinois in the
early decades of the nineteenth century, however, had
come from the South.   Ohio by 1803 had a population large enough to be admitted as a State.   Indiana
was admitted in 1816, and Illinois in 1818.   Improvements in transportation were also of great importance
in bringing many people to the Lakes region.

The first trip of the Walk-in-the-Water, the first
steamer on Lake Erie, 1818, marked the beginning of
a new era of travel on the Great Lakes.   Before the
coming of the steamboat, the emigrant to the West
by way of Lake Erie had the choice of three routes
of travel.   He could make the voyage in a schooner,
slow, often storm-tossed and wind-bound, with little
accommodation for passengers; he could make his
way on foot or horse through the dark and almost
roadless woods of Canada, his way frequently beset
by robbers; or he could go along the south shore of
Lake Erie and through the Black Swamp of northwestern Ohio.[7]   The Walk-in-the-Water reduced the
time for Lake travel between Buffalo and Detroit from
five or ten days to forty-four hours and afforded much

5. *N. Y. Col. Docs.*, II, 663.
6. Winsor, *The Westward Movement*, 299, 503.
7. *Mich. Hist. Colls.*, XIV, 537.

more comfortable quarters for travelers than did the schooners. Subsequent steamers shortened the time still more, furnished more comfortable quarters, ensured greater safety, and lessened the cost of transportation. The steamboat greatly facilitated the westward movement of population in the Lakes region. It is fortunate for Detroit that it was chosen as the western terminus for the initial attempts at steam navigation on the Lakes, and that the city for many years continued to be the chief western terminus for the traffic on Lake Erie. Thousands of settlers passed through the city on their way to the interior of the State and the West. Many were attracted by the commercial possibilities of the city and remained to build up its enterprises.

After 1825 the Erie Canal, combined with the steamers on the Lakes, was perhaps the greatest factor in bringing people to Michigan and Detroit. Preparations had been made to handle the rush of settlers that was sure to follow the opening of the canal, and before the season of 1825 was over, three steamers (the Superior, the Henry Clay, and the Pioneer) were running on Lake Erie. The number of steamers on Lake Erie increased rapidly. By 1826 there were six steamboats on the Lake, all engaged in the passenger and packet trade. In each new steamer was embodied many improvements. The carrying capacity was being enlarged constantly, the speed increased, and the cost of passage thereby reduced.

Many changes took place in New England that brought on unrest and consequent migration. Navigation on the Lakes by steam was cheap, and the easy transportation furnished by the Erie Canal brought the products of Ohio, Indiana, and Michigan into competition with those of the East. This competition, constantly becoming more severe, was felt especially by the small farmers on the crystalline uplands of New England and by those farmers of New York whose lands lay at a considerable distance from the Canal. The very taxes that the New York farmer paid for the building and upkeep of the Erie Canal lowered the value of his products. Many farmers in New England were compelled to leave their mortgaged farms and seek employment in the growing factory towns. Some turned their attention to the grazing industry or sold their farms to others who were going to engage in this business. Sheep raising especially was profitable after the passage of the tariff laws, particularly those of 1824 and 1828.[8] Thousands left their old homes in both regions and sought cheaper and more productive lands in the Territories and States to the west.

The cheap lands of Michigan and the ease and cheapness of transportation brought an influx of settlers that completely changed the aspect of things and made Southern Michigan a part of "Greater New England." Every addition to the population of Southern Michigan had its effect in swelling the size and increasing the importance of the growing metropolis on the eastern border.

In 1820 the American frontier (density six to eighteen persons per square mile) bordered the southern shores of Lake Ontario and Lake Erie as far west as

8. *Ibid.*, XXXVIII, 543 (Fuller).

Cleveland, and thence followed an irregular line toward the mouth of the Missouri River. An area of similar density was located in southeastern Michigan, with the nucleus at Detroit. Connecting the Detroit settlement and the settlements in Ohio was a thinly settled area (two to six persons per square mile) bordering Lake Erie. By 1830 the frontier had enveloped the settlements in southeastern Michigan.[9]

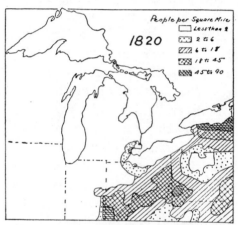

DISTRIBUTION OF POPULATION IN THE
LAKES REGION IN 1820
(*From Statistical Atlas, Ninth Census, XVI.*)

Behind the economic conditions and the improvements in transportation already noted, another factor, inherent in the habits of the people, was very important in furthering emigration. "Nothing," says Daniel Blowe in 1820,[10] "has tended so much towards the rapid progress of the Western Country as the strong

9. *Twelfth Census, Statistical Atlas,* Population Maps of 1820 and 1830.
10. Blowe, *Emigrant's Directory,* 63.

disposition to emigration among the Americans themselves. Even when doing well in the southern or
eastern States they will break up their establishments
and move westward with an alacrity and vigor no
other people would do unless compelled by necessity.
. . . In this way it is that the Western States have
advanced in population and prosperity with rapidity
unparalled in the history of mankind."

In 1825, the year of the opening of the Erie Canal,
Niles' Register reported,[11] "Emigration is powerful to
the west. The vessels on Lake Erie are hardly able
to carry the passengers and their goods, though the
steamboats convey three hundred persons westward
every week. The destination of the people is chiefly
Ohio and Michigan." On July 23, 1825, it was estimated that four thousand persons had arrived at
Detroit since the opening of navigation, and the sum
of $60,310 had been received at Detroit for land sold
in that district alone since the first of May.[12]

The next year saw an increase in transportation
facilities, and *Niles' Register* for June 3, 1826, reported,[13]
"The Steamboat Henry Clay, *the first vessel for the season*,
arrived at Detroit from Buffalo, May 8. She had two
hundred passengers, chiefly emigrants. . . . There
are now *seven* steamboats on Lake Erie, last year,
at this time, there were only three."[13] Eventually arrangements were made for the shipping of household
effects, implements, and live stock. In 1831 one paper
reported,[14] "The steamboats and all other water crafts

11. *Niles' Weekly Reg.*, XXVIII, 161.
12. *Ibid.*, 324.
13. *Ibid.*, XXX, 341.
14. *Ibid.*, XL, 285.

on the lake [Erie] are filled with men, women, and
children, beds, cradles, kettles, and frying pans."

Between 1830 and 1840 the population of Detroit
increased from 2222 to 9102, or 309 per cent. After
a time the great movement of people ceased to occasion surprise, and although settlers still came in large
numbers there were fewer comments about the migration. In 1831 the sale of public lands in the Detroit
District amounted to $48,727 between March 1 and
May 28. In one day the sales amounted to $5,600.[15]
Two years later the receipts at the Detroit office were
$79,000, and at Monroe, $90,000.[16]

The Black Hawk War temporarily checked emigration to Michigan. The seat of war was in Illinois
and Wisconsin, but all southern and western Michigan
for months was kept in a state of suspense and alarm.[17]
With the quieting of the Indians, however, the movement of emigrants assumed greater proportions than
before.

In 1833 the Detroit *Courier* noted the arrival of
seven steamboats between May 1 and May 7, with a
total of 2,610 passengers. It was reported that steamboats often left Buffalo before the appointed time in
order to avoid the pressure of persons wishing to take
passage.[18] Besides those carried by steamboats, many
came by land. About 1837 it was estimated that on
an average twenty teams of horses, two hundred yoke
of oxen, and eight hundred persons came through

15. *Ibid.*, XL, 293, quoted from Detroit *Courier* of May 28, 1831.
16. *Ibid.*, XLIV, 373, quoted from Detroit *Journal*.
17. *Mich. Hist. Colls.*, II, 295.
18. *Niles' Weekly Reg.*, XLIV, 198.

Canada each month and crossed the river by ferry.[19]

In 1844 the Michigan papers estimated that twenty thousand people had come to the State during the past season of navigation.[20]

In 1827 Congress granted the Military Reserve to to Detroit, the post having been abolished that year, as before noted. Lots in this Reserve were sold at very low prices,[21] and a large area was added to the business portion of the city. The razing of the fort marked the close of the long history of Detroit as a military post. With the rapid relative decline of the fur trade and the destruction of the last emblem of militarism, the traces of the ancient regime had nearly disappeared. Many things in the life and manners of the people, however, and many features of the city, indicated that primitive conditions had not passed away entirely.

The principal street, Jefferson Avenue, was lined on both sides with low French houses, "whose unpainted fronts and mosscovered roofs," as one writer puts it, "looked as though they had braved the storms of a century." Here and there along the avenue a newly painted shop showed the presence of emigrants from the East. There were only two brick buildings on the street.[22] Not a street had been paved or macadamized. Sidewalks were few. There were four churches, but not a public school.[23] A few impoverished Indians still lived near the city. Annually many

19. McCabe, *Directory of Detroit* (1837), 35.
20. *Niles' Weekly Reg.*, LXV, 352.
21. Leonard, *Industries of Detroit*, 17.
22. *Mich. Hist. Colls.*, XVIII, 462 (Mrs. Stewart).
23. *Ibid.*, II, 567; *Mag. West. Hist.*, III, 539.

bands came from the Upper Lakes on their way to
Malden to receive their presents from the British
Government. The banks of the river at such times
were lined with their canoes.[24]

In 1827 a franchise was granted providing for a
water system. The installation took place that year.[25]
Previous to this improvement, water was carried from
the river in pails and barrels.[26] Buckets hung on a
wooden yoke, a contrivance used in the French period,
were much used. A few men earned their living by
hauling water in barrels from the river. The introduction of a water system changed this primitive
method for part of the city. Water now was raised
from the river to a reservoir on the bank, from which
it reached a small part of the city through pipes made
from logs. The Detroit River has ever been the chief
source of the water supply for the city. The mantle
rock under most of the city is stiff impervious clay.
The water in wells was (and is) inferior in quality,
because it is not filtered naturally but is merely the
run-off. Besides, very few wells gave a supply
throughout the summer. There are few or no springs
within the city limits.[27] Until after 1833 there was
no fire department. For a time buckets were used.
When an alarm was sounded, every male who had a

24. *Mich. Hist. Colls.*, XVIII, 463. In 1836 over 4000 American
Indians received presents from the British on Drummond
Island at mouth of St. Mary's River. The practice prevailed at Malden for several years after this date.
(Campbell, *Pol. Hist. of Mich.*, 406).
25. *Rept. of Bd. of Water Com.* (1853), 28.
26. See Chapter VI.
27. *Rept. Bd. of Water Com.* (1853), 126; Sherzer, *Geol. of Wayne
Co.*, map.

bucket rendered what assistance he could and formed a "bucket brigade."[28]   Later an ordinance required each family to keep on the premises a cask containing a certain amount of water, and so arranged with poles for handles that it could be brought into immediate use in case of fire.[29]   About 1833 fire protection was furnished by a hand force-pump.[30]

Detroit continued to ship many furs, but with the settling of Southern Michigan and the destruction of the forests, lumber and agricultural products became the basis of trade. The first shipment of flour from Michigan took place in 1826, when two hundred barrels were sent to the East from Monroe.[31]   Detroit was a center of flour manufacturing in Southern Michigan, and the "banks of the river were studded with grist mills."[32]   Tobacco was raised in the surrounding region, one hundred hogsheads were sold to a firm in Baltimore in 1827. Improvements in transportation enabled perishable goods to enter more extensively into traffic, and white-fish came to be an article of export, selling for six to seven dollars per barrel in the eastern markets. The first oysters were received at Detroit from the East in 1826, an event which reflects the rapid development of trade and transportation.[33] During the winter months Detroit was almost as isolated from the shores of the Atlantic as in the

28. *Mich. Hist. Colls.*, II, 567; Mitchell, *Detroit in History and Commerce*, 15.
29. *Rept. of Bd. of Water Com.* (1853), 27.
30. *Mich. Hist. Colls.*, II, 567; Mitchell, *Detroit in History and Commerce*, 15.
31. Campbell, *Pol. Hist. of Mich.*, 416.
32. Roberts, *Sketches of City of Straits*, 10.
33. *Niles' Weekly Reg.*, XXIX, 310.

French period. Travel in the winter months was almost entirely by sled. In December 1833 a ton's weight of powder and soldier's clothing left Rome, N. Y., for Mackinac. From Rome the freight was carried by sled to Buffalo and thence along the south shore of Lake Erie to Detroit. Here it was delayed until April 10, for the opening of navigation. The cost of transportation from Rome to Mackinac was $250.[34]

The great influx of settlers to Detroit and vicinity was not alone from the Eastern States. A foreign element about 1830 began to appear in the population of the city. In 1827 there were thirty-nine foreigners not naturalized in Detroit. By 1833 there were enough Germans in Detroit to form a religious organization.[35] The city was growing rapidly, and the value of property was increasing at an astonishing rate. A lot near the business center was reported to have sold for $12,000 in 1836. "The purchaser had since been offered $20,000," says the report,[36] "but was holding it in expectation of getting $25,000. Eighteen large brick stores were in process of building on Jefferson Ave."[36]

The year 1837 marked about the beginning of the era of internal improvements in the Northwest, and Michigan had many canal and railway projects under contemplation. A Detroit newspaper of that year announced that seven railroads had been chartered to run into the city and that two were already in course of construction. These were the Detroit and St.

34. *Mich. Hist. Colls.*, XIII, 520.
35. *Ibid.*, XXXVIII, 551.
36. Gilman, *Life on the Lakes*, 51, 57.

Joseph and the Detroit and Pontiac. Roads and
turnpikes had been laid out and some had been constructed.[37] Most of the important ones centered at
Detroit. The Detroit-Chicago Road had been completed.[38] Wayne County alone had a population of
23,400; Washtenaw, 21,817; Oakland, 20,163; Lenawee,
14,504. These were the more populous counties in the
State, within the sphere of the commercial control of
Detroit. Detroit in 1837 had four banks, whose capi-
tals totalled $2,250,000; there were also in the city[39]

27 drygoods stores,	8 jewelry shops,
25 grocery and provision stores,	4 printing offices,
	2 daily newspapers,
10 commission houses,	4 weekly newspapers,
14 hardware stores,	1 semi-weekly newspaper,
3 markets,	1 tri-weekly newspaper,
8 drug stores,	1 educational magazine,
4 hotels,	37 lawyers, and
3 book stores,	22 physicians.
7 clothing stores,	

The factories in Detroit were chiefly of the metal
and woodworking industries. The American Fur Company still had an agency, but few furs were collected.
The business interests were mostly commercial, forty-
seven Lake vessels being owned in Detroit. There
were 3900 feet of docks; and three steamers, besides
several sailing vessels, arrived and departed daily during the season of navigation. A steam ferry carried

37. See Chapter X.
38. *Ibid.*
39. McCabe, *Directory of Detroit* (1837); *Mich. Hist. Colls.*, X,
    102; *Ibid.*, X, 189 (quoted from Blois' *Gazetteer*).

people to and from Windsor. The sewage system of the city was fairly extensive, but the streets were still in a primitive condition.[40] A steam pump now elevated the water to the reservoir, and iron pipes had replaced the wooden ones formerly used. Detroit was fast acquiring the appearance of a modern city, and the foundations were being laid for its future greatness. Many of the leading manufacturing and mercantile firms of the present time date from about 1840.

The first public school in Detroit was opened in 1838, the sessions being held in the second story of an old frame building. The first story was used for a grocery store.[41] Other public schools were soon opened. Many private schools existed, both for primary and secondary instruction. A directory of the city for 1837 lists five private colleges and seminaries. St. Phillip's College gave a "course of instruction embracing the foreign languages, classics and every branch of learning requisite for a polished and refined education." In the St. Clair Seminary, studies embraced "all the attainments which are necessary for society." Besides these, there were the Detroit Female Seminary, the Catholic Theological Seminary, and the St. Anne's Classical and Mathematical Academy.[42]

Among the public buildings, there were: a state house, city hall, eight churches, four banks, four hotels, a United States land office, three city markets, a theatre, a museum, a state penitentiary, a govern-

40. *Mich. Hist. Colls.*, X, 98.
41. *Ibid.*, 91.
42. McCabe, *Directory of Detroit* (1837), 18, 104; Haskell and Smith, *Gaz. of U. S.* (1843).

ment magazine, and a mechanic's hall.[43]   The city
hall was a brick structure, one hundred by fifty feet.
The first story was occupied by a city market and the
city clerk's office.   It was erected in 1835, and cost
$20,000.[44]   In 1840 there were eleven commission
houses engaged in foreign trade, with a capital of
$123,000.[45]   Detroit had now assumed importance as
a jobbing center, having parts of Indiana, Illinois,
Wisconsin, and Canada as its territory, besides its own
logical hinterland within the State.   This business increased for ten or fifteen years, when the rivalry of
Chicago and Milwaukee began to be felt in Indiana,
Illinois, and Wisconsin.   The city, however, still continued to be the jobbing center for a large part of Michigan.   A contemporary writer said,[46] "Nearly all the
merchants in the interior of the State depend upon
Detroit for occasionally replenishing their stock and
many buy all their goods there."   The exports were
mainly agricultural products, showing that the manufacturing industries were supplying merely the markets
of the State.   Among the exports were ashes, beef,
pork, cranberries, flour, wool, wheat, lumber, staves,
and fish.

By 1837 thirty-nine counties had been organized in
Michigan.   There were two chartered cities, and
twenty-three incorporated villages.   Of the estimated
56,450 square miles in the State, 25,636 had been
surveyed.   Land offices were established in Detroit,
Kalamazoo, Monroe, Flint, and Ionia.   Forty-five

43.   Haskell and Smith, *Gaz. of U. S.* (1843).
44.   McCabe, *Dir. of Det.* (1837), 105.
45.   Haskell and Smith, *Gaz. of U. S.* (1843).
46.   Hunt's *Merchant's Mag.*, XX, 278 (Seaman).

"wildcat banks" had been organized, and twenty-four railroads had secured charters. Four State lines of railroads had been provided for, and under the internal improvement system many canals and river improvements had been proposed.[47]   The Central Railroad had been completed from Detroit as far as Ypsilanti, and the Detroit and Pontiac as far as Royal Oak.[48]

The inflation in the value of real estate noted in a preceding page[49] was only a local manifestation of conditions prevailing throughout the Territory.   Such inflation and such advances in all lines of activity were in part an expression of the "boom period" just preceding the financial panic of 1837.   Towns were being laid out in various parts of the State.   A company would purchase a tract of land by the acre at the Government price.   If the land could be located along some river or lake the prospects were good that lots could be sold readily.   The tract was surveyed and laid out as a city or village, with streets, and spaces for public squares and buildings.   As business became more prosperous for the speculator, time was not taken to survey the land.   Cities were planned on paper only, and hundreds of lots were sold from such plans.   After the survey or prospectus was made, then came the time for advertising.   The city was announced as the future metropolis of its section.   Many tracts were bought, laid out, and sold without any of the parties ever having seen the land.   Frequently, when claims were examined the investors were sur-

47. See Chapter X.
48. *Mich. Hist. Colls.*, X, 98 (quoted from Blois' *Gazetteer*).
49. Page 181.

prised to find the "city" located in the middle of some
vast swamp or on some small stream that would never
be able to float even a stick of cordwood. A contemporary writer in the *North American Review* said,[50]
"No one can travel through Michigan at the present
time without being astonished at the spread of speculation. The hardy yeoman who emigrates to this
country with limited funds, with purposes of purchasing and improving a farm is soon infested with
the epidemic-speculating-mania; and betakes himself
to his paper and pencil instead of uprooting the oaks
or following the plow through the mellow soil."

Detroit was the center of speculation. "At the
hotels were gathered animated crowds from all quarters of the country speculating in land. . . . Auc-
tioneers were 'knocking down' lots to eager buyers, and
happy was he who secured one with fine water privileges at a price a thousand fold beyond the first
price a few days ago."[51] The Detroit *Journal* well
describes the conditions in the city in 1835. "Buying
and selling," it says,[52] "is the order of the day. Our
city is filled with speculators who are all on tip-toe.
Several snug fortunes from $10,000 to $20,000 have
already been made. Governor Cass has disposed of
the front part of his farm as far back as Larned Street
for $100,000. Extensive improvements are rapidly
making in Detroit. Our city authorities are authorized
to obtain a loan of $100,000."

Another phenomenon of this period of speculation
was the creation of the so-called "wildcat banks."

50. *N. Am. Rev.*, XLIV, 55.
51. Hubbard, *Memorials of a Half Century*, 95.
52. Quoted in *Niles' Weekly Reg.*, XLVIII, 273.

Their existence was an answer to the call of the democracy of the frontier for a "square deal" and the aboli-
tion of the banking monopoly.   When the State was
organized in 1837 eight banks were in existence, and
before the State was formally admitted seven more
were chartered.   The population of the State in 1837
was only about 150,000.   With a bank for every
10,000 persons it would seem that Michigan had
banking facilities enough.   The period of speculation,
however, had created a great demand for money, and
this resulted in exorbitant interest rates.   More
money was wanted.   Many could not see why any
corporation should have a monopoly of the issue and
reap great profits; so the democracy of the frontier
demanded that all have similar privileges.   In 1837
the State Legislature, responding to popular demands,
passed the General Banking Law.   Monopoly was
abolished.   Judge Cooley estimated that more than
one hundred thousand dollars in bills were issued.
Provisions had been made to protect the holders of
these issues, but the wide distribution of the banks
and the poor means of communication and travel made
it easy to evade the banking laws.   Many reserves
were pooled and carried from one bank to another.
After the banking commissioner had examined one
bank, the specie was hurried to another to be there
when he arrived.   One bank when first examined
showed the requisite reserve, but when examined a few
days later it was found to have $34.30 in its vaults,
with which to cover an issue of twenty thousand
dollars.[53]

---

53.   *Mich. Hist. Colls.*, XV, 209 (Utley).

The storm burst when the banks ceased to redeem their issue. Wrecked banks were on every hand, and it was said that the engravers of the bank notes, Rawdon, Wright, and Hatch, never received their pay for engraving most of the bills. The collapse of these banks cooled the fever of speculation, and the prices of land and products fell. Men whose property a few weeks before was figured at hundreds of thousands of dollars were now unable to buy provisions for their families. To add to the depreciation of real estate the actual settlers, having developed an aversion to all strangers for fear they were speculators, did not welcome newcomers.[54]

Trade was much hindered for want of money. Some companies used due bills. At Detroit, wooden bowls were used for small change. "Cut money" was another form of specie.[55] "Shin-plasters" were issued by the city. At times there was not enough money for the city to pay the laborers at work on city improvements.[56] The period of stagnation lasted until 1845. During 1838, 1839, and 1840, times grew harder and harder and then at last began to improve. By 1845 business and financial conditions were normal again.

' Detroit was becoming truly cosmopolitan by 1850; as its size increased, it drew people from wider and wider areas. Of the 21,000 people in the city in 1850, 11,000 were native born, and 10,000 were foreign born. Every State east of the Mississippi was represented. The major lines of movement of the emigrants are well shown in the make-up of the native-

54.   *Ibid.*, IV, 174 (Trowbridge).
55.   *Ibid.*, I, 382.
56.   Leonard, *Industries of Detroit*, 17.

born population. Of the 11,055 born in the United
States, 6,323 had been born in Michigan. Of the
4,732 remaining, 4,173 had been born in Ohio, New
York, Pennsylvania, New Jersey, or the New England
States. The numbers furnished by each of these States
were as follows:[57]

New York	2,620;	Connecticut	224;
Ohio	305;	New Jersey	83;
Massachusetts	296;	New Hampshire	80;
Vermont	281;	Maine	70;
Pennsylvania	276;	Rhode Island	21.

New York had been the great hive, having furnished
twenty-four per cent of the American born, and nearly
sixty-three per cent of those born outside of Michigan.
Few had come from the States south of Pennsylvania
and Ohio;

161 had come from Virginia,	6 from Louisiana,
98 from Kentucky,	6 from Alabama,
24 from Tennessee,	4 from Mississippi,
15 from North Carolina,	2 from Florida, and
13 from Georgia,	12 from South Carolina.

It seems probable that most of the 161 native-born
Virginians had resided in Ohio before coming to
Detroit.

In 1850 the chief foreign elements in the population
of Detroit had come from Ireland, Germany, England,
and Scotland. In order of numbers these were; Ireland, 3289; German Empire, 2855; England and Wales,
1245; Scotland, 474; and France, 282. There were

57. DeBow's *Review*, XIX, 262.

only seven Austrians, four Spaniards, and four Italians in Detroit. The foreign-born made up about 47 per cent of the total population of the city.[58]

With the growth of population in the Lake States and the development of cities at many points Detroit came to have many rivals. The early start that Detroit had in its founding had little or no effect upon its later growth. Its real growth and development began only after emigration from the East set in. The Easterners laid the foundation of the greatness of Detroit. Characterized by activity and energy, a liberal public spirit, and a high order of intelligence, they built the stores, factories, wagon roads, and railroads; founded schools, academies, and colleges; settled the lands back from the rivers; and carried the products of the growing settlements, both raw and manufactured, to the markets of the East. The steady growth and continued prosperity of the city from the time the British withdrew from the Lakes region to the present day are due largely to the Americans who came from States to the east. But these same hardy citizens came by thousands to find homes in the other Lake States, where Cleveland, Toledo, Chicago, Milwaukee, and many smaller cities grew up and competed with Detroit for the trade and commerce of the Lakes.

As early as 1835, a rival to Detroit sprang up in Michigan. Many far-sighted men thought they saw at Monroe a most eligible point for a large city. Governor Cass and others in 1836 bought large tracts of land at and near the head of navigation on the Raisin

58. *Ibid.*

River.   Monroe at that time had brilliant prospects.
A canal had been projected to be built across the
State from the headwaters of the Raisin River.   The
Southern Railroad was to have Monroe as its eastern
terminus, where it would connect with vessels on Lake
Erie.   A line of steamers for a time made Monroe a
port of call on the route between Buffalo and Chicago.
Thousands of emigrants landed at Monroe on their
way to the interior of Michigan and to Illinois and
Wisconsin.   Until about 1856 the prospects of Monroe
were bright.   Its friends had failed, however, to take
account of the development of the railroad.   The death
blow to the aspirations of Monroe was struck when in
1856 the Lake Shore and Michigan Southern Railway
made connections with Buffalo along the south shore
of Lake Erie.   The railway steamers on Lake Erie
were withdrawn, and Monroe declined in importance.[59]
In 1910 Monroe was the thirty-fifth city in size in
Michigan, with a population of 6893.[60]

Between 1850 and 1860, many writers on commercial
subjects saw in Toledo a formidable rival of Detroit
and other Lake cities.   In fact many thought Toledo
would rival Chicago as a commercial and industrial
center.   Andrews, in 1851, said,[61] "Toledo is in one
respect more advantageously situated for an extensive lake commerce than perhaps any other western
port."   The two canals centering on Toledo made
it the depot for the trade of the Miami, Maumee, and
Wabash valleys and since this trade was increasing
yearly it was "almost tantamount to saying that it

59.   *Mich. Hist. Colls.*, VI, 369.
60.   *Thirteenth Census* (1910), II, 920.
61.   Andrews, *Exec. Doc*. 112, *32nd Cong., 1st Session*, 185.

must need be ultimately the great meeting-place and mart for the immense products of all that region."[62]

A writer in *Hunt's Merchant's Magazine* in 1854 says,[63] "Chicago and Toledo, it will be presumed, have no rivals on the lakes in the great advantage of holding the shortest and cheapest channels of the trade connecting them to the great rivers of the plain, and the great cities of St. Louis and Cincinnati bordering these rivers. . . . Toledo by means of her canals with the Ohio, and Chicago by her canal to the Illinois will command the heavy freights exchanged between the great river region below Cairo and the Lakes region. . . . How extensive this communication will soon become, the most sanguine will fail duly to estimate."

J. B. Scott, an able writer on commercial topics, as late as 1862 prophesied for Toledo the highest rank among the Lakes cities. "Twenty years ago," he says,[64] "it was generally believed that our largest interior cities would grow up on our interior rivers. Experience has shown that our interior commerce prefers to concentrate on the borders of our Great Lakes. Between 1850 and 1860 the growth of the ten largest lake cities has been twice as great as the ten largest river cities. Of the largest lake cities Chicago and Toledo show the greatest growth." Between 1850 and 1860 Toledo advanced in population from 3,800 to 13,700; Detroit, from 21,000 to 46,000; Buffalo, from 42,000 to 81,000; Milwaukee, from 20,000 to 45,000; and Chicago, from 30,000 to 109,000. Both Toledo

62. *Ibid.*
63. *Hunt's Merchant's Mag.*, XXXI, 403, 405.
64. *Ibid.*, XLVII, 403.

and Chicago in this decade trebled in population. It was on the basis of the figures of this decade that Mr. Scott based his conclusions. In 1910 Toledo stood sixth in size among the Lake ports. Chicago had a population of 2,185,000; Cleveland, 560,000; Detroit, 465,000; Buffalo, 424,000; Milwaukee, 301,000; and Toledo, 224,000.[65] The advantages of Toledo in position, as compared with the other Lake ports, were much overestimated. Here again the railroad was underestimated, and the importance of lake and canal transportation was overestimated. With the development of the trunk lines, Toledo became a way-station on the great east and west lines of railroads. The railroads gave to inland cities, like Indianapolis, commercial advantages not dreamed of in the days when canals and rivers were the chief highways. When Toledo ceased to be one of the main termini for lake shipping its growth became less rapid. It is too far from the deep waters of the Lake to be a port of call for modern vessels plying between ports on the Upper Lakes and those of Lake Erie. The small schooners of early days could sail almost anywhere in Maumee Bay, but modern freighters are confined to dredged channels. The muddy water of the Maumee River is, therefore, one cause of the slower growth of Toledo than of many of the other Lake cities.

Detroit, on the other hand, has come to be the terminus for many railways in Michigan, and some of the through lines between the East and West cross the river at this point by tunnel and ferry. It is on the

65. *Thirteenth Census*, V, Part I, 430–433; *Stat. Abstract of U. S.* (1911), 55.

25

route of all vessels plying between Lake Erie and the Upper Lakes. Since the Detroit River flows from a lake, it carries little sediment, and bars are few. The channel is more than thirty feet deep, and the channel bank is near the shores of the river. Vessels of large tonnage find no difficulty in reaching the docks of the city.

Since 1850 the growth of Detroit has been rapid. Only one of the larger cities in the United States showed a greater percentage of increase than Detroit from 1900 to 1910. In this decade Atlanta showed an increase of 72.3 per cent; Detroit, 63 per cent; Denver, 59.4 per cent; Cleveland, 46.9 per cent; New York, 38.7 per cent; Chicago, 28.7 per cent; and Toledo, 27.8 per cent.[66]

Since 1850 there has been a decrease in the percentage of foreign-born in Detroit. In that year the foreign-born constituted 47.3 per cent of the population; in 1880, 39.4 per cent; and in 1910, 33.6 per cent.[67] In 1910 native-born whites of native parentage made 24.7 per cent of the population, and native-born whites of foreign or mixed parentage, 40.4 per cent.[68] The parentages of native-born are not given in the data for 1850 and 1880. With the increase in size of Detroit there has come an increase in the area from which the population is drawn. The city has become more cosmopolitan. In the data of the foreign-born for 1850, nine foreign countries were represented; in

66. Dept. of Commerce and Labor, *Census Report* (1910), 108–134.
67. DeBow's *Review*, XIX, 263; *Tenth Census Rept.*, Part I, 542, 551; *Thirteenth Census Rept.*, II, 948.
68. *Thirteenth Census Report*, II, 948.

1910, nineteen were designated. In 1910 every State in the Union had representatives among the native-born. One person of the 465,000 had been born in Alaska, thirteen in Washington, eleven in Florida, and 260 in Maine. The near-by States, and particularly those to the East, furnished the larger numbers. From New York had come 5968; from Ohio, 3405; Pennsylvania, 1199; Indiana, 859; Illinois, 871; and Wisconsin, 307. The city now draws a larger percentage of its population than formerly from outside the State. In 1850, 30 per cent of the population had been born in Michigan, in 1880 about 46 per cent, but in 1910 only about 9 per cent.[69]

The change in the composition of the population of the cities of the United States is one of much importance to their social, political, and economic development. In many if not most of our cities the foreign element, instead of scattering throughout the city, segregate in particular portions and there form colonies, speak their own language and have their own schools and churches. Under such conditions they tend to resist the forces working for assimilation and amalgamation, a fact which makes the source of the immigrants a matter of grave concern. The following table shows the nativity of the population of Detroit in 1850, 1880, and 1910:[70]

---

69. *Ibid.*
70. DeBow's *Review*, XIX, 263; *Tenth Census*, Part I, *Population*, 542–551; *Thirteenth Census*, II, 948. Canada and those European countries that have been important contributors are the only ones considered.

	1850.	1880.	1910.
Total population...................	21,019	116,340	465,766
Native born......................	11,055	70,695	303,331
Foreign born.....................	9,927	45,645	156,565
Not designated...................	137	....	5,870
Country of Birth:			
Germany.....	2,851	23,769	44,674
Canada....	....	10,754	41,945
Russia...........................	....	77	18,644
Austria...........................	7	557	14,160
England and Wales...............	1,245	4,200	9,202
Hungary..........................	....	64	5,935
Italy.............................	4	127	5,724
Ireland...........................	3,289	6,775	5,584
Scotland..........................	474	1,783	3,320
Belgium..........................	....	240	2,237
Turkey...........................	....	....	686
France...........................	282	721	637
Sweden...........................	....	55	601
Switzerland.......................	....	421	595
Greece...........................	....	....	584
Netherlands......................	....	275	584
Denmark..........................	....	71	411
Norway...........................	....	27	225
Poland...........................	....	1,771	....

In the sixty years since 1850, there has been a slow but steady increase in the percentage of foreign-born from the countries of Southern Europe. For example, in 1850 there were four Italians in Detroit, making .089 of one per cent of the population. Thirty years later Italians constituted about one per cent of the population, and numbered 127. In 1910 the percentage was one and five-tenths, and their number 5724.[71] On the other hand, many of the countries of Northern Europe show a relative decrease in their representation. In 1850 one person in seven in Detroit had been born in Ireland. In 1880 the proportion was one in twenty, and in 1910 only one in eighty. Germans since the middle of last century at least have been numerous among the foreign-born of Detroit. In 1850 they composed 13.5 per cent of the population of the city; in 1880, nearly 20 per cent; and in 1910, nearly

71. *Ibid.*

10 per cent. Both English and Scotch born show a lower percentage in the population of 1880 and 1910 than in 1850. In 1850 there were 7 Austrians in Detroit; in 1910 there were 14,160. Another rather large element in the foreign population in 1910 were the Russians, most of them Russian Jews and Poles, who made about 4 per cent of the total population. In 1910 the foreign-born from Northwest Europe and Austria, mostly of Teutonic origin, constituted nearly 18 per cent of the total population of the city, or about one-half of the foreign-born. If to these are added those born in Canada, the percentage amounts to 27 per cent of the total population, or three-fourths of the foreign-born. The presence of so large a number of people who represent the ideals of society of the city and government under which the city has developed, seems to insure for the future a continuation of these ideals.

In 1910 Detroit was a city of 465,766 people, and if the many suburbs are included the total population was more than 500,000. The city extends for eleven miles along the Detroit River, with a width of about four and one-half miles. The influence of the river in determining the general shape of the settlement still persists. The area of the municipality is about forty square miles. The average density of population, therefore, is about 11,600 people to the square mile. As in most large American cities, the relatively low average density is due to the inclusion of many thinly settled districts on the outskirts of the municipality.

About the city are scattered many suburbs, whose

existence is due largely to the same factors that have developed the population group within the political boundaries. These suburbs have grown up about some factory or group of factories, along some important line of transportation, or simply as residential districts. Suburbs about Detroit have their greatest development along the Detroit River, again emphasizing the control of the waterways.

Unlike most of our large cities, modern Detroit started with a definite plan, the work of Augustus B. Woodward just after the great fire in 1805. The old town, most of whose business streets were only twelve to fifteen feet wide, was destroyed by the fire. This gave an opportunity for development along any desired plan. The Woodward plan, said to be "similar to that of Byzantium," was on a grand scale, characteristic of the man and of his time.[72] Though the plan was not carried out fully, the topography in and about the city made easy the adoption of its leading features. The broad, flat surface of the lake plain imposed no restrictions nor problems. Today avenues one hundred twenty to two hundred feet wide radiate from the center of the business section. This gives large, open spaces in the crowded sections, and facilitates communication with the outlying parts of the city. Few cities give such an impression of openness and light in the business districts.

The business section of Detroit naturally grew up about the nucleus of the old town, with one side extending along the river front. During the first half of the nineteenth century, when commerce was the

---

72. *Tenth Census*, XIX, Part II, 601.

chief interest and occupation of the people, the river front was the most active part of the city. When railroads were constructed their termini were placed on the river front. Thus for many decades there has been a tendency to concentrate commerce and trade along the river. Indeed, concentration has gone so far that within the last decade or two many "sky scrapers" have been built to provide room and reduce ground rents.

The residence section has grown up about the business center. In the early decades of the nineteenth century the best residences were only ten or fifteen minutes walk from the center of the city. As the town grew, and more business was centered in the business sections, the value of land increased, ground rents became higher, and only business houses came to occupy the central sections. Residential quarters were driven farther and farther from the center. The well-to-do left first. They went to the outskirts, or to the suburbs of the city. The old mansions came to be tenement houses; for by crowding, the laboring people were able to reduce the rent per occupant. As a result of this process the worst housing conditions are to be found about the business section, in a belt about one-half mile wide. There are relatively few tenement houses in the city, however. Instead, along miles of streets may be seen one and two story cottages and houses, the majority of which have garden plots. In the building operations for 1912, out of the 395 permits granted, 158 were for residences, 99 were for two family flats, 35 for flats, tenements, and terraces, and the remainder for business places.[73] Detroit leads the large cities of the country in the relative number of home owners. The percentages of the population owning homes in the larger cities of the country are as follows: Detroit, 39.1; Cleveland, 37.4; Milwaukee, 35.9; Buffalo, 32.9; Chicago, 26.4; San Francisco, 24.1; St. Louis, 22.8; Philadelphia, 22.1; and New York, 12.1.[74]

Factories, whose raw products are to be received and manufactured wares distributed largely by rail, are located at various parts of the city, back from the river. There is hardly what one may call a factory section. Such a wide distribution of factories tends to minimize crowding of the population, and also tends to prevent congestion on city transportation lines. Ship yards, dry docks, grain elevators, lumber yards, iron furnaces, and a few other plants are located along the river front. Belt lines connect the many railways with the larger plants.

Detroit has abundant transportation facilities. Seven railways on the American side of the Detroit River center here. Three roads lead to the East through Canada, and are connected with Detroit by car ferries and a tunnel. Eight interurban lines lead out from Detroit, bringing various cities in the southeastern part of Michigan in close touch with the city. About thirty passenger boats make regular stops at the docks of Detroit during the season of navigation, furnishing cheap and efficient communication with all the important cities on the Great Lakes. Like most

73. *Board of Com. Rept.* (1912), 47.
74. *Thirteenth Census* (1910), quoted in *Municipal Manual of Detroit* (1912–13), 203.

of the cities of the country having water transportation, Detroit has allowed most of the waterfront to be taken over by the railways and steamboat lines. Freedom of traffic is thus greatly curtailed.[75]

The total length of tracks of electric railways, including both city and interurban lines, is about 780 miles. These radiate from the center of the city in many directions. Cross-town lines and belt lines connect many of these radiating lines. As yet, congestion is not great enough to demand through-routing of cars; nor is there, at present, need of sub-ways, elevated lines, or commutation service. Nor are the dimensions of the city large enough to demand rapid transportation. The city may be crossed in most directions by street railway in thirty to fifty minutes.

The water supply of the city is taken from Lake St. Clair. Up to within the last few decades the river furnished the water for domestic, fire, and sprinkling purposes. With the concentration of the people along the river front to the northeast of the center of the city, it became necessary to move the intake further up stream. The present source of water is by no means free from possible contamination. In the not far distant future, as population increases along St. Clair River and Lake St. Clair, Detroit will be obliged to adopt some means of water purification. As in the case of most river towns, the drainage and sewage of Detroit is run into the river. This, too, will need to be rectified in the near future.

The people of Detroit are well provided with parks and recreation grounds. The parks number about

75. *Transp. by Water, Rept. Com. of Corp.*, II, 196.

thirty, varying in size from one-half acre to 707 acres, the area of the Belle Isle Park. The total acreage of the parks is about twelve hundred. Belle Isle, the largest park, owes its attractiveness to its situation in the Detroit River, and to the large natural forests covering about two hundred acres. The many attractive islands and natural parks easily reached by excursion steamers from Detroit furnish recreation grounds for thousands during the summer months.

Detroit today is one of the great modern cities of the country, in close touch with all the commercial sections of the world, and sustained by varied, well-founded manufacturing and commercial interests.[76]

76. The development of the means of transportation and the manufactures will be discussed in the succeeding chapters.

CHAPTER IX

Detroit and the Development of Navigation

I. *The Development of the Carrying Agent and Facilities for Transportation*

THE navigation of the waterways of the St. Lawrence River system by white men began long before the founding of Detroit. The south shore of Lake Superior as far west as the Apostle Islands had been visited in 1629. In 1669 Joliet coasted along the shores of Lake Erie. By 1670 the French explorers, traders, and missionaries had navigated all the Great Lakes and knew all the portages within the St. Lawrence Basin, and those that led across the divide to the tributaries of the Mississippi. The British in 1685 and 1686 sent parties to trade in furs with the Ottawa Indians about the north and east shores of Lake Huron. From 1682 to 1701 the mission and post at Michilimackinac was the rendezvous of the French traders and missionaries; but with the founding of Detroit the latter became the chief collecting and distributing point for the commerce of the West, and for one hundred years it remained the most important trading station on the Great Lakes. For many decades in the second century of its existence it was one of the most important cities in the Lakes region. Each improvement in the carrying agent made possible an increase in the commerce of Detroit, but just how much cannot be determined. When other centers of trade and commerce began to be developed, the benefits came to be shared by other cities. The vast commerce of the Lakes today, and the growth in the past, is in part both the result and the cause of the development of the carrying agents. In a discussion of the development of the carrying agent, three stages or eras are recognized: the canoe era, the sailboat era, and the steamboat era.

For one hundred and fifty to two hundred years after the French landed on the shores of the lower St. Lawrence and built their first permanent settlement, the birch-bark canoe was the chief carrying agent used, and for the first seventy-five years was almost the only means of conveyance for men and goods on the lakes and rivers of the interior of North America. The "dugout" was used only to a limited extent. The canoe carried Champlain along the Ottawa River on his expedition to Georgian Bay (1615). Nicolet in 1643 used it to visit the falls at the Sault, and the various tribes of Indians at the foot of Green Bay. Marquette and Joliet floated down the "Father of Waters" to the mouth of the Arkansas in a bark canoe built by the Indians of the Marquette Mission. The canoe and the waterways made possible the advance into the interior, that has ever excited the admiration of the readers of French history. The canoe was as necessary as the waterways to success of the French in their interior exploration. Its light draught enabled the explorers and traders to navigate relatively small streams so that the length of portage between the navigated waterways was short.[1]

1. See Chapter I.

Long before the coming of the French to the Lakes region, the Indian had evolved the birch-bark canoe. It safely may be said that ninety-five per cent of all journeys of the Indians in the Great Lakes region were made on the water courses, and the birch canoe was almost invariably the carrying agent.[2] The French improved the canoe by making it larger and stronger. The canoes built by the French and used by the fur traders were on the average thirty-five feet long, five feet wide, and three or four feet deep. They could carry a load of three or four tons besides the crew of six or eight men and provisions weighing upward of one thousand pounds. Such a craft could be carried over portages by two men.[3] They were seaworthy considering their size. Moreover they were made from materials at hand in the forest, in a few days, and required few tools for the construction. For all these reasons the canoe was for several years the sole carrier used on the lakes and rivers of the Lakes region, and it remained for many decades the only carrier on some of the shallow rocky rivers where frequent portaging was necessary.

At Detroit during the latter part of the French period, Campbell tells us,[4] "every farmer had his canoe, and generally several." Some were dugouts but "there were many birch bark canoes and elm bark canoes in use." For "long voyages large sized bark canoes brought from the upper country were used for heavy loads."

The birch-bark canoe was used even as late as the

2. Winsor, *Narr. and Crit. Hist.*, I, 294.
3. Henry, *Travels in Canada*, 15.
4. *Mag. West. Hist.*, IV, 375 (Campbell).

early part of the nineteenth century. Crooks, the
partner of Astor in the American Fur Company, frequently made the trip between Buffalo and Mackinac
by canoe. Governor Cass made a four months' trip
of four thousand five hundred miles from Detroit, a
three months' journey of fifteen hundred miles, and a
two months' journey of one thousand miles, coasting
all the Upper Lakes and descending the Mississippi
River to the Ohio, in bark canoes.[5]

Indispensable as the canoe was for certain kinds of
routes of traffic, it had some defects. It was easily
injured; in approaching a shallow, gravelly, or stony
shore great care was necessary. Again, the bark became brittle when dry and peeled readily. The cold
of winter contracted the bark and caused it to split.
The bark canoe was, therefore, short lived. When the
canoes were to be left for several days or weeks they
usually were buried. Still again, the cost of transportation by canoe was very high.[6] In the Indian trade
in which profits were great and the goods handled
were costly according to bulk, the canoes could be used
with profit; but other commodities could not stand
this costly method of transportation.

5.   Trip made about 1820. *Mich. Hist. Colls.*, I, 383; *Mag. West.
     Hist.*, X, 389.
6.   In 1815 in discussing means of getting effects of the British
     army from Michilimackinac to Montreal, the Commis-
     sariat of the British army estimated that "the whole ex-
     pense attending on a canoe to Michilimackinac" could
     not "be estimated at less than 275 pounds currency."
     Each canoe could take sixty-five "canoe pieces" of 90 to
     100 pounds each. *Mich. Hist. Colls.*, XVI, 100 (*Ottawa
     Papers*, May 12, 1815). If the currency is reckoned at
     par with sterling, the cost per ton was 85 to 90 pounds
     sterling, or about $450.

For these reasons wherever cŏnditions were suitable, as on the large rivers and lakes, larger and stronger boats than the canoe came to be built. There were several types of these semi-primitive craft: the pirogue, the batteau, and the durham boat.

The pirogue was a large "dug-out." It usually was made by splitting the dug-out lengthwise, using the halves for siding, and inserting planks for the bottom and ends.

According to Brodhead, the first large plank batteau was built at Montreal about 1671. It was two or three tons burden and was used to carry provisions from Lachine to Grenadier Island, a few leagues above the site of Ogdensburg, New York.[7] The batteau as usually constructed was pointed at both ends and with sides straight up and down. The bottom was made flat with a slight inclination upward at each end. It was navigated by five men and propelled by four oars or a square sail when the wind was aft. Sometimes the boats were towed by men walking along the shore. Where the water was shallow and swift "setting poles" were used for pushing the crafts. The crew camped on shore for the night. The craft could carry about three tons, or thirty barrels of flour. It was the only boat used for many decades on the St. Lawrence to carry the bulky articles between the head of La Chine Rapids and Kingston. Several boats usually made the trip in company so that the crews could assist one another at the difficult places in the river. The freight charges were gauged by the price paid for a barrel of

7. Brodhead, *Hist. of State of N. Y.*, II, 188.

rum, the rate for which from La Chine to Kingston was $3.50.[8]

Cadillac soon after the settlement of Detroit provided batteaux for the traffic of the Detroit settlement. In the *Cadillac Papers* (Canadian Archives) is written,[9] "I could not send any of our oxen or calves to France until after barges had been built on which I believe they (the men) are going to work at once. One of the barges will be on Lake Frontenac (Ontario) and the other at Detroit in order to facilitate the conveyance of hides and wool, which could not be affected by the canoe transport. Three barges will also serve for other large skins, for beaver skins and other small furs which will be conveyed at less expense in this way. They will serve for everything in general that is included in trade, and they will be capable of sailing two thousand leagues in the surrounding districts."

The batteaux were used by the French on the St. Lawrence above Montreal, on Lake Erie before sailing vessels were built, and on the Ohio River and its tributaries. All during the French period and the early part of the English period, batteaux on Lake Erie carried goods between Detroit and the portage at Niagara.

After 1812 Durham boats, from which the keel boat of the Ohio and Mississippi rivers was copied, came into use.[10] These crafts were first used on the Lakes by the United States troops in the War of 1812. The Durham boat was flat-bottomed, had a keel and a

8.   Kingsford, *Hist of Canada*, VII, 26.
9.   *Mich. Hist. Colls.*, XXXIII, 136.
10. Ringwalt, *Dev. of Transp. System in U. S.*, 13.

centerboard, and was decked at bow and stern. A running-board extended along the whole length of the sides. On this the crew walked while poling the boat. Sails were used when the wind was fair. At other times men on shore drew the craft through swift waters by means of a tow line. This craft could carry 350 barrels of flour down stream, but only eighty up.[11] Unlike the traffic along the Ohio and Mississippi, the chief movement of goods was upstream on the St. Lawrence. Many furs were carried down to Montreal and Quebec, but the great quantities of provisions and munitions of war carried upstream to the Lakes region made a strong balance for the up-river traffic. The flatboat, which could move only with the current, was not used.

These primitive types in transportation gave rise to a distinct type of river-men. The Canadian voyageur became indispensable to the fur trade wherever that trade was carried on in connection with the waterways. These river-men found occupation about the Great Lakes, far north along the waterways of Canada, along the Missouri River, and even on the Pacific Coast. Waterway, canoe, and voyageur were necessary for the fur trade, that industry so long the prevalent one in the interior of the North American continent. Hubbard describes the voyageurs as he saw them on the Upper Lakes in 1835:[12] "The class of men known as coureur de bois, or voyageurs were extinct at Detroit sometime before . . . 1835; but at Mackinaw and Lake Superior they found some of

11. *Ibid.*, 26.
12. Hubbard, *Mem. of a Half Century*, 150.

their old employment, and retained a good deal of their ancient character. They manned the Mackinaw barges (batteaux) and canoes of the fur-trader that plied along the northern waters for the Hudson Bay Company. A wierdness was often enhanced by the dash of Indian blood. Picturesque, too, were they in their red flannel or leather shirts and cloth cap of some gay color, finished to a point which hung over to one side with a dependent tassel.

"They had a peculiar love for their occupation and muscles that seemed never to tire at the paddle and the oar. From dawn to sun set they would ply these implements, causing the canoe to fly through the water like a thing of life. . . . The labor at the oar was relieved by song to which each stroke kept time with added vigor."

The prelude to the advent of the sailing vessel as a factor in the commerce of the Lakes was the building of two vessels by La Salle about 1677 to 1678. La Salle first built a small vessel of about ten tons burden at Fort Frontenac (Kingston) on Lake Ontario, in which he set sail from the east end of Lake Ontario on November 16, 1678, for Niagara River. He carried with him the equipment for a second vessel, which he intended to build on the river above the falls. This vessel, the Griffin, built on Cayuga Creek, was launched in 1679, and was the first to navigate the Upper Lakes. The building of these two vessels was part of La Salle's scheme to dominate the fur trade of the Upper Lakes and of the whole interior of the continent. The motive involved in the building of these vessels was to reduce freight costs and thus cheapen the cost of goods to the Indians.[13] Before beginning the construction of the Griffin, the French, suspecting that the English would lose no time in stirring up the Iroquois against any such bold attempts to usurp the trade of the Lakes, visited the Senecas, and after making handsome presents, got their consent to build a "great wooden canoe" above the falls by means of which, they said, they would be able to supply them with European commodities cheaper than the English at New York or Boston could.[14] With the sinking of the Griffin sank the hopes of La Salle to control the Lake trade. The French made no further attempts at the construction of sailing vessels on the Lakes above the falls for several years. On Lake Ontario, however, within a few years they built many sailing vessels as adjuncts of the fur trade. Although batteaux were much used on the St. Lawrence River and Lake Erie, these sailing vessels on Lake Ontario were a great aid to the traffic between Detroit and Montreal.

It is said that Cadillac owned a sloop of ten tons to ply between Detroit and Niagara, and that he probably used this vessel when he visited Quebec in 1705.[15]

In 1726 when the French got permission to build the second fort at Niagara they also secured the right to build two barks on Lake Erie. These two vessels were constructed in 1726,[16] and were used to carry goods between the Niagara Portage and Detroit and Michilimackinac.

In preparation for the final struggle (French and

13. See Chapter II.
14. Brodhead, *Hist. of N. Y.*, II, 324.
15. Ross and Catlin, *Landmarks of Wayne Co. and Detroit*, 560.
16. *N. Y. Col. Docs.*, IX, 958.

Indian War), both French and British saw the need of vessels on the Lakes to control the Indian trade and to protect the political interests of each nation. Pownall of England in 1754 says,[17] "The navigation of the lakes would establish a mart where the Indians of every nation would resort. . . . If the Indian trade of the Hudson Bay Company, which is, as it were, only on the outskirts of the continent, is found so beneficial, what might this be that is in the very heart of it. The back settlements in time will want a vent for their products." He pointed out that if the English were masters of the Lakes, and consequently had the friendship of the Indians, the French could have little communication between Louisiana and Canada, and no effectual communication with most of the forts they had built "up and down the country."

After taking possession of the Lakes region in 1763, the British built two vessels on the Lakes above the falls. One, the Gladwin, besides being engaged in the regular carrying trade of the Lakes, served a good purpose in keeping open the route between Detroit and Buffalo during Pontiac's siege. The other was lost in 1763. Batteaux, however, continued to be used in much of the carrying trade because of lack of sailing vessels.

In 1764 Sir William Johnson saw the need of increasing the shipping on the Lakes, and in that year in his report to the Lords of Trade wrote that several vessels were needed on Lake Huron and Lake Erie to protect the "persons and property of his Majesty's subjects," for in open boats they were exposed to great risks in

17. *Ibid.*, VI, 895.

navigating the Lakes, and were obliged to put to shore every night and even during the day in stormy weather."[18]

The suggestion seems to have met a response, and boat building at His Majesty's yards at Detroit was active during most of the period of British occupation. Between the years 1774 and 1782, nine vessels, ranging in size from 18 tons to 136 tons burden were launched at the Detroit yards. These vessels were not only for defense and for the carrying of supplies to the garrisons at the posts, but were also engaged in the regular carrying trade of the Lakes. Soon after 1763 the British Government sought to control the traffic on the Lakes, and by the year 1776 it was entirely in the hands of the King's service.[19]

No vessels except those belonging to the King were allowed to navigate on the Lakes, though small sloops were owned by various individuals. This move on the part of the Government seems to have been prompted by the fear that the Americans might get a foothold and compete with the British subjects in the fur trade. Especially was this notion entertained after 1783. About 1784, Haldimand wrote to Lord Sydney,[20] "The navigation of the lakes by the King's vessels only is an object so nearly connected with the entire preservation of the fur trade, that I have withstood various applications for building and navigating vessels upon the Lakes. No precautions that could be taken would be effectual in preventing a great

18. *Ibid.*, VII, 600.
19. *Mich. Hist. Colls.*, XIX, 674.
20. *Ibid.*, XX, 278.

part of the furs from going directly into the American states.

"I would therefore recommend by all means that a sufficient number of King's vessels be kept on the lakes and all other craft prohibited, not only for the foregoing reasons, but in events to preserve a superiority upon these waters."

This Government monopoly, however, served to hinder free intercourse with the East. The vessels were small, and when engaged in the King's service neglected the commercial interests of the Lakes. The growing trade in peltries soon outstripped the carrying capacity of these vessels.[21] Although from time to time special permission was given to private vessels to carry peltries "with orders not to quit company with the King's vessels with which they were to sail except in the stress of weather,"[22] every year saw larger quantities of fur unable to reach the market because of lack of transportation facilities. In 1785 conditions were more acute, and a petition was sent to General Haldimand describing the situation of the merchants at Detroit stating, "if more vessels were not employed by the government, or permission given to transport their own property in crafts of their own, the trade of the place would suffer materially, and would probably cause the fall of some of the first houses concerned in supplying the merchandise at Detroit." Because of poor transportation facilities, "one thousand packs of furs and peltries," they said, "which used annually to be remitted to Montreal have this year from an inability

21. *Ibid.*, XI, 424.
22. *Ibid.*

to supply the trader in time been sent to New Orleans;" upward of fifty batteaux which left Detroit in the fall loaded with goods for the Indian trade were frozen up before they reached their destination, and many traders after a fruitless attendance returned unsupplied.[23] The number of vessels was increased, and by 1788 it was reported that there were five small sailing vessels on Lakes Erie and Huron and one of considerable burden still on the stocks. Some of the smaller ones carried only from four to ten batteau loads.

With the transfer of the posts to the Americans in 1796, on the Lakes there soon appeared vessels built in yards of the United States. It took many years, however, to overshadow the shipping owned by the British. The first American-built boat on Lake Erie was a craft of thirty tons, built in 1795, by Captain Lee. It had no crew; the passengers assisted in navigating the vessel. A year later the Erie Packet was built at Erie and used in local trade.[24] The first American schooner built on the Lakes was launched at Four Mile Creek near Erie, Pennsylvania; it was called the Washington.[25] In 1798 a sloop was constructed by E. Beebe at Erie; it was used in the trade between Buffalo and the ports on Lake Erie.[26] This was the beginning of the trade that taxed the capacity of the vessels on Lake Erie far on into the next century. Slowly but surely the shipbuilding industry grew. Between 1800 and 1805 six schooners and three sloops were built on the Lakes. During the War of

23. *Ibid.*, XI, 461.
24. Plumb, *Hist. of Navigation of Great Lakes*, 12.
25. *Mich. Hist. Colls.*, XXIX, 519; *Ibid.*, XXI, 43, 352.
26. Plumb, *Hist. of Navigation of Great Lakes*, 12.

1812 there was great activity at the yards on Lake
Erie, making preparation for the final struggle which
should determine the supremacy of the Lakes. In
1818 the first steamer appeared, but sailing vessels continued to be in the majority as late as 1886 or '87.[27]
The number of sailing vessels in service on the Great
Lakes by decades, starting with 1870, is as follows:

    1870—1545 sailing vessels, tonnage 254,820
    1880—1415 sailing vessels, tonnage 302,260
    1890—1236 sailing vessels, tonnage 320,000
    1900— 813 sailing vessels, tonnage 333,906.

In 1906 there were only 511 sailing vessels with a tonnage of 268,580.[28] No statistics are available to show
the relative importance of the various lake ports in
these decades in the construction of sailing vessels or
in the tonnage registered.

The steamboat era on Lake Erie began with the
Walk-in-the-Water, built at Black Rock near Buffalo
in 1818. An issue of the Detroit *Gazette* for 1818
contains the item:[29] "The Erie steamboat from Buffalo arrived on her first trip on the 22 of August."

The Walk-in-the-Water was 135 feet long, 32 foot
beam, 8.5 feet draught, and had a low pressure square
engine. The engine was transported from New York
to Albany in a sloop, thence overland in wagons to
Buffalo. On the trip from Buffalo to Detroit the
Walk-in-the-Water burned on the average 30 to 40
cords of wood. The fare from Buffalo was $6 to

---

27. *Trans. by Water, Cen. Rept.*, 122.
28. *Transp. by Water, Census Rept.*, (1906), 122.
29. Quoted in *Niles' Weekly Reg.*, XV, 92.

Erie, thirteen to Cleveland, fifteen to Sandusky, and $18 to Detroit.[30]

Flint describes this first steamer as follows:[31] "A fine vessel of 330 tons with two masts and rigged for taking advantage of the wind in the manner of the ocean crafts. The interior of this vessel is elegant and the entertainment is luxurious."

The average speed of the Walk-in-the-Water was eight miles per hour, and it took from thirty-six to forty-nine hours to reach Detroit from Black Rock; frequently the time was two to three days. There was no harbor at Buffalo at the time, so Black Rock was used as the eastern terminus.[32] The power of the engines was so low that no headway could be made against the strong current of the Niagara River. The passage to Lake Erie from Black Rock was accomplished by what was familiarly called the "horned breeze,"—several yoke of oxen.[33]

The cabins were on the upper deck. There were six berths on each side of cabins, with a walk of eight or ten feet between berths.[34] Compared with the luxurious steamers of today the 'Walk-in-the-Water was small indeed, but at that time it was heralded as the greatest advance of the age. Small as it was, the travelers of that time saw in it a great advance over the small slow-going, unreliable, uncomfortable schooners.

The movement of the Walk-in-the-Water was

30. Morrison, *Hist. of Steam Navigation*, 366.
31. Thwaites, *Early Western Travels*, IX, 314 (Flint).
32. *Mich. Hist. Colls.*, XIV, 536.
33. *Ibid.*, VI, 480.
34. *Ibid.*, XIV, 536.

scheduled and announced in the newspapers of the day much as are the ocean liners of our time. The first trip to Mackinac in 1819 was advertised in the New York papers. Said the New York *Mercantile Advertiser*,[35] "The swift steamer Walk-in-the-Water is intended to make a voyage early in the summer from Buffalo on Lake Erie to Michillimackinac on Lake Huron. The trip has so near a resemblance to the famous legendary expedition in the Heroic Ages of Greece that expectation is quite alive on the subject. Many of our most distinguished citizens are said to have already engaged their passage for this splendid adventure." The round trip from Buffalo to Mackinac took on the average twelve days.

The Walk-in-the-Water was used mostly for carrying emigrants and their effects, and provisions and Indian goods, to the West and bringing in return furs and peltries. Detroit for most of the trips was the western terminus. An occasional trip was made to Mackinac. There was so little traffic at that early period that a dividend was paid the owners only after three years. After three years of service the Walk-in-the-Water was wrecked during a storm on Lake Erie.

In 1822 the Superior was built to replace the Walk-in-the-Water; in 1824 the Chippewa and in 1825 the Henry Clay and Pioneer were added. All were used in carrying emigrants to the West. Detroit was the western terminus for most of these vessels.

The growth of the steam-shipping was slow. By 1825, seven steamers had been built. In 1826, four

35. DeBow's *Review*, IV, 386.

were built. This was incident to the opening of the
Erie Canal. By 1830, eleven had been launched, and
by 1840, seventy-two. After 1852 the number launched
increased rapidly. In 1853, twenty-nine went into
service; in 1854, thirty-one. The banner year up to
1880 seems to have been 1864, when one hundred fifty-
seven steamers with a total tonnage of 70,669 were
launched. The number constructed during each ten
year period after 1840 is as follows:[36]

> 1841-1850, inclusive,   96
> 1851-1860, inclusive, 249
> 1861-1870, inclusive, 611
> 1871-1880, inclusive, 660
> 1881-1890, inclusive, 1419

Since 1890 there has been a decline in numbers,
but an increase in the tonnage of the vessels built
per year.

The number, gross tonnage, and average tonnage of
steam vessels in service on the Great Lakes since 1870
are as follows:[37]

1870.	Number of steam vessels.	Gross tonnage.	Average tonnage.
1870	625	136,980	219
1880	912	209,465	230
1890	1507	648,725	430
1900	1719	1,106,842	644
1906	1824	1,838,136	1,008

36. *Tenth Cens., Spec. Rept. on Steamboats*, 11; *Trans. by Water,
    Cens. Rept*. (1906), 128.
37. *Transp. by Water, Census Rept*. (1906), 122.

These figures show that while the number of vessels
has increased to nearly threefold, the average tonnage
in 1906 was nearly five times that of 1870. The
average steamer in 1906 was nearly five times as large
as the average in 1870.

There have been great changes and improvements
in the steamer during the ninety or more years since
the appearance of the early steamers on the Lakes.
The hulls have been improved in shape and in size,
the spars and rigging have been reduced, and sails are
no longer to be seen, except on some small barges.
Great improvements have been made in the engines
and boilers. The consumption of fuel has been reduced, and speed and efficiency have been increased.
The screw propeller as a means of locomotion has
replaced the paddle-wheel, except on some of the
passenger vessels.

The first vessel on the Lakes equipped with a screw
propeller was the Vandalia, sloop-rigged, of 150 tons,
built on Lake Erie in 1842. In 1843 the Hercules and
Sampson were constructed. These marked a great
advance in steam navigation.[38]

The use of the propeller allowed the placing of the
engine in the rear part of the boat, making it possible
to have one large hold for the cargo. This greatly
facilitated loading and unloading the cargo. The reduction of the size of the engine gave greater carrying
capacity, and other improvements have increased the
efficiency of the engines and the speed of the vessels.
In 1860 began the era of the screw propeller in vessels
of one thousand tons or more.[39]

---

38.   Morrison, *Hist. of Steam Navigation*, 372.
39.   *Ibid.*

Since the early eighties, steel has come more and more to be a factor in the construction of vessels. In 1875 there were sixteen iron vessels on the Lakes, with an aggregate tonnage of 15,585. In 1885 there were thirty-four metal vessels. In 1890 there were eighty-eight; in 1900, 318; and in 1906, 543. With an increase in numbers there likewise has come an increase in size. In 1875 the average tonnage per vessel was 974; in 1885, 1001; in 1895, 1582; in 1906, 3811. In 1907 there were nine vessels that were 7,000 tons or more in capacity. These vessels if loaded to their maximum draught (nineteen feet), are capable of carrying fourteen thousand tons of coal, the equivalent of about three or four hundred railroad car loads.[40]

With the increase in experience in building, and increase in traffic, came specialization in types. Today there are packet steamers, passenger steamers, ore vessels, lumber vessels, coal vessels, tugs, sand-scows, oil-vessels, ferry boats, and car ferries, each built for a special line of traffic and not generally used in other lines of traffic. By far the larger number of steamers on the Lakes are the "bulk-cargo" crafts. These vessels carry cargo-lots of a single commodity. They maintain no regular schedule, though they operate over only a limited number of routes. This type is increasing in importance in the transportation of coal, iron, wheat and lumber.

The increase in size of vessels, both sailing and steam, improvements in engines and boilers, and specialization in types, combined with improved facilities for handling the cargoes at the docks have reduced greatly the

40. *Transp. by Water, Census Rept.;* 124, 126.

cost of Lake transportation.   Detroit, along with the
other Lake ports, has directly and indirectly reaped the
benefits of the lower freights.

In shipbuilding Detroit has been, for as far back as
there are available statistics, among the more important ports and customs districts of the Lakes.   For a
time the Detroit region owed its importance in shipbuilding to the great quantities of ship timber (oak)
in the immediate vicinity of Detroit.   For many years
Michigan supplied much oak timber as well as iron
to the shipyards in the East.[41]   By 1880, however, ship
timber was scarce in Michigan, nearly all the large
timber had been used, and in the three large shipyards at Detroit only short timbers were being used.[42]
For the years 1880 to 1889, inclusive, Detroit stood
fifth among the customs districts of the Lakes region
in the number of vessels constructed.   In 1880 it was
second among the Lake districts.[43]   In the total number and tonnage of vessels constructed for the years
1887, 1888, and 1889 it stood third among the shipbuilding districts.   The data for these three years for
the leading three districts are as follows:[44]

District.	No. of vessels.	Tonnage.
Huron	92	61,424
Cuyahoga	58	77,343
Detroit	50	53,515

41. *Tenth Census* (1880), *Spec. Rept. on Shipbuilding*, 171.
42. *Ibid.*
43. *Eleventh Census, Transp. by Water*, 266.
44. *Ibid.*, 267.

Of late years the Detroit region has occupied a high rank in the building of steel steamers. In 1910 there were constructed at the Detroit shipyards nine steel steamers with a total tonnage of 37,275. At the Cleveland shipyards nineteen steamers were built with a tonnage of 79,442; at Newport News, seven steamers with a tonnage of 34,900; and at Baltimore, eight steamers with a tonnage of 27,800.[45] These were the leading four shipbuilding districts in the United States for that year. Detroit stood second in the list in number of steamers and tonnage. In 1912 Detroit led all other shipbuilding districts of the United States in the number and tonnage of steel steamers constructed.[46] This was an exceptionally prosperous year for the Detroit yards. In 1911 Detroit was seventh in rank in the number of vessels and second in rank in tonnage of vessels built.[47] In 1913 Detroit was fifth in order of number of vessels and fourth in tonnage of vessels constructed.[48]

Although consecutive authentic data regarding the registered shipping and transportation facilities at the various ports are lacking for the decades until about 1890 the occasional report obtainable indicates that Detroit has been among the foremost Lake ports in registered tonnage. The position of the city on one of the main routes of the Great Lakes has always insured it abundant transportation facilities, potential facilities at least. Evans in 1818 wrote,[49] "Detroit has

---

45. Bureau of Commerce and Labor, *Rept. of Com. of Navigation* (1910), 217.
46. *Ibid.* (1912), 239.
47. *Ibid.* (1911), 287.
48. *Ibid.* (1913), 203.
49. Thwaites, *Early Western Travels*, VIII, 222 (Evans).

a central situation for the fur-trade in the Northwest and there is a considerable commercial connection between this place and Chicago and Green Bay." The "permanent" registered tonnage for the Lake ports for 1815 was for Owsego, 295 tons; Sackett's Harbor 317.6, Erie 27, Detroit 159.[50] (No returns for Buffalo Creek and Genesee). According to these data, Lake Ontario was much more prominent in the commerce of the Lakes than was Lake Erie. The Lake Ontario region was much better peopled at this time than were the lands about Lake Erie. Migration to northern Ohio and Indiana had hardly begun and much less so to Michigan. Moreover, much of the shipping of both Lakes Erie and Ontario had been destroyed during the War of 1812.

By 1820 the Lake Erie ports had become more populous, and began to assume some importance in the Lake shipping. The permanent registered tonnage for the Lake ports for the year ending December 31, 1820, was as follows:[51]

Genesee	313.6,
Oswego	260,
Sackett's Harbor	424,
Buffalo	no returns,
Cuyahoga (Cleveland)	195,
Sandusky	126,
Detroit	393,
Michillimackinac	no returns.

50. *Am. State Papers, Com. and Nav.*, II, 40.
51. *Ibid.*, 518, 519.

Detroit at this time stood second in rank among the ports from which there were returns.

With the settling of the Detroit region and Michigan by Americans, Detroit became the western terminus for many sailing vessels and steamboat lines. Between April 8 and 19, inclusive, in 1830, there arrived at Detroit fourteen steamboats and schooners, and from June 19 to 25, inclusive, in 1832, the entrances were eight steamers and eight sailing vessels.[52] These vessels were employed in the transfer of both passengers and freight, ·the latter consisting of grain, lumber, meat, fish, flour, hides, and skins.[53]

In 1837 there were registered at the Lake Erie ports 145 schooners, 58 sloops, 2 brigs, and 2 sailing vessels besides 47 steamboats.[54] The vessel interests at Detroit owned 42 schooners, 37 sloops, 3 brigs, and 17 steamers, most of which were registered in the Detroit district.[55] The total tonnage of the Lake Erie ports was about 24,000, that of Detroit 6700.[56] Detroit had 38 per cent of the registered vessels on Lake Erie and 28 per cent of the registered tonnage. It held second rank among the Lake Erie ports[57] in registered tonnage. In 1838 Detroit had steamboat lines to Buffalo, to Fort Gratiot (Pt. Huron) and to Chicago. Steamers on these traffic lines stopped at all the cities and vil-

52. Palmer, *Early Days in Detroit*, 46.
53. *Ibid.*
54. *Niles' Weekly Reg.*, LI, 352.
55. MacCabe, *Directory of Detroit* (1837), 10.
56. *Niles' Weekly Reg.*, LI, 352.
57. Some writers consider Detroit a Lake Erie port. In the early part of the nineteenth century, when its commerce was almost wholly with the cities to the south and east, it may be considered so, very properly.

lages en route.[58]   It is reported that in 1846 the trade of the Lakes required 60 steamers, 20 propellers, 50 brigs, and 270 schooners.[59]

In 1849, 43 steamers registered from Detroit, 42 from Buffalo, and from all the Lake ports 140.   Detroit, therefore, owned 30 per cent of the number of vessels on the Lakes.[60]   Andrews lists the steamers registered at the Lake ports in 1852 as follows: Detroit 47, Buffalo 42, Cleveland 13, Mackinac 12, Presque Isle 7, Chicago 4, Toledo 4, Sandusky 1.[61]

Detroit and Buffalo at this time were termini for the more important steamer lines on the Lakes.   Commerce on the Lakes in the early fifties was mainly the transfer of emigrants and manufactured goods and package freight westward and the carrying of grains and lumber eastward.[62]   The great commerce in iron ore and coal is of more recent development.   Since the days of the Walk-in-the-Water, Detroit has been one of the great centers for Lake steamer lines.   In 1857 three of the largest steamers on the Lakes ran daily between Detroit and Buffalo during the season of navigation, making the voyage one way in fifteen hours.   Six small steamers from Detroit were in the Lake Superior trade.   Two steamers ran between Detroit and Green Bay, four between Detroit and Port Huron, two to Toledo, one to Saginaw, two to Cleveland.   Steamboat lines also were established from Detroit to Sandusky, to Port Sarnia, to Dunkirk,

58. *Mich. Hist. Colls.*, XXXVIII, 595 (Chase).
59. DeBow's *Review*, I, 158 (Editor's note).
60. *Ibid.*, II, 448.
61. Andrews, *Trade and Com. of British Colonies with the U. S.*, Exec. Doc. 112, 32nd Congress, 51.
62. *Ibid.*, 55.

where connections were made with the New York and Erie Railway, and to Ogdensburg. Besides these there were numerous barges and schooners not running on any schedule.[63]

In 1870 there were eight lines of steamers from Detroit to the various Lake ports, and on many of the lines steamers left Detroit daily. More than seventy steamers in these lines used Detroit as a terminus or touched at Detroit.[64]

The leading five lake ports in total passenger traffic on the Lakes in 1889, with the regular, excursion, and ferry passengers, were as follows:[65]

	Total passengers.	Regular passengers.	Excursion passengers.	Ferry passengers.
Detroit.....................	406,317	233,196	173,121	*
Pt. Huron.................	349,199	81,924	16,347	250,925
Gd. Haven...............	329,870	177,302	8,960	143,608
Toledo.....................	257,046	*	257,046	*
Sandusky..................	173,696	57,260	43,530	72,906

The total passenger traffic for the whole Lakes in 1889 was 2,235,993; of the total Detroit had about 22 per cent.[66]

The increase in population in the Lakes region, the reduction in cost of transportation, the greater per capita wealth, and the greater leisure have contributed toward increasing the passenger traffic. The total number of passengers reported from the different districts on the Great Lakes in 1906 was 16,300,000.

63. Roberts, *Sketches of the City of the Straits*, 20; Disturnell, *Trip Through Lakes and St. Lawrence Valley* (1857), 135.
64. Farmer, *Map of Michigan* (1870).
65. Not separately listed. (*Eleventh Census* (1890), *Transportation by Water*, 339).
66. *Ibid.*

Of this number Detroit was credited with 7,400,000, or about 45 per cent of the total. These figures included passengers carried by ferries, excursions steamers, and by passenger and freight vessels, these not being separately listed.[67] The remarkable showing made by Detroit in the passenger business is due to the location of the city on a large navigable river

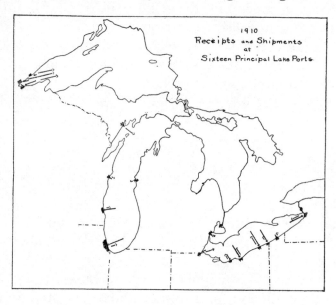

between Lake Erie and the Upper Lakes. The city park on Belle Isle, Windsor opposite, many recreation parks on the islands in St. Clair and Detroit rivers and in Lake Erie, and the several lake cities to which steamer lines extend from Detroit, all contribute to give Detroit a great passenger traffic.[68]

67.   *Transp. by Water, Census Rept.* (1906), 144.
68.   Evans comments on this as early as 1818. See Thwaites, *Early Western Travels*, VIII, 222 (Evans).

Detroit reaps only indirectly the benefits of facilities for transportation offered by the "bulk cargo" carriers of the Lakes. The mines, the forests, and the grain fields of the Great Lakes region are the sources from which most of the commodities carried on the Lakes originate. In 1898 coal, iron ore, lumber, grain, and flour constituted nearly 92 per cent of the total traffic

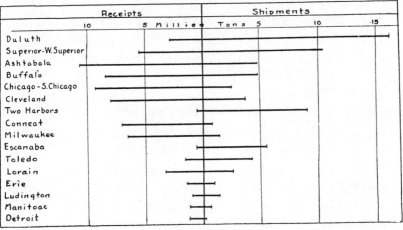

TRAFFIC IN ALL COMMODITIES IN 1910 AT THE PRINCIPAL LAKE PORTS
(*Data from Monthly Summary of Commerce and Finance, December, 1911, 960*)

of the Lakes.[69] Moreover, local traffic on the Great Lakes is small; nearly all the commodities are carried from one end of the Lake system to the other. Coal, which constitutes almost entirely the west bound traffic, is carried from the ports of Lake Erie to the ports on the western shores of Lakes Michigan and Superior. Iron ore, mined in the Superior region, goes mostly

69. Tunell, *Stat. on Com. of Lakes*, 55th Congress, 2nd Session, H. D. No. 277, 9.

to the south shore of Lake Erie and to Chicago. Most of the grain is shipped from Chicago, Milwaukee, Duluth, and Superior to Buffalo. Lumber is no longer an important commodity in the commerce of the Lakes. Detroit, being situated on the border of a region which neither originates nor consumes much of any of these commodities, has little traffic in them, and consequently little of the traffic of the Lakes. In 1889 Detroit was surpassed by sixteen of the Lake ports in tonnage of freight received and shipped. Only 764,553 tons of freight out of 51,200,000 for the whole Lakes passed over the docks at Detroit.[70] In 1906 Detroit stood twenty-first in rank among the Lake ports in total freight handled.[71] The 60,000,000 tons of freight that pass the city yearly[72] transported mostly in "bulk cargo" carriers, is no index of the importance of the city in the commerce of the Lakes. The facilities for transportation offered by the 20,000 to 30,000 vessels (estimated) that pass Detroit yearly must be considered merely as "potential" facilities in Lake transportation for Detroit.

70.   *Eleventh Census* (1890), *Transp. by Water*, 321.
71.   *Transp. by Water, Census Rept.* (1906), 134.
72.   *Ibid.*, 153.

CHAPTER X

DETROIT AND THE DEVELOPMENT OF WATER TRANS-
PORTATION

II.—*Waterways and Water Routes*

THE surface levels of the Great Lakes form a series
of great steps, the highest step being Lake Superior, 602 feet above sea level. Between the Lake
Superior level and the Huron-Michigan level is a fall
of twenty feet, the greater part being at the Falls
of St. Mary's River. Lake Erie lies about eight
feet below the level of Lake Huron; but this slight
fall is distributed fairly uniformly over about ninety
miles and hence there is little or no hindrance offered
by strong currents to navigation in the strait between
Lakes Huron and Erie. From Lake Erie to Lake
Ontario there is a fall of 325 feet within a distance of
about twenty-five miles. More than 160 feet of this
fall occurs at Niagara Falls. Here is offered the
greatest obstacle to navigation in the whole St. Lawrence River Basin. Lake Ontario lies 246 feet above
tide water in the estuary of St. Lawrence, about three
hundred miles distant. In this distance are many
rapids, the current is swift throughout, the channel
shallow and beset with many sunken ledges of rock.
The many rapids in the St. Lawrence River, the falls
at Niagara, and the falls in the St. Mary's River are
formidable barriers and tend to restrict the deep

water commercial activities of Detroit to Lakes Michigan, Huron, St. Clair, and Erie, and the waterways between Lake Huron and Lake Erie. Moreover, the many Lake harbors in their natural conditions were ill-adapted to the requirement of modern Lake transportation, so that improvements were necessary before there could be freedom of communication between the various Lake cities. Most of the Lake cities are located at the mouths of streams which carry great quantities of silt. Deposition of this silt takes place where the streams enter the Lake. In time, through continued deposition and the action of waves on the deposits, bars are formed. Even the small steamers in the early steamboat era found difficulty in entering most of these harbors. Darby, who made a tour of the Lakes in 1819, comments on the Walk-in-the-Water and the harbors as follows:[1] "I did not see her (Walk-in-the-Water), but learned at the town of Erie that she had gone up and had performed well, though drawing too much water to suit entirely the navigation of Lake Erie, she stranded in seven feet of water on the Erie bar. A more fatal fault in construction of any vessel to be used on Lake Erie could not be easily committed than that of too great draught of water. The harbors are few, narrow, and difficult to enter, and the immediate shores dangerous in the extreme. With the exception of Niagara River below Bird Island, Put-in-Bay, and Detroit River there exists no harbor in Lake Erie that can be safely entered in a swelling sea in a vessel drawing seven feet of water. To the number of vessels which are actively

1. Darby, *Tour from New York to Detroit* (1819), 207.

employed I am convinced that there are as many wrecked on Lake Erie as on the coast of the United States."

To overcome these many obstructions to navigation in the Great Lakes and the St. Lawrence River, both the Canadian and United States Governments have spent large sums of money in improvements. Up to and including the appropriations for 1907 (these are the latest data available), the United States has spent nearly $98,000,000 in the Great Lakes region and St. Lawrence River, distributed as follows:[2]

Lake Superior (including "Soo" Canals)...	$29,000,000
Lake Huron and Lake St. Clair..........	11,000,000
Lake Michigan.......................	24,000,000
Lake Erie...........................	26,000,000
Lake Ontario........................	4,600,000
St. Lawrence River..................	700,000

Appropriations for some of the rivers are not included.

The Canadian Government up to 1912 has spent over $128,000,000 in all to improve the St. Lawrence River and the Canadian side of the Lakes.[3]

The many improvements in the Lakes region and along the St. Lawrence, together with the Erie Canal and the many canals leading from the Great Lakes to the Ohio and Mississippi rivers, have greatly extended the area commercially in touch by water with Detroit. Most important of the improved waterways on the

2. *Transp. by Water, Census Rept.* (1906), 152.
3. Canadian Govt. Pub. (1912), *Navigation, Railways, and Steamboat Lines*, 59.

growth of Detroit in population and manufactures are the St. Lawrence, the Erie Canal, and the Great Lakes.

DETROIT AND THE ST. LAWRENCE ROUTE

Many of the early French navigators experienced difficulties of navigation in the Lower St. Lawrence, and have left detailed accounts of the obstacles encountered.   Talon in his voyage in 1665 made a series of observations and sent them back to France, a copy of which was given to each vessel leaving Rochelle and the ports of Normandy for the St. Lawrence.   He writes,[4] "As I am aware of the great dangers in navigating the St. Lawrence I reflected considerably in order to ascertain the measures to be adopted to improve it, so as to diminish the difficulties the captains of ships experience in steering securely through it. . . " The thick fog and stormy weather, the many shoals and sunken rocks, the strong currents, and lack of anchorage, all make the navigation of the estuary of the St. Lawrence River very difficult.   In the earlier days of navigation a voyage to Canada was considered "much more dangerous than to any other part of America."   An entrance to the estuary was never attempted except during the summer months, and even with fair wind and weather the vessels almost never sailed at night.[5]

From Quebec to Montreal the navigator, before improvements were made, found even greater difficulties. The high tide at Quebec occasions so strong a current

4.   *N. Y. Col. Docs.*, IX, 35.
5.   *Ibid.*, V, 728 (Colden).

that "a boat of six oars," says Colden, "cannot make way against it." Above Three Rivers the current is so strong that it requires a strong and fair wind to carry the sailing vessels against the stream. Being in the belt of the westerly winds, the prevailing winds were adverse to the up-passage of sailing vessels. From Montreal to Lake Ontario, the early navigators had hard work to stem the current.[6]

During the French period nothing was done to improve the navigation of the lower St. Lawrence. In 1763 the British took over the control of Canada, but they likewise neglected the waterways for many years. Not until after Haldemand assumed control of the Province of Canada in 1778, was the improvement of the St. Lawrence undertaken. Soon after this date a canal was dug between St. Louis and St. Francis lakes. This was the forerunner of the canals of Canada. The improvement of the channel of the St. Lawrence began as early as 1779. To facilitate the passage of canoes and batteaux, obstructions such as trees, stones, and logs were removed to provide for a deep channel along the shores. Projecting points of land were crossed by small canals.[7]

A canal at Coteau du Lac across a point that projects into Coteau Rapids was completed for traffic in 1781. The original canal had three locks and was six feet wide at the gates. In 1801 it was widened to nine and one-half feet at the gates; and in 1817 a second canal was built at this point, four hundred feet long and four feet deep.[8]

6. *Ibid.*
7. Kingsford, *Hist. of Canada*, VII, 21.
8. *Ibid.*, 22.

About 1782 two other canals were constructed on the St. Lawrence, one six hundred feet long at Cascade Point to avoid Mill Rapids, and the other at Split Rock around Point au Buisson. These two shorter canals were replaced in 1806 by a canal 1600 feet long, twenty feet wide at the gates, and nine and one-half feet deep, to connect the St. Lawrence with the Ottawa River. These canals mark the real beginning of the improvement on the St. Lawrence. Since 1806 they have been increased in size, number, and capacity.[9] Between 1814 and '17 the three canals, Cascade, Split Rock, and Coteau du Lac, were enlarged. They continued to be the only channels by which access to the western lakes and Detroit by way of the St. Lawrence was obtained until October, 1845, when the Beauharnois Canal was opened.[10]

The La Chine Canal near Montreal was begun in 1821 and completed in 1825. The locks were made one hundred feet long, twenty feet wide and five feet on the sills.[11] Up to 1842 there had been no such a thing as a canal system in Canada. In that year a unified system was adopted along the St. Lawrence. The locks were to be forty-five feet wide and have nine feet of water on the sill. At a later date the locks were made forty-five feet wide and with fourteen feet of water on the sills.[12]

The great difference in level between Lake Erie and Lake Ontario always has been, even after the building of the Welland Canal, a serious obstacle to traffic

9. *Ibid.*, 23.
10. *Ibid.*, 22.
11. *Ibid.*, 21, 25.
12. *Ibid.*, 24.

between Detroit and Montreal or Quebec. During the French period, after about 1702, the Niagara Portage was used by most of the traders and travelers passing between the Upper Lakes and Montreal. About 1718 many families of Seneca Indians lived along the portage, where they cultivated the soil and acted as porters for the French traders, taking their pay in furs and Indian goods. The road along which the goods were carted was in the upland to the east of the gorge and falls. It led from Lewiston up over the two-hundred-foot cliff of the escarpment and thence southward to a point about two miles above the falls to a landing called Duncan's House. The total distance along which goods had to be carted or carried was about eight miles.[13]

To the costly furs this break in transportation had no great deterrent effect. It precluded, however, almost any bulky commodity from getting an outlet from the Upper Lakes to the markets to the east.

In 1817 Samuel Williams, in discussing the export trade of the Lake Country, writes,[14] "From the lakes the export trade, except in furs is inconsiderable because there is yet no channel through which the productions of the country can be conveyed to market. The Cataract of Niagara presents an insuperable obstacle to navigation between the Upper Lakes and Lake Ontario."

To William Hamilton Merrit, a resident of St. Catherines, Ontario, is due the "bold and workmanship idea of making a ship canal from Lake Erie to

13. *N. Y. Col. Docs.*, IX, 885; *Doc. Hist. N. Y.*, II, 458.
14. *Niles' Weekly Reg.*, XI, 321.

Lake Ontario."[15]   As early as 1816 a joint commission
of both houses of Upper Canada (now Ontario) reported on the project of a canal at the Falls, and a
bill was introduced to authorize a survey. But no
immediate action followed. In 1823 another commission reported favorably on the plan, and two years
later a company was incorporated by the legislature
for the construction of a canal. Work was soon begun.
By 1829 the project was so far completed that two
schooners, each of eighty-five tons burden, passed
between Lakes Erie and Ontario.

For many years before improvements were made
there were only 10.25 feet of water over the sills of
the locks and 24 out of the 27 locks were 150 feet in
length. In the enlarged canal the dimensions of the
locks are 270 feet by 45, with 14 feet of water over the
sills. The present canal is 26.75 miles long, has 26
locks, and the total lockage is 326.75.[16] The great
length, the large number of locks, the great lockage to
overcome, the small size of the locks, and the shallow
water in the locks have been serious defects, making
it impossible to use the canal as an important part of
the Great Lakes transportation routes. Even the
present dimensions of the locks restrict the size of
vessels that may pass from the Lakes to the ocean
and have given rise to a particular size of vessel,
called the "Canalers," intended for traffic on the Upper
Lakes, Lake Erie, and Lake Ontario. Harbor improvements on Lake Ontario also have been planned
with these limitations in mind, the harbor improve-

15.   Hall, *Travels in Canada and U. S.* (1827), I, 215.
16.   Canadian Govt. Pub. (1912), *Navigation, Railways, and
        Steamboat Lines*, 39.

ments being designed to give facilities for vessels drawing fourteen feet of water.[17]

The specifications for the various St. Lawrence canals in 1912 between Lake Erie and deep water at Montreal are as follows:[18]

Canal.	Dimensions.		Locks.			
	Length, miles.	Width, feet.	No.	Lift, feet.	Width, feet.	Depth on sill.
La Chine.................	8.5	150	5	45	45	14–18
Soulanges................	14	164	5	84	45	15
Cornwall.................	11	164	6	48	45	14
Farrand Pt...............	1	154	1	3.5	45	14
Rapide Plat..............	3.7	152	2	11.5	45	14
Galops Pt................	7.3	144	3	15.5	45	14
Welland (New)...........	27	156	26	326.8	45	14

The commerce of Detroit far into the nineteenth century was largely along the St. Lawrence River route. There was little communication between the cities on the Atlantic seaboard and the Upper Lakes previous to 1820 or 1825. However, in the matter of rum for the Indian trade, most of which was obtained from the West Indies, the Mohawk Route had the principal part of the Detroit trade, because New York, Boston, and other ports engaged in this trade were open at all seasons and, moreover, were nearer both the West Indies and Detroit markets than were Montreal and Quebec.[19] For 125 years the merchants of

17. *Transp. by Water*, II, *Cens. Rept.*, 242.
18. *Atlas of Canada*, Plate 22; *Blue Book Amer. Shipping* (1910), 463; Canadian Govt. Pub. (1912), *Navigation, Railways, and Steamboat Lines*, 29–39.
19. *Mich. Hist. Colls.*, XXIV, 406; *Mem. of Montreal Merchants* (1792); See Darby, *A Tour from N. Y. to Detroit* (1819), 188.

Montreal supplied the post at Detroit with most of the goods for the Indian trade and took in return the furs and peltries of the forests.   In 1788 the amount of goods recorded arriving at Detroit for the Indian trade was valued at sixty thousand pounds (sterling) and twenty thousand pounds worth were consumed in the settlement.   The large Detroit merchants had agents in Montreal to whom they sent their furs and peltries.   The agents shipped these to London and sold them on "the account" of the Detroit merchants. Goods from Europe were ordered through the agent on "the account" and risk of the merchant at Detroit.[20] Before these many improvements along the St. Lawrence were made, commodities for Detroit had to be carried in batteaux from Montreal to Kingston.[21] This passage was long and tedious, although the navigation of this part of the river was much aided by canals that had been built across the points and around the rapids of the St. Lawrence.   Hall describes the slowness of travel along this part of the St. Lawrence about 1827.   " 'Tis a sad waste of life," he says,[22] "to ascend the St. Lawrence in a batteau.   After admiring the exertion with which the Canadian boatmen, who seem to have exclusive possession of this employment, force the long flatbottomed boats against the rapids, there is nothing left but to gaze listlessly on the descending current and its low wooded shores. . . .   It cost us fifteen hours to row from Coteau du Lac to Cornwall."   At Kingston the goods were transferred to sailing vessels, which in the course of from four to

20.   *Mich. Hist. Colls.*, XI, 631.
21.   *Ibid.*, III, 125.
22.   Hall, *Travels in Canada and U. S.* (1827), 96.

ten days, made the voyage from Kingston to Lewiston or Queenstown. After a land carriage of eight miles the batteaux again were made use of and being poled, towed, or sailed, reached deep water in the upper part of the Niagara River. Here vessels were again employed, which, after another journey of four to ten days, or even more, finally reached Detroit. Liancourt reported that because of this costly means of transportation, such goods as woolen blankets, coarse cloth, worsteds, and others sold at Detroit for three times the price charged at Montreal.[23] Although tedious and costly, this route between the ocean and the Lakes region was considered by many writers even as late as 1852 to be the most feasible. Just previous to the opening of the Erie Canal, ex-President Dwight of Yale University, in discussing the outlet for the products of Western New York and the Lakes region, said of the St. Lawrence River,[24] "This has ever appeared to me the cheapest, safest, and most unembarrassed passage for the produce of all the country that borders the Great American Lakes. The ordinary price for transporting a quarter cask from Montreal to Queenstown is but a single dollar. Whenever a regular trade is established between this country and Montreal, and a regular transportation around the Niagara Falls, the cost will be reduced. Thence merchandise of all kinds may be conveyed in ships of convenient size to the south end of Lake Michigan, and with the exception of a short land carriage to the western end of Lake Superior, a tract consisting of

23. Liancourt, *Travels in N. A.*, I, 330:
24. Dwight, *Travels in New Eng. and New York*, IV, 124.

31

242 HISTORICAL GEOGRAPHY OF DETROIT

from 400,000 to 500,000 square miles will hereafter empty its produce upon the ocean through the St. Lawrence River."

Andrews in his report on the commerce of British colonies with the United States in 1852 shows the importance of the St. Lawrence at that date as an artery of commerce. "The River St. Lawrence and the lakes," he writes,[25] "must be the principal channel for the commerce of the country on both sides of these waterways, the American side as well as the Canadian, both for the export and the import trade. As long, therefore, as the British hold their present possessions they must exclusively enjoy that trade. . . . The St. Lawrence being the shortest and deepest channel with which these countries can be supplied with foreign commodities, the Canadians will therefore have the supplying of the Americans, who inhabit the country on their frontiers, with British and other foreign manu-factures secured to them. This frontier will prove a door always open to the introduction of British manu-.factures, in spite of the most rigid enactments of the American government to the contrary." In another section in his report he writes,[26] "Notwithstanding the opinion that may be entertained adverse to that mighty river as a channel of communication between the West and the Atlantic, it is nevertheless certain to be more used and to increase in importance in proportion to every material stride in the prosperity and advancement of the country bordering on the lakes."

25. Anderson, *Trade and Commerce of British Colonies with the U. S.*, Exec. Doc. 112, 32nd Congress, 23.
26. *Ibid.*, 5.

This prediction was made before the great trunk lines of railroads linked the Lakes with the Atlantic seaboard and shortly after the many improvements along the St. Lawrence had been completed, and the Great Lakes region given a deep waterway to the ocean for vessels of that period. Many vessels on the Lakes took advantage of the St. Lawrence Route to the ocean. It was thought at that time that such an intercourse between the Lakes and ocean meant a new era for Lake commerce. Detroit was pointed out as being admirably situated for foreign trade, its importance being greatly enhanced by its imminent and extensive relations with the regions to the north and west.[27]

With the increase in importance of the railroads between the Lakes and the American seaboard and the increase in the size of vessels navigating the Lakes, the canals of the St. Lawrence came to be used less and less and the St. Lawrence failed to become the favorite route expected.

DETROIT AND THE MOHAWK ROUTE

With the increase of American settlers at Detroit after 1796, the commercial relations of the city began to be deflected toward New England and New York. As long, however, as the chief business of the city continued to be the trade in furs, and as long as the majority of the mercantile establishments remained in the hands of the English and the Scotch, the major part of the trade of Detroit flowed along the St. Law-

27. Hunt's *Merchant's Mag.*, LI, 405; *Ill. Hist. Colls.*, IV, 244.

rence route.   The many improvements made along the
St. Lawrence tended to keep the traffic along this
important line of communication.   From time to time,
however, as the American frontier moved westward,
improvements were made in American territory that
tended to deflect some of the traffic eastward across
the State of New York.   Not until the Erie Canal,
and more especially the railroads, became important
factors in transportation, did Detroit and the other
portions of the Lakes region sever almost entirely their
commercial relations with the lower St. Lawrence.

In 1794 the Legislature of New York appropriated
money for the construction of a road six rods wide
from old Fort Schuyler (Utica) westward to the Genes-
see River.   Until after 1797, however, the road was
little better than an Indian path.   At that date a
lottery was authorized by the State to obtain money
for its improvement.   In 1799 a stage began to run
over the road.   In 1800 the road was made into a
turnpike, and the same year was extended to Buffalo.[28]
This road and a turnpike in the southern part of the
State near the boundary line of Pennsylvania were,
until the opening of the Erie Canal, the only outlets
for the traffic of Detroit to the Atlantic seaboard
across the State of New York.[29]

In 1817 a regular line of wagons and packets was
established between Detroit and New York.   The cost
of carriage, as advertised, was in no case to exceed
$4.50 per one hundred pounds.[30]   Packets carried the

28.   Thwaites, *Early Western Travels*, VII, 41 (Butterick).
29.   *Doc. Hist. of N. Y.*, II, 691; Thwaites, *Early Western Travels*,
        VIII, 118 (Evans).
30.   *Niles' Weekly Reg.*, XIV, 14, Feb. 28, 1818.

goods and passengers between Albany and New York.
Between Albany and Buffalo, covered wagons "with
tires as broad as a Quaker's hat" and drawn by ten
to a dozen horses were used.   These wagons frequently
traveled in caravans of a hundred or more.   From four
to six weeks were consumed in the journey from New
York to Buffalo.   Packets were used on Lake Erie
between Buffalo and Detroit.[31]

Some of the cities on the Atlantic seaboard recognized the importance of deflecting products of the
Lakes region to their markets.   Boston, New York,
Philadelphia, and Baltimore all were interested in the
trade with the West.   The Erie Canal is a memorial
of the endeavor of the State of New York to direct
the Lake trade to its port on the Atlantic seaboard.   •

Work was begun on the Erie Canal in 1817.   In 1825
the canal was opened for traffic.   Long before its completion the immense influence it would exert on the
commercial and economic affairs of the Lakes region
was recognized by all.   Flint, writing in 1818, commented on the importance of the canal as follows:[32]
"The New York canal is a work not only interesting
to a large portion of the United States . . . but
also to Upper Canada. . . .   Should the government of Britain continue to neglect the inland navigation of Canada and persist in excluding the colonies
from the advantages of free trade . . .   new interests must arise in the Upper Province of Canada.
England may still give Canada lands gratis, . . .
but she cannot shut the eyes of her subjects to the

31. *Mich. Hist. Colls.*, XXII, 369.
32. Thwaites, *Early Western Travels*, IX, 315 (Flint).

facilities to be derived from an uninterrupted route to the port of New York, which is free to all flags of all nations and open to the sea at all times of the year." Darby comments as follows:[33] "If such a channel of commerce was open the consequences would be, not only to secure to the U. S. the benefits of the produce of its own industry, but also to secure the moral attachment of the inhabitants of some of its remote, and as matters now stand most detached parts above the falls of Niagara."

These predictions proved not amiss. The whole Lakes region felt the stimulus of this shorter outlet to the sea. Immigration was greatly accelerated. The farmers now for the first time had communication with the East, such that farm products could be transported profitably for five hundred or more miles. Products from Western Pennsylvania, Northern Ohio, and Eastern Michigan began to find their way to the markets of New York. Distance was declared to be "conquered by science" and in the neighborhood of the Lakes was "no longer a thing to be regarded." "Detroit," said a writer in *Niles' Weekly Register*,[34] "is virtually nearer the city of New York than Cumberland, Maryland, is to Baltimore." The facilities for transportation offered by the Erie Canal aided greatly the development of manufactures in the Lakes region. The real development of the manufacturing industries at Detroit dates from about the time of opening of the Erie Canal.

During the season of navigation of Lake Erie and

33. Darby, *A Tour from New York to Detroit* (1818), 189.
34. *Niles' Weekly Reg.*, XXIX, 180.

the Erie Canal, the transportation facilities were much increased, but for the winter season, Detroit was almost "as far" from the Atlantic seaboard as in the French period. Compared with our modern time of dispatch, the transit was exceedingly slow, in either summer or winter. A merchant of Detroit, to lay in a stock of goods from New York, required from three to six months from the time he set out from Detroit to the arrival of the goods. It was customary for many of the merchants, who made their own purchases, to leave Detroit in February or March, cross Ontario to Buffalo in a French "carry-all," and after a journey of some two or three weeks reach New York where their purchases were made. As soon as the ice had gone from the Hudson River and Erie Canal, the goods were dispatched by canal boat to Black Rock, which point they reached some time in June. From there steamers on Lake Erie carried them to Detroit. This was the way Detroit received its merchandise until the late forties when a railroad was built which connected Buffalo with the Atlantic seaboard. As late as 1845 or '50 goods were bought from New York merchants at twelve, eighteen, and even twenty-four month's credit.[35]

DETROIT AND THE IMPROVEMENTS OF NAVIGATION ON LAKE ERIE AND THE UPPER LAKES

In the earlier periods of settlement in the Lakes region, when Ohio, Indiana, Illinois, and Michigan had nearly all the people in the Old Northwest, most

35. *Mich. Hist. Colls.*, XXII, 369.

of the eastbound traffic of the Lakes was in articles destined for the markets in the East, and the westbound traffic was emigrants and their household effects and provisions. The commerce on the Lakes northbound from Detroit was mainly in provisions and supplies for the forts and in goods for the Indian trade.[36] The spread of population westward and the peopling of the regions about the shores of Lakes Michigan and Superior made the improvement of the harbors of Lake Erie and the Upper Lakes and of the connecting rivers between these Lakes imperative.

Government aid to the improvement of navigation on the Great Lakes dates from 1825, in which year money was appropriated for the improvement of the harbor at Erie. By 1851 the Government had spent about $2,791,000 in improvements on the Great Lakes.[37] For several decades the improvements were not made with regard to any definite plan. The amount of appropriation and the magnitude of the work carried out depended mostly upon the political influence of the congressman in whose district the port or river was located. The engineers in charge of work on the Great Lakes at length came to see that a unified plan was necessary, and recommendations were made to the Rivers and Harbors Committee in Congress. Their plan found its expression in the Rivers and Harbors Act of July, 1892, in which appropriations were made for the improvement of the connecting waters between the Lakes from Chicago and Duluth to Buffalo, by excavating channels to the

36. DeBow's *Rev.*, IV, 386.
37. Andrews, *Trade and Commerce of Br. Colonies with U. S.*, Exec. Doc.112, 32nd Congress, 1st Sess., 53.

minimum depth of twenty feet and a minimum width of three hundred feet. Such channels were believed at that time adequate to meet all demands for many years to come. Each succeeding year, however, saw larger and larger vessels built and vessel interests called for larger and deeper channels. To meet the demand, Congress by the Act of March, 1905, authorized a preliminary examination and survey with a view to enlarging the channels to the depth of twenty-two or twenty-five feet. The next year the board of engineers made a report in which they suggested that the contemplated improvements must be deferred, that the advantages would not warrant the cost of improvement.[38]

In pursuance of the plan of 1892 for a uniform channel, appropriations have been made from time to time and the work has gone on, until now vessels loaded for twenty feet of water may enter or leave any of the important ports on the Lakes and pass through all the connecting waters in safety.[39]

The most important and most expensive of the many improvements is the excavation of the canals about the Falls of the St. Mary's River (at Sault Ste. Marie). On these canals and on the Hay Lake and Neebish channels in the St. Mary's River the Government has spent, up to and including the appropriations for 1907, more than $17,000,000.[40] Attempts were made at an early date to overcome the difficulties at the Falls. In 1797 the Northwest Fur Company

38. *Transp. by Water, Cen. Rept.* (1906), 153.
39. *Ibid.*, 154.
40. *Ibid.*, 154.

constructed a canal on the Canadian side of the river
with locks 38 feet long, 9 feet high, and about 9 feet
wide. A tow path along the canal was made for
oxen to pull the batteaux and canoes used in the fur
trade.[41] Detroit probably profited little from this
canal, for the Northwest Fur Company was a British
company with headquarters at Montreal, and Detroit
was at this time in the hands of the Americans.

The growing trade of Lake Superior about the middle
of the nineteenth century, at a time when Detroit was
active in Lake Superior traffic in iron ore and copper
ore, called for some means of avoiding the rapids. In.
1850 the Chippewa Portage Company built a tramway
along the side of the rapids and connected the upper
and lower boat landings. During the first year the
company transferred three thousand tons of freight.
This could be considered only as a temporary make-
shift. Shortly after, agitation became so active that a
bill was introduced into Congress December 10, 1851,
by Mr. Felch, asking that the Government grant "to
the State of Michigan the right of way and donation
of public lands for the purpose of constructing . . .
a ship canal around the Falls of St. Mary's."[42] The
right of way was granted through the military reserva-
tion and 750,000 acres of public land were donated to
the State.[43] Work was begun in 1853 and completed
in 1855. This canal provided for the passage of vessels drawing 11.5 feet of water. In 1881 the Wietzel
Lock (canal) was opened for navigation to accom-

41.   *Mich. Hist. Colls.*, XVIII, 639.
42.   *Cong. Globe*, XXIV, Pt. I, 33, 1532, 1717, 1731.
43.   DeBow's *Review*, 519.

modate the increasing Lake shipping, and in 1896 the
Poe Lock was placed in commission. The Poe Lock
permits the passage of vessels drawing 20 feet of
water. The chambers are 800 feet long and 100
wide. A new lock is now under construction.[44]

In the early decades of American control of the
Lakes when the people of the Lakes region were to be
found mainly about the shores of Lake Erie, Detroit
was a western terminus for the Lake traffic. At this
period manufactures were little developed, the business
of the city was chiefly commercial. The opening of
the St. Mary's Canal, the exploitation of the Lake
Superior iron deposits, the growth in population of
the Upper Lakes ports, and the settlement of the upper
Mississippi Valley have all contributed toward a new
routing of traffic on the Lakes, a great change in kind
of commodities handled, and a tremendous increase in
the amount of traffic.

The Great Lakes today are great and important
water routes for inland commerce. Our domestic commerce is certain to remain the more important of our
commercial transactions, but it seems quite clear that
could an adequate route to the ocean be provided, the
Great Lakes traffic would be benefited greatly. From
time to time, chiefly between 1830 and 1850, canals
have been opened between the Lakes region and the
Ohio and Mississippi rivers. These canals have done
much to develop some of the Lake cities, but no
definite influence has been traceable on the growth of
Detroit. It seems very probable that a Lakes-to-the-

44. *Transp. by Water, Rept. Com. Corp.* (1909), II, 205, 206;
Transp. by Water, Cen. Rept., 153.

Gulf Waterway would benefit Detroit but little. For over fifty years the city has enjoyed the advantages of a fourteen foot channel to the ocean by way of the St. Lawrence, yet seems to have taken little advantage of it.

CHAPTER XI

The Development of Land Transportation of Detroit

FROM the founding of Detroit in 1701 until the coming of American settlers early in the nineteenth century, there was little need of roads in southeastern Michigan, for most or all of the people lived along the larger navigable waters. Indeed, this was the situation until after 1820.[1] To this time communication with the interior was chiefly along two trails used by the Indians after 1796 in going to Malden to receive their annual presents from the British. One led up the St. Joseph River from Lake Michigan, thence overland to the Huron River, and along the latter to Lake Erie. This was the St. Joseph trail. The other trail skirted the southern end of Saginaw Bay and extended thence to the Rouge River, and along this stream to the Detroit River.[2] This was the Saginaw trail. What the people of Detroit needed was ready communication with the frontier in Ohio.

In the treaty of Brownstown, made November 25, 1808, the Indians granted to the United States a tract of land two miles wide, extending westward and northward from the Connecticut Western Reserve to the foot of the Rapids of the Miamis of the Lakes, with the

---

1. *Mich. Hist. Colls.*, VI, 484 (Campbell).
2. *American St. Papers, Miscellaneous*, II, 597.

understanding that a road should be built along it. In 1811 the president authorized a party to survey and mark this road and six thousand dollars were set aside to cover the expense. But the War of 1812 prevented the carrying out of the provisions of the treaty. Another cause for delay undoubtedly was the great expense necessary to construct the road across a great swamp, the Black Swamp, then in existence in northern Ohio. National aid to internal improvements was not then in vogue in Congress. The Black Swamp "consisted of a slightly elevated basin of impervious clay upon which rested a thick stratum of fertile black loam. The surface was so level water could not escape except by evaporation.[3]" All north central Ohio for fifty miles to the south of Toledo and one hundred miles to the southwest is glacial lake bottom (lakes Maumee, Whittlesey and Warren). The slope of the surface is, on the average, only about four or five feet per mile, toward Lake Erie. The streams draining the region are few, many are intermittent, the gradient of all is low. The smaller discharge their water into the Lake through sand bars, the larger are drowned for five or ten miles in their lower courses. The area even at the present time is difficult to drain. In the early days before portions were cleared of forests and ditches opened up, the drainage lines were choked with aquatic vegetation and driftwood. The impervious clay cited above is the characteristic fine-grained deposits of glacial lakes. This morass was about thirty miles wide and interrupted all land communication between the settlements in Michigan and those of

---

3. *Ibid.*, II, 573.

Ohio.[4] Gov. Cass (of Michigan Territory) said in 1817,[5] "To reach the Territory of Michigan from any (settled) part of the state of Ohio, this swamp must be crossed. No description can convey to a person who is unacquainted with it, an adequate idea of the difficulties to be surmounted before a tolerable road can be found through this country." Since Detroit was surrounded, on the American side of the river, by flat lands (lake bottom), which before being deforested and drained were swampy and little cultivated, much of the food consumed in the settlement had to come from Ohio, by lake during the season of navigation or by land through the Black Swamp. It was during the off-season of navigation that the Black Swamp was the most difficult to cross. It is reported that at times the supply of food was very low and prices soared frightfully.[6]

At the opening of the War of 1812, Gen. Hull built his famous military road across the "Black Swamp." The road was poorly located and not constructed to meet the requirements of even the slight traffic of that time. One writer claims that the want of a suitable road through the Black Swamp cost the United States Government ten to twelve million dollars in the War of 1812. During the war flour was sold at Detroit for fifty dollars a barrel.[7] Hull's road seems not to have been used much after the passage of the army, and soon it was overgrown with brush. A writer said

4. See Darby, *A Tour from New York to Detroit* (1818), 188.
5. *Ibid.*, 596.
6. *Mich. Hist. Colls.*, V, 540 (Rev. W. Fitch).
7. *Ibid.*, VII, 53 (Bliss); *Am. State Papers, Miscellaneous*, II, 593 (Gov. Cass).

of it in 1820,[8] "Not a solitary traveller finds his way
along that avenue; it is principally indicated by the
broken remnants of buggies, wagons, and gun carriages, scattered remains of flour barrels, and the
mouldering skeletons of horses and oxen, remaining as
they were left just visible above the surface of the
mud and wet which destroyed them." About 1816 the
soldiers stationed at Detroit began the construction
of a road from Detroit to the Black Swamp.[9] By
January, 1818, they had reached within ten miles of
the Black Swamp. The following summer the road
reached the Maumee River, but was not constructed
farther.[10]

Many men who had seen service in the late war
urged Congress to provide for a continuation of the
road to the eastward. Appeals were made both by
civil and military officials in the Northwest who urged
that such a road was necessary to bring the region
into contact with the rest of the Union, to facilitate
the settlement of the Territory, to increase land sales,
and to give the people already there an outlet for their
products. Governor Cass showed that such a road
could be made a branch of the Cumberland National
Road, thus bringing Detroit into direct communication with the Capitol.[11] In 1823 Congress, stirred to
action by the many appeals, granted land for the
construction of a road from the Connecticut Reserve

8.   *Amer. State Papers, Miscellaneous*, II, 593.
9.   Thwaites, *Early Western Travels*, VIII, 209 (Evans); Farmer,
       Hist. Detroit and Mich., 925.
10. *Mich. Hist. Colls.*, XXXVIII, 559 (Fuller); *Niles' Weekly
       Reg.*, XIII, 312.
11. *Amer. State Papers, Miscellaneous*, II, 596.

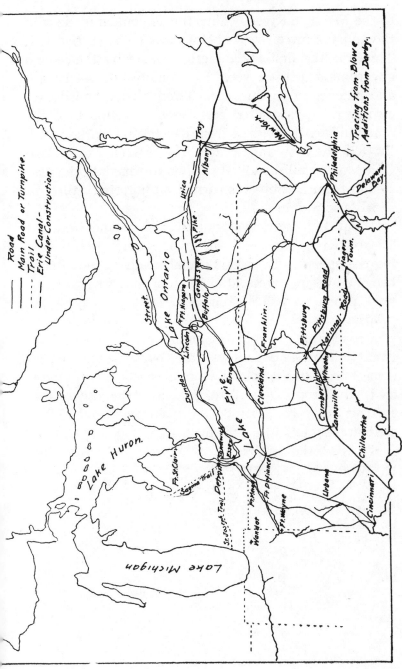

ROADS AND TURNPIKES IN 1820 BETWEEN GREAT LAKES AND COAST

to the Maumee River. Thus the agreement made with the Indians fifteen years before was to be carried out. This was the first regular grant made by the federal government with a view to promote the settlement and defence of Michigan.[12] Twenty thousand dollars also were appropriated for the improvement of the road built by the soldiers from Detroit to the Maumee.[13] In 1827 the first stage coach line between Detroit and Ohio was established.[14] Previous to this date the mail to and from Detroit was carried on horseback through the Black Swamp.[15]

About 1820 settlers began to push inland from the Detroit River[16] and with the great immigration following the opening of the Erie Canal, roads to the interior became absolutely essential. After 1825 several roads were projected to lead out of Detroit. Congress appropriated three thousand dollars for the laying out of a road from Detroit to Chicago.[17] Two years later twenty thousand dollars were appropriated for the construction of this road. Two more roads were authorized, one from Detroit to Saginaw, the other from Detroit to Fort Gratiot.[18] Fifteen thousand dollars were appropriated for the surveys of the latter two.[19]

By 1832 the settlement of Western Michigan had

12. *Mich. Hist. Colls.*, VII, 52.
13. *Ibid.*, 53; *Niles' Reg.*, XXVI, 280; *Ibid.*, XXIX, 128.
14. *Mich. Hist. Colls.*, XXXVIII, 559 (Fuller).
15. McCabe, *Directory of Detroit* (1837), 14.
16. *Mich. Hist. Colls.*, II, 38; *Ibid.*, III, 565 (Drake).
17. Farmer, *Hist. of Detroit and Mich.*, 925; *Mich. Hist. Colls.*, IV, 399; *Ibid.*, V, 151; *Ibid.*, VII, 54 (Bliss); *Ibid.*, XXXVIII, 594 (Chase).
18. *Ibid.*, XXXVIII, 559.
19. *Ibid.*; *Niles' Weekly Reg.*, XXXII, 62; Farmer, *Hist. Detroit and Mich.*, 925.

progressed so far that $3500 were appropriated for the survey of a road to the mouth of the Grand River.[20] Work on these roads progressed slowly. By 1831 the Chicago Road had been graded to Saline. Beyond this point settlers seeking land in the interior of the state followed a wagon track or an Indian trail.[21] By 1833 the Chicago Road was completed. From Ypsilanti the Territorial Road passed through Ann Arbor, Jackson and Marshall to St. Joseph.[22] By 1834 four other important roads radiated from Detroit.[23] About this time Michigan became interested in several railroad projects and the opening of other through wagon-roads received less attention. Although these early wagon-roads were constructed very poorly, the few and small settlements along the routes not warranting the expenditure of much money, they made known the real character of the country. Along them thousands of settlers passed from Detroit to the interior in search of fertile land. Back along them the farmer kept in touch with the outside world and sent his produce to the market at Detroit. Many descriptions of the difficulties of travel on these early dirt roads have been handed down. "Everybody, old and young, who has ever studied the topography of Michigan," says one writer,[24] "knows that for miles in every direction around Detroit lies a heavily timbered, level, muddy plain, where the soil is alluvial on the surface and a

20. *Mich. Hist. Colls.*, IV, 399; *Niles' Weekly Reg.*, XXXII, 62; *Mich. Hist. Colls.*, XXXVIII, 559 (Fuller).
21. *Mich. Hist. Colls.*, I, 48.
22. Latrobe, *The Rambler* (1835), 183; *Mich. Hist. Colls.*, VI, 238 (Fisher).
23. *Mich. Hist. Colls.*, XXXVIII, 560 (Fuller).
24. *Ibid.*, XXII, 348.

cold, squeezy, heavy clay beneath, through and over which even now transit is almost impossible. But no one but the early pioneers of the region can tell the horrors of travel over the same region forty years ago. Through a forest where elm, beech, walnut, maple, fir, and basswood sprang to the very skies, shutting out the midday sun, a black, sticky road was cut, and when the rush of emigration commenced in 1830 all those highways were cut up with slough holes, dug-ways . . . through which it seemed impossible to drag a stage coach or a heavy laden wagon. Except the road through the Black Swamp, from Toledo to Lower Sandusky, there were no more fearful and horrible roads to be found than these leading out of Detroit in 1833 to 1837." Not infrequently three days were required for an emigrant wagon to reach Ypsilanti from Detroit, a distance of twenty-eight miles.[25] Farmers carrying produce from Ann Arbor to Detroit by way of Plymouth Four Corners (now Plymouth), almost thirty-five miles, would need nearly a week to make the journey and return.[26]

Stage lines were established along most of these roads shortly after their completion.[27] A stage line was established from Detroit to Romeo in 1830.[28] Mitchell's Tourist's map of 1835 shows two stages out of Detroit, one through Ypsilanti, Coldwater, Niles, Michigan City to Chicago, over which stage coaches made three trips a week; and a second through Monroe

25. *Ibid.*
26. *Ibid.*
27. See map.
28. *Mich. Hist. Colls.*, XXXVIII, 559 (Fuller).

and Toledo to Lower Sandusky.[29]   In 1837 the Western
Stage Company of Detroit advertised five lines of
stages, on most of which conveyances left Detroit
daily.   One route extended through Monroe, Toledo
and Perrysburg to Lower Sandusky, requiring two
days for the journey.   The Western route led from

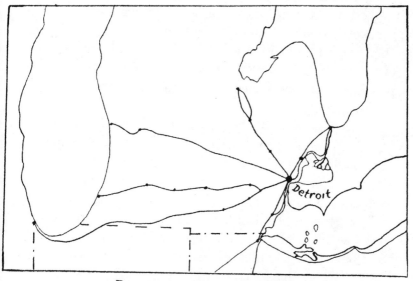

ROADS FROM DETROIT IN 1835
(*From John Farmer's Map of Michigan*)

Detroit to Chicago by way of Ypsilanti, Clinton, Jones-
ville, and Niles.   Another on the Territorial Road
passed through Ann Arbor to St. Joseph.   A fourth
led to Flint River (now Flint) through Pontiac and
Grand Blanc.   On the route to Ft. Gratiot stages left
Detroit every morning.[30]   By degrees the railroads

29.   *Ibid.*, XXXVIII, 594 (Chase).
30.   McCabe, *Directory of Detroit* (1837), advertisement.

were extended in Michigan, in many cases along or near the stage roads, and these supplanted the stages.[31]

Until the coming of the railroads in Southern Michigan, the roads just described served as the only outlets for the surplus agricultural products of the interior. Detroit, the nucleus from which these roads radiated, became the focus toward which the surplus products moved in search of a market. It was not only a market but also a supply station for a large part of the region touched by these roads. The large number of stage lines connecting it with the interior emphasizes its importance as a "Gateway" to Southern Michigan.

In 1826 work was begun on the Atlantic seaboard on the Baltimore and Ohio Railroad, the first important line to be built in the United States. Four years later, in Michigan—a place an eastern paper described as being "so far we seldom hear of it,"—the Detroit and St. Joseph Railroad Company was incorporated. In 1834 the route for this railway was surveyed, and by 1836 several miles of track had been built. In March, 1834, the Detroit and Pontiac Railroad Company was granted a charter "to transport property and persons by the power and force of steam, of animals or of any mechanical or other power or of any combination of them."[32]

With the people of the western country internal improvement was a mania, but a mania based on their economic needs. They sought markets. Roads must

31. See map.
32. Campbell, *Pol. Hist. of Mich.*, 418; Leonard, *Industries of Detroit*, 18; *Mich. Hist. Colls.*, IX, 273.

be built, canals dug, and railroads constructed to give them an outlet for their products and a return route for their purchases. Nor was this all. The spirit of their environment was progressive. They had a broad outlook on life; the vastness of their enterprises and their craze for speculation well illustrate this.

In 1837, the year Michigan was admitted as a State, a vast system of internal improvements was proposed. Three main lines of railroads were projected: one from Port Huron to Grand Haven, a second from Detroit to St. Joseph, and the third from Monroe to New Buffalo.[33] These were known as the Northern, Central, and Southern routes. They were to connect the navigable waters of Eastern Michigan with those of the western side of the State and Lake Michigan. At that time few dreamed of the possibilities of railroads. Waterways were considered the ideal means of transportation. The idea that steam railways would be organized and combined into great systems did not occur to the average citizen until the middle of the nineteenth century. Besides these railroads, many canals were planned, as well as improvements on some of the principal rivers. A loan of five million dollars was arranged for, to carry on these enterprises. Railroads which had been started by private companies were taken over by the State.

Following the panics of 1837 and 1839 the State began to feel that it had undertaken enterprises far beyond its means. To make matters worse, the Morris Canal and Banking Company, which was to furnish the five million dollars, was unable to meet its

33. *Mich. Hist. Colls.*, XXII, 487.

promises.[34] A disastrous bankruptcy of the State seemed exceedingly imminent. Resolutions were offered in the State Senate to "enquire into the expediency of bringing in a bill to repeal the act to provide for further construction of further work of internal improvements." The bill passed, with but two Senators dissenting.[35] The work on canals and rivers was abandoned soon after and the work on the railroads was much reduced. According to a report of the Board of Internal Improvements in 1839, the State was giving aid to

the Southern Railroad;
the Central Railroad;
the Northern Railroad;
the Kalamazoo-Clinton Canal;
the Sault Ste. Marie Canal;
the Saginaw Canal;
the improvement of Grand River;
the improvement of the Kalamazoo River; and a survey of the St. Joseph Railroad.

The total expense for the year 1838 had been $530,496.77. Contracts had been let to the amount of $1,200,000.[36]

By 1840 the Central Railroad had been completed by the State as far as Ann Arbor. It had an immediate influence on the development of the region along the route. "Already," says one writer,[37] "many thriving towns and settlements have been established along the line in anticipation of the ultimate completion." The Erie and Kalamazoo had been completed

34. *Ibid.*, XIII, 338.
35. *Ibid.*, I, 47.
36. *Rept. of Bd. of Internal Improvements, Mich.* (1839), I, 12.
37. Farmer, *Hist. of Detroit and Mich.*, 215.

from Toledo to Adrian, a distance of thirty-three miles. On the Havre Branch, a line to connect the Southern Railroad with the Erie and Kalamazoo, work was progressing rapidly. The Ypsilanti and Tecumseh Railroad was completed for twenty-five miles. The Detroit and Pontiac was in operation as far as Royal Oak, thirteen and one-half miles. The Allegan and Marshall, the St. Clair and Romeo, the Port Sheldon Railway, and the Shelby and Detroit roads all were under construction.[38]

By 1842 the Central Railroad had reached Jackson; the next year, Kalamazoo. About this time an eastern paper cited the central route across Michigan as an illustration of cheap traveling with great speed. "Persons can now go," it says,[39] "from Detroit to Jackson, 80 miles, by railroad in 6 hours; from Jackson to St Joseph, 120 miles, by stage in 26 hours; St. Joseph to Chicago 69 miles by steamboat in 7 hours. The whole distance of 269 miles in 36 hours and for only $8.50." In 1846 Michigan, dissatisfied with State ownership, sold the Central Railroad to the Michigan Central Railroad Company. By the terms of the contract, the railroad was to be pushed to the west with all speed. In 1849 the railway reached Lake Michigan.[40] Connections were made with Chicago by a line of steamers.[41] In 1852 the Michigan Central reached Chicago, and gave that city its first railroad connection with Detroit. The significance of bringing Michigan and

38. Tanner, *Canals and Railroads of U. S.* (1840), 215; Haskell and Smith, *Gazetteer*; *Mich. Hist. Colls.*, IX, 273.
39. *Niles' Weekly Reg.*, LXIV, 272.
40. *Ibid.*, LXXV, 256.
41. *Ibid.*, LXXV, 256.

Detroit into communication by rail with the city which later became the greatest railroad center of the country, if not of the world, seemingly was not recognized by the people of Michigan at the time. Many were indignant, "deeming it an unjust robbery that the millions they had spent fostering railroads should become a benefit to the great city of Illinois."[42] Detroit for a time was the eastern terminus of the Central Railroad. Connections with Buffalo were made during the season of navigation by steamers belonging to the Michigan Central Railroad. This means of communication with the East continued until 1854, when the Great Western Railway was opened through Canada between Windsor and Niagara Falls, a distance of 229 miles. The first train reached Windsor January 17, 1854.[43] This was the last link in the railroad connections between the East and Detroit. Detroit now had communication at all seasons with the Atlantic seaboard.

From the first, the Michigan Central Railway was a paying venture. In 1838, when the equipment consisted of only four small locomotives, five passenger cars and ten freight cars, and the line only to Ypsilanti, twenty-four miles from Detroit, the railway carried 29,000 passengers.[44] The net receipts for the year were $37,283.[45] Andrews, commenting in 1851 on its influence in developing the territory it served, said,[46] "From Detroit to New Buffalo the Central

42. Ross and Catlin, *Landmarks of Wayne Co. and Detroit*, 499.
43. *Ibid.*, 503; Roberts, *Sketches of City of Straits*, 54.
44. *Mich. Hist. Colls.*, XXII, 488.
45. Hunt's *Merchant's Mag.*, XII, 387.
46. Andrews, *Trade and Commerce of Brit. Colonies with U. S.*, Exec. Doc. 112, 32nd Cong., 1st Sess., 57.

Railroad has done more to develop the matchless resources of this state, and urge it forward to its commanding position, than any other route. Cities, villages, and large flouring mills are springing into existence everywhere along the line of this road, depending upon it as an avenue for their business to the lakes."

The Michigan Central and the Great Western formed important links in a trunk line along "the great railroad route" between the densely settled, commercial, manufacturing East and the thinly settled agricultural central West, the route, that students of transportation, even before the middle of last century came to recognize ultimately must develop.[47]   Indeed these two railroads, along with the Lake Shore and Michigan Southern which connected Chicago with Buffalo in 1853, and the Pittsburg, Ft. Wayne and Chicago which reached Chicago in 1856, were among the chief agencies in bringing about the shifting of traffic routes whereby New Orleans lost and New York, Boston, and Philadelphia won in the dominance of the traffic with the central West.   The situation of Detroit along the great transportation belt, which has since 1869 become an ocean to ocean route, has no doubt been an important factor in its growth in population and industries, particularly since the Detroit River occasions a break in rail transportation, only partially overcome by car-ferry (since 1867) and tunnel (since 1910).[48]

The Detroit and Pontiac Railroad by 1843 had been

47.   Hunt's *Merchant's Mag.*, XII, 325; *Ibid.*, XXVII, 438.
48.   See p.

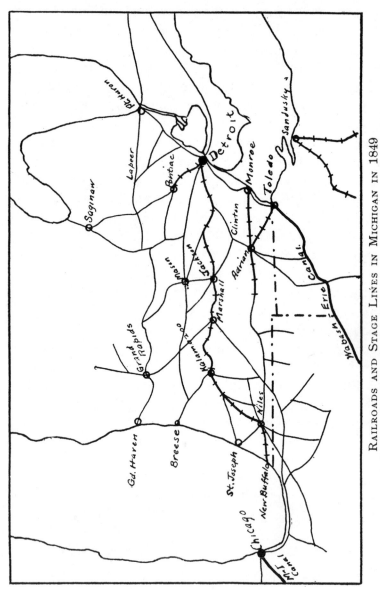

RAILROADS AND STAGE LINES IN MICHIGAN IN 1849

(*From Mitchell's Traveller's Guide, Pub. by Thomas Cowperthwart & Co., Philadelphia. The light lines are Stage Lines*)

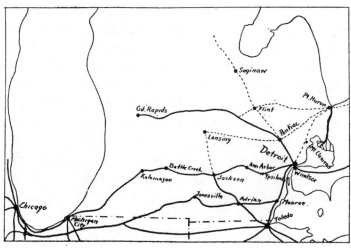

RAILROADS OF MICHIGAN IN 1857
(*After J. Disturnell*)
Heavy lines, completed.
Dotted lines, projected.

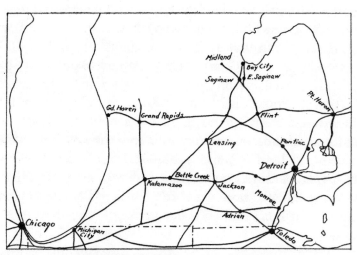

RAILWAYS OF MICHIGAN IN 1869
(*From Colter's Map of Michigan*)

constructed as far as Pontiac.[49]   In 1848 (April 3d) the Oakland and Ottawa Railway Company was incorporated.   The line built by this company was to extend from Pontiac to Ottawa County in the western part of the State.   The construction of this line was slow, however.   In 1855 the Detroit and Milwaukee Railway was organized and authorized by the Legislature to take over both of the above lines.   By July 1, 1856, the line had reached Owosso and by September, 1856, it was completed as far as Mill Point (now Spring Lake), where steamer connections were had with the cities on Lake Michigan.   In 1858 it was extended to Grand Haven.[50]   This road brought Detroit into touch with one of the most fertile parts of the State and rich also in resources of lumber, coal, and gypsum.   The population of the section tributary to the road in 1854 was 241,000 and the acreage of improved land 820,000 acres.   At Grand Haven the road was connected by car-ferry with Milwaukee, from which city railroads radiated westward.[51]   This line is now the Detroit, Grand Haven, and Milwaukee Railroad, operated under the Grand Trunk System.

By 1857 there were four railroad lines leading westward from Detroit: the Michigan Central; the Detroit and Milwaukee (nearly completed), the Detroit, Monroe and Toledo (62 miles built); and the Detroit and Port Huron (under construction).[52]   During the decade 1850 to 1860, several trunk lines were formed in

49.   *Niles' Weekly Reg.*, LXIV, 345.
50.   *Mich. Hist. Colls.*, IX, 273, 275 (Percival).
51.   Roberts, *Sketches of City of Straits*, 52.
52.   Disturnell, *A Trip Through Lakes of N. A.*, 135; *Mich. Hist. Colls.*, VII, 71.

Eastern United States by the consolidation of many
short lines. This was one of the more important
movements in the history of railroads in America.
By such consolidation Detroit was brought into connection with most of the railways then in existence
in the eastern portion of the country, and the Michigan Central gave Detroit access to a large mileage
focusing on Chicago from the north, west and south.
By 1885 ten railways led from Detroit:[53]

Lake Shore and Michigan Southern;
Wabash, St. Louis and Pacific;
Detroit, Monroe and Toledo;
Michigan Central;
Pere Marquette;
Detroit, Grand Haven, and Milwaukee;
Detroit and Bay City;
Detroit, Lansing, and Northern;
Grand Trunk (to Port Huron);
Grand Trunk (Gt. West. Div.)

Today, connections with such railway centers as
Chicago, St. Louis, Cincinnati, Pittsburgh, and Buffalo
give Detroit access to all parts of the United States,
Mexico, and Canada, that may be reached by rail.
The Grand Trunk gives Detroit a direct route to the
best part of Ontario and Quebec. The Canadian
Pacific puts Detroit in communication not only with
east Canada, but with Manitoba and the immense
territory to the west.

The benefits of increased transportation facilities
that accrued to Detroit and Southern Michigan by

53. Weeks, *Directory of Detroit* (1885), data from several pages.

the extension of wagon roads were greatly increased by the growth of the railroad mileage radiating from Detroit. Michigan in the decade between 1830 and 1840 increased in population 180,628. From 1840 to 1850 the increase was 185,387, from 1850 to 1860, 351,459, from 1860 to 1870, 434,946.[54] The railroad mileage at these decades was as follows:[55]

> 1840—35 miles
> 1850—342 miles
> 1860—779 miles
> 1870—1638 miles

The population data for Detroit during these decades likewise show rapid increases.[56] Statistics show that the agriculture in Michigan from 1850 to 1870 advanced rapidly. The statistics for 1850, 1860, and 1870 are as follows:[57]

	Area in farms.	Improved farms.	Farm values.
1850...................	4,383,890 acres	1,929,110 acres	$51,872,446
1860...................	7,030,834 acres	3,476,296 acres	160,836,495
1870...................	10,019,142 acres	5,096,939 acres	398,240,578

In 1870 the area in farms was 2.3 times that in 1850, and the acreage of improved farms 2.6 times that of 1860. The value of farm property, however, by 1870 was 7.7 times that of 1850. These great advances in acreage and value of farm property are due chiefly to

54. *Stat. Abst. U. S.*, 1913, 26.
55. Poor's *Manual of R. R. of U. S.* (1876), 97; *Stat. Abst. U. S.* (1913), 262.
56. See p.
57. No data are obtainable for 1840 on the items given in this table.

increased facilities for reaching markets, reduction of freight rates, and an increased return for labor expended on the farm.

In 1837 the cost by wagon of transporting material from Detroit to Marshall was $2 per cwt. ($40 per ton). The Michigan Central in 1848 carried wheat from Kalamazoo to Detroit for $6.04 per ton.[58] Assuming the cost of raising wheat to be $15 per ton and the cost of hauling on dirt roads 25 cents per ton-mile, wheat selling at $1.00 per bushel can be raised profitably only within 72 miles of a market. With a rail rate of 4 cents per ton-mile the area for profitable wheat-raising has a 450 miles radius. At a distance of 100 miles from market, under the first conditions, wheat, if raised, is raised at a loss of $7 per ton, under the second conditions, with freight rates at 4 cents per ton-mile, the profits at 100 miles are $14 per ton. With a decrease in freight rates the profits of wheat-growing, and farming in general, became greater, the total value of farm products increased, and the value of farm property would show a similar advance. This expansion of market area and increase of wealth of producers meant much to Detroit, the natural market for most of Southern Michigan.[59] It was reported that in 1849 two-thirds of the exports of the State and three-fourths of the imports for the State passed through Detroit.[60]

The railroad undoubtedly has been the greatest single factor in the development of manufactures at Detroit, particularly so in the recent decades since

58. *Mich. Hist. Colls.*, XXXVIII, 603 (Chase).
59. *Tenth Census*, XIX, Pt. II, 604.
60. Hunt's *Merchant's Mag.*, XX, 278.

Detroit has come to rely so little on the Lake transportation.[61]   The capital invested in manufactures and
the value of products turned out by decades for 1840
to 1870, inclusive, are as follows:[62]

MANUFACTURES OF WAYNE COUNTY.

	Capital invested.	Value of product.
1840 (1)...	$275,810	not stated.
1850 (2)...	1,066,255	$1,966,000
1860 (3)...	4,137,766	6,498,593
1870 (4)...	14,732,160	26,217,685

The position of Detroit, sixty miles northeast of
the west end of Lake Erie, is such that the shortest
railroad route between Detroit and Buffalo is across
Southern Ontario.   To use this route both the Detroit
and Niagara rivers must be crossed.   The Suspension
Bridge was constructed in 1855 to overcome the break
in the land route at Niagara River,[63] but the bridging
of the Detroit River, owing to the immensity of Lake
traffic and the lowness of the lands on each side of
the river, is not feasible.   For thirteen years after the
Great Western Railroad reached Windsor, ferry-boats
were used to transfer freight across the Detroit River.
This was both an expensive and a slow process.   The
increase in traffic, due to the spread of railroads and
the closer settlement of the region to the west of

61.   See p.
62.   Data for Wayne County must be used, for statistics on the
        manufactures of cities were not taken by the census
        bureau until 1880.
                (1). Comp. Sixth Census, 333.
                (2). Comp. Seventh Census, 259.
                (3). Eighth Census, M'f'res., 272.
                (4). Comp. Ninth Census, 828.
63.   Flint, *Railroads of U. S.*, 167.

Detroit, led the Great Western Railroad in 1867 to introduce car-ferries.[64] Car-ferries are still used on the Detroit River by some of the railroads. As early as 1871, the construction of a tunnel beneath the Detroit River received consideration. In 1872 and 1873, a shaft was sunk and a lateral bore made, but the work was soon abandoned because of sulphur water and quicksand.[65] The unfavorable conditions of the rock discouraged the engineers, who made an attempt at Stoney Island in 1879.[66] Nothing further was done in tunnel-making until 1906, when the Michigan Central Railroad began work on a tunnel which was opened for traffic July 1, 1910. This tunnel is unique in its construction. Profiting by the experiences of the earlier engineers, no attempt was made to excavate a bore beneath the river. Instead, a trough was dredged in the bottom of the river from shore to shore, and a steel cylinder, constructed in sections at a shipyard, was sunk so as to rest in the trough, and covered with cement and stone. Approaches were excavated beneath Detroit and Windsor. The total cost of construction was $8,500,000. This tunnel has greatly reduced the time for and expense of the transportation of through freight taking the route by way of Detroit. Before its construction and use there was much delay in breaking up trains, loading and unloading car-ferries and the reassembling. In the winter, ice in the river—and during the season of navigation the heavy traffic passing up and down the river—interfered with the passage of the car-

64. *Ibid.*
65. Sherzer, *Geology of Wayne Co.*, 24.
66. *Ibid.*; *Mich. Pamphlets 1850 to 1877*, XIX, 106.

ferries.   Trains now pass through the tunnel in the time it formerly took to load the car-ferries.

Interurban railroads are projected from large population centers wherever the density of population in the neighboring rural districts is sufficient to furnish a large passenger traffic, or where there are other cities within fifty or one hundred miles.   Both these conditions exist in the region about Detroit.   Within a radius of seventy-five miles of Detroit are Port Huron, Flint, Jackson, Ann Arbor, Pontiac, Adrian, and Toledo, cities of ten thousand people and over.   Within

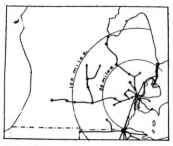

INTERURBAN LINES CENTERING AT DETROIT,
WITH A FEW CONNECTING LINES

a radius of one hundred miles there are also Bay City, Saginaw, East Saginaw, Lansing, and Battle Creek. Within the hundred mile radius of Detroit there are large areas in which the density of rural population is from forty to one hundred people per square mile. All the above-named cities, except Adrian, and most of the lesser cities and towns are connected with Detroit by interurban lines which furnish hourly and in some cases half-hourly service.   On all the lines fast "limited" cars are run.   In 1911 more than 260 passenger cars and 40 express (freight) cars ran daily over these various electric lines.[67]   The several lines radiating from Detroit have extended the area from which "shoppers" come to the city.   Many of the merchants in the smaller towns report a loss of trade.   Since many of the interurban lines parallel the steam railways, some of the latter have been forced to grant commutation fares to and from Detroit.   This has been beneficial to the retail business of the city.   The many interurban lines and the commutation service on the steam railways are important factors in extending the residence area of the business people of Detroit. Many of them now live from ten to twenty miles from the city, passing to and from their places of business daily.[68]

---

67.   Sherzer, *Geol. of Wayne Co.*, 26.
68.   The dates of construction of the various interurban lines out of Detroit are as follows:

Detroit to Wyandotte....................1891.
Rapid Ry. to Mt. Clemens...............1894.
Rapid Ry. to Pt. Huron.................1899.
Detroit to Pontiac.....................1895.
Shore line to Mt. Clemens..............1897.
Detroit to Ann Arbor...................1897.
Branch to Saline.......................1899.
From Ann Arbor to Jackson..............1901.
Flint line from Detroit............1898 to 1900.
Orchard Lake Division..................1898.
Flint to Saginaw (Since about 1908)........   ?
Detroit to Toledo......................1901.

(Data furnished by A. D. B. VanZadt, Publicity Agent of Detroit United Railway.   As to the data above he says, "It is not possible to give you the specific dates in the construction of all these properties as most of these interurban lines were built by smaller companies whose interests were later purchased by the Detroit United Railway.")

The Michigan United Railway, since April, 1911, has been running cars over the Detroit United Railway between Jackson and Detroit.[69]   Both the Michigan United Railway and the Detroit United Railway connect at Jackson with the Michigan United Railway lines from Kalamazoo and Lansing.

69.   Sherzer, *Geology of Wayne Co.*, 25.

CHAPTER XII

THE DEVELOPMENT OF MANUFACTURES AT DETROIT

MANUFACTURING industries commonly come late in the economic development of a region. This is well illustrated in the industrial development of eastern United States. Our forefathers for the first few decades after their settlement along the Atlantic coast gained a living by exploiting the furs, the fisheries, and the forests. What tillage was done was mainly exploitive. Where conditions were favorable, agriculture later came to dominate, and it in turn, after many decades, was overshadowed in importance by the factory and the work-shop.

On a developing frontier the same stages in the evolution of the industries are experienced; but while the older regions take scores of years to pass from the exploitive to the manufacturing stage, the frontier will in the course of a few years, or at most decades, pass through all the stages and come to possess industries as highly specialized as any to be found in the older regions.

The hunter and trapper are commonly the first to arrive on the frontier. Then comes the pioneer settler, half farmer and half hunter. He is soon replaced by the real agriculturist.[1] In time, with further increase

1. Ogg, *Fordham's Personal Narrative*, 1817–1818, 125; Blowe, *Emigrant's Directory*, 105; Dwight, *Travels in New Eng. and N. Y.*, II, 458 to 463; Thwaites, *Early West. Travels*, IX, 232 (Flint).

of population, a village is started which under favorable conditions may become a town, and later a city. Village, town, and city have their own respective types of industries.

The Detroit region has passed through all these stages, but its development has some peculiarities owing to the fact that for the first hundred years it was a mere adjunct of the fur trade. For nearly one hundred years its industries suffered arrested development. It was not until the early part of the nineteenth century, after the coming of the Americans, that its real industrial development began.

The commerce and industries of the settlement during the French regime have been discussed in a previous chapter.[2]   Under the British they remained almost unchanged, except that ship-building was introduced. This industry was stimulated by their desire to keep and control the inland waters.   Records show that from 1769 to 1794 there were turned out of the King's shipyard at Detroit many vessels varying in size from 18 to 136 tons burden.   From 1772 to 1782 eight vessels were built and repaired.[3]   Large rafts of logs to be used for the planking were brought from the river La French, and masts and beams from the forests bordering Lake Huron.[4]   The cost of construction was great, as all the rigging, lines, and iron had to be brought from England.[5]   In 1794 a sloop of forty-seven-foot keel, nineteen-foot beam and seven-foot hold was laid down in His Majesty's dock yard

---

2. Chap. IV.
3. *Mich. Hist. Colls.*, XXIV, 12; XXIII, 343, 353.
4. *Ibid.*, XVII, 594.
5. Liancourt, *Travels in N. A.*, I, 289.

at Detroit to cost "1,901 pounds 12s. 4 d.-half penny
Currency Dollars at five shillings.[6]" The upkeep of
these early Lake vessels was also great. They were
constructed of unseasoned timber, and at most lasted
for only eight or ten years. Frequent overhauling was
necessary.[7] The ship yard at Detroit, being the only
one on the Upper Lakes, therefore kept very busy.

In the early period of American occupation of the
Detroit region the condition of the manufactures was
little improved. Their primitive character at the close
of the first decade of the nineteenth century is well
shown by the following data:[8]

MANUFACTURES AT DETROIT 1810.

Products.	Amount.	Value.
Flax and hemp goods—yards	421	$316
Woolen goods in families—yards	1,300	1,300
Hats—number	400	2,800
Liquors—gallons	8,200	6,000
Soap—pounds	37,000	4,750
Candles—pounds	6,500	2,356
Hides, tanned—number	1,100	6,600
Saddles and bridles—number	60	720

6. *Mich. Hist. Colls.*, XXIII, 344.
7. Liancourt, *Travels in N. A.*, I, 289; *Mich. Hist. Colls.*, XVII, 349.
8. *Amer. State Papers, Finance*, II, 811. These are the earliest data of manufactures at Detroit. Statistics of manufactures of cities did not again become a part of the reports of the census bureau until 1880. Between 1810 and 1880 the reports give statistics only for the states and the counties. It will, therefore, be necessary to use the statistics for Wayne County between 1810 and 1880 to trace the development of manufactures at Detroit. Since Detroit, as will be shown in later pages, completely dominated the manufactures of Wayne County during the later decades, it is very probable that it did in the decades between 1810 and 1880. The early statistics are incomplete and the system of enumeration differed from that followed in later decades. The data for the various census years, therefore, are difficult to compare.

There were 120 spinning-wheels and 6 looms in operation in homes and factories. The other factories were 2 tanneries, 1 hat factory, 2 distilleries, 4 candle and soap factories, and 4 gristmills.[9] The total value of manufactures for Detroit was $24,742. This was sixty-seven per cent of the total for the State, and less than two-hundredths of one per cent of that of the United States.[10]

Descriptions of these early industries are lacking, but judging from the amount of the product turned out, they were all small; many were carried on in the homes. The industries were called upon to supply only the local needs of the people. The raw materials used—flax, hemp, wool, furs, corn, barley, fat, and hides—were of local production.

The census report for 1820[11] gives returns for three counties in the State—Oakland, Crawford, and Wayne. The boundaries of these counties were very different from those now bearing the same names. In Oakland County there was produced ten thousand dollars' worth of lumber in two sawmills, employing in all seven men. In Crawford County, the manufactures were bar-lead, traps, tomahawks, and other articles for the Indian trade. Wayne County shows the greatest value and variety of manufactures. Complete returns of the value of products produced in the county are not given.

9. *Ibid.*
10. *Ibid.*, 712.
11. Enumeration began Aug. 1, 1820. The data are for the year ending Aug. 1, 1820. ·

MANUFACTURES OF WAYNE COUNTY 1820.[12]

Articles.	Value of material used.	Men employed.	Capital employed.	Wages paid.
Cooper's ware	$100	1		
Flour and meal	(6,500 bu.)	3	$1,600	$180
Flour and meal	(5,000 bu.)	2	$5,000	$300
Hats	$6,500	6		$2,500
Leather	$950	4	$3,000	$500
Leather		2	$5,000	$400
Lumber	$37	2	$500	$125
Saddles	$2,000	4		$800
Saddles		2	$2,500	$300
Tinware	$1,000	2	$500	
Whiskey	(grain used 2,160 bus.)	3	$1,000	$210

Leather and lumber are the only manufactured products to which values are assigned. The leather was valued at $2,500 and the lumber at $500.

The incompleteness of the returns in 1820, and the fact that no returns for Wayne County in 1810 are given, makes anything more than a general comparison with the industries of the previous decade impossible. In the data for 1820 textile products are not included, but a new industry, the manufacture of tin, has been introduced. No advance apart from the introduction of the manufacture of tinware seems to have been made in the ten years preceding 1820.

There are many reasons for the retarded development of manufactures at Detroit in the early decades of its existence as an American town. The abundance of cheap land and the great productivity of the land per unit of labor, caused many settlers in the West to prefer agricultural pursuits to the manufacturing industries.[13] Bradbury, writing in 1810, says in this

12. American State Papers, Finance, IV, 221; Also in 4th Census Rept., 1820.
13. Thwaites, Early Western Travels, IX, 238 (Flint); Quart. Jr. Econ., XVII, 117.

regard:[14] "There is no part of the world where labor
finds a better market than in the Western Country.
This results from a state of things that will not admit
of a speedy change. A very moderate sum of money
enables a man to procure one or two hundred acres
of land; the savings of two or three years will enable
a working man to effect this, if he is prudent; and
although he can cultivate only a small part of it, and,
perhaps, for the first two or three years not more than
will maintain his family, yet the accumulation of
property by the regular and rapid advance in the
value of land, forms more than the savings of the
laborer and the mechanic." Because of these conditions even when the laborers went to the towns they
were continually returning to the farm as soon as
they had saved a little money. The density of population had not yet become great enough to leave a surplus of workers beyond those on the farms.

Capital was lacking in the West. The withdrawal
of laborers from the towns meant the withdrawal of
their savings to be invested in lands. Much of the
money invested in lands went to the Government,
and was therefore taken from the West. It took
many years for the farmers to accumulate a surplus.
There was little flow of capital to the West, there
being few economic prizes to offer. The Easterners
were content, therefore, to invest their money at
home.

Transportation facilities were poor and the market
for manufactured goods was confined to the immediate
region. The frontier was as yet only thinly peopled.

14. Thwaites, *Early Western Travels*, V, 285.

The aggregate purchasing power was therefore small. Life on the frontier was semi-primitive. Purchases were limited to the necessities of life, and since many of the manufactures were carried on at home, there was little need to go outside the household for clothing and foods. Most of the houses and barns were built of rough logs. The forests furnished an abundance of these.

The completion of the Erie Canal, the introduction of the steamboat on the Great Lakes, the opening of the Lakes-to-Ohio and Mississippi canals, and the building of railroads, all within the course of twenty or thirty years, did much to improve the conditions for the growth of manufactures. The spread of the cotton culture in the South and the resultant stimulus to the industries in the Ohio and Upper Mississippi valleys had some effect, though indirect, upon the economic conditions of the Lakes region. The increasing population in the territory enlarged the market for the products of Detroit and furnished a surplus of workers for the factories. Skilled mechanics of various trades became more numerous, the increasing population and enlarging markets making a division of labor more possible. The standard of living was raised, due to a certain extent to a closer contact with the outside through the various agencies of transportation and communication, but to a large degree, no doubt, to the increase of wealth. The per capita purchasing power was, therefore, increased.

From 1835 to 1837 was the great period of speculation[15] and of rapid flow of capital to the West. The

---

15. Page

rising prices seemed to assure the borrowers an easy burden, and the high interests that soon came to be paid assured the lenders a good reward. It was the capital of the East that built the canals and railways in the West and linked the Great Lakes with the American seaboard.

The ingenuity of the American people had much to do with the rapid development of manufactures when once their activities were directed to these industries. Flint says,[16] "The habits of the American people are peculiarly favorable to the adoption of manufacturing pursuits. Their well known spirit of enterprise and the circumstance of almost every man's being able to handle the axe, the saw, the hammer, and the joiner's plane must give faculty to the acquisition of mechanical labor. From 1820 to 1840 the increase in variety and value of manufactures was considerable. The data for Wayne County in 1840 are as follows:[17]

MANUFACTURES OF WAYNE COUNTY, 1840

Product.	Value of product.
Products of flour, grist, and saw mills	$116,375
Leather	81,370
Various metals (not stated what these were)	45,500
Machinery	21,760
Hats and caps	12,000
Brick and lime	8,040
Granite and marble	7,000
Carriages and wagons	5,075
Tobacco	5,000
Precious metals	5,000
Confectionery	3,000
Hardware and cutlery	1,250
Earthenware	1,100

16. Thwaites, *Early Western Travels*, IX, 275 (Flint).
17. *Comp. Sixth Census* (1840), 322 to 333. Data "corrected by the Dep't. of State in 1840," printed in 1841. Date of close of census year not stated. No data are available for 1830, no provision having been made by Congress for

Values were not given for many of the products. There were also produced in Wayne County $22,614 worth of timber, forty tons of pot and pearl ashes, 76,000 pounds of soap, 56,000 pounds of candles, 8,000 gallons of whiskey and 194,000 gallons of beer. The manufacturing plants listed were 8 flour mills, 3 grist-mills, 28 sawmills, 2 breweries, 1 distillery, 3 tanneries, 2 fulling mills, and 5 furnaces for making cast iron. The number of soap and candle factories was not given.

Few quantitative statements can be made as to the advance in manufactures during the twenty years following 1820, the data for both 1820 and 1840 being so incomplete and indefinite. Leather had increased in value of product from $2,500 in 1820 to $81,370 in 1840. The number of men employed in the tanneries had increased from 4 to 21 in the same period. In the value of timber produced in Wayne County, there had been an advance from $500 in 1820 to $22,614 in 1840. The leading products manufactured in 1840 according to value were leather, flour, lumber, metals, machinery, and alcoholic drinks. These for the most part are representative of primary manufactures or of manufactures in their early stages of development.

The tanning of leather, up to the last half century, depended largely upon the use of oak or hemlock bark. Since the finished product, leather, could stand the cost of transportation much better than the bulky

the taking of the industrial statistics. (*Tenth Census, Manufactures*, page vii.) Wayne County was organized with boundaries as at present in 1826. (Sherzer, *Geology of Wayne County*).

bark, the tanning industry was located near the oak and hemlock forests. The forests of Southern Michigan, containing large stands of oak and hemlock, furnished one of the essentials for the location of tanneries. The tanneries of Wayne County produced forty per cent of the leather of the State. Tanning was a simple operation requiring no machinery and little skill and labor. Layers of bark were put between layers of hides in pits or vats, and the whole covered with water. The tannin in the bark did the work. The tanneries were small. In 1810 the two tanneries in operation in Detroit had a total output of 1,100 hides.[18] In 1840 in Wayne County there were only three tanneries in operation, employing in all twenty-one men, and producing $81,370 worth of leather per year.[19]

Flour milling is an industry representative of all the higher stages of social development. It was one of the first industries on all the American frontiers. At Detroit a flour mill was erected as early as 1703 or 1704. Because of the low gradient of the streams, however, most of the power used was from windmills. Weld in 1716 reported that the French ground their grain by windmills.[20] In the earlier years of the development of industries at Detroit the flour mills supplied chiefly the local markets. Soon after the development of the region by the Americans, flour became an article of export. In 1808 Thos. Emerson and Company of Detroit shipped a large consignment

18. *Amer. State Papers, Finance*, II, 811.
19. *Comp. Sixth Census*, 322.
20. Ross and Catlin, *Landmarks of Wayne County and Detroit*, 257.

to Fort Wayne,[21] and in 1826 two hundred barrels were shipped East from Monroe by vessel and through the then newly completed Erie Canal.[22] By 1831 it became the practice of merchants at Montreal and Quebec to purchase American flour in the Western Country for exportation to the West Indies.[23] In 1841 the exports of flour from Detroit amounted to 180,000 barrels valued at $900,000.[24] Only a small part of this, however, originated in Wayne County, for the output in 1840 was only 20,100 barrels valued at $116,375.[25]

The lumber industry of Wayne County in the early decades of the nineteenth century depended on the pine timber in the forests of southeastern Michigan. A dense "hardwood" forest covered most of the section south of a line extending from Port Huron to Grand Haven, but most of the sandy tracts in this area had heavy stands of pine trees. The great pine forest area in Michigan lay to the north of a line from Port Huron to Grand Haven. The mills of Wayne County on the west bank of the Detroit River, obtained their logs from a large area bordering Lake St. Clair, St. Clair River, and Lake Huron. In 1810 lumber was not listed among the manufactured products of Detroit nor of the Territory of Michigan. There was little call for lumber in the early settling of the region. The French used hewn timbers for the construction of their buildings. It is probable that

21. Roberts, *Sketches of Detroit*, 18.
22. Campbell, *Pol. Hist. of Mich.*, 416.
23. *Niles' Weekly Reg.*, XLI, 165.
24. Hunt's *Merchant's Mag.*, VI, 341.
25. *Comp. of Sixth Census*, 322 to 333.

the British used hewn timbers also in the buildings they erected. Hewn timbers or lumber sawed by hand was used in the construction of the vessels during the British occupation of Detroit. The early American settlers commonly lived in log houses for the first decade or two after settling in Michigan, but with the increase of wealth and the development of higher standards of living, frame houses and barns came to be the dominant types. The first steam sawmill in Detroit was built in 1832 by the "Detroit Steam Mill Company."[26] By 1840 twenty-eight mills were reported in operation in Wayne County. The products of these mills found a ready sale in the farming region of southeastern Michigan. After 1825 the Erie Canal furnished an outlet for lumber to the East. Shingles and lumber to the value of $75,000 were shipped from Detroit in 1841.[27]

The iron industry in Wayne County in 1840 owed its existence to the abundance of wood, from which charcoal was made, and to deposits of bog iron ore. It is reported that there were fifteen blast furnaces in Michigan in 1840, five of which were in Wayne County. Many of these alleged furnaces were doubtless foundries. Others were true blast furnaces producing cast iron from bog ores.[28] The rich ores of the Northern Peninsula of Michigan were not yet used. Much pig iron was brought from Ohio and Pennsylvania. In 1840, 420 tons of iron were produced in Wayne County, sixty-four men were employed, and 377

26. *Mich. Hist. Colls.*, II, 410.
27. Hunt's *Merchant's Mag.*, VI, 341.
28. *Tenth Census, Manufactures*, 843, 845.

tons of fuel used.   The capital invested was $32,300.[29]
The machinery produced at the foundries and machine
shops supplied the market in the surrounding region.

Alcoholic drinks, beer and whisky, were made from
the local products of the farm: barley, rye, corn, and
hops. Such industries are particularly adapted to
regions with poor transportation facilities.   The finished product found a ready sale in the local markets
and much was shipped outside the county.   It is reported that in 1841, 12,000 barrels of whisky were
shipped from Detroit, valued at $7,800.[30]

The industrial development of the region was hindered greatly by the lack of factory workers.   The
rapid settling of the region to the west of Detroit
drew men to the lands.[31]   Until there should come a
surplus of workers upon which the industries could
draw, the chief interests of the city would be commercial; manufacturing would be of secondary concern and only such as would supply the most pressing
local needs of the people.   A writer who visited Detroit about this time remarks,[32] "Some large iron
foundries have lately been erected and set in motion
here; but commerce rather than manufactures is likely
to be for a long time the distinguishing occupation of
the whites of Detroit."

During the twenty years from 1840 to 1860, however, the leading economic activities at Detroit had
shifted from commerce to manufactures.   The in-

---

29.   *Comp. of Sixth Census*, 322.
30.   Hunt's *Merchant's Mag.*, VI, 341.
31.   See Chapter VII.
32.   Buckingham, *The Eastern and Western States of America*,
        III, 388.

creasing transportation facilities furnished by the railways to the East and the West broadened the sphere
of commercial relations for the city. Raw products
could be derived from a wider area, the manufactured
articles could reach a much larger market. The number of purchasers had increased, the purchasing power
per capita was greater, and the people were depending less and less upon supplying their own wants.
More and more they came to enjoy the benefits of
co-operative exchange. The excellent transportation
facilities furnished by the lakes and rivers north of
Detroit enabled the city to continue in the manufacture of lumber. This is the chief reason for the
great importance that the lumber and wood industry
had in Detroit and Wayne County in 1860. The completion of the St. Mary's Canal in 1855 furnished an
outlet for the copper and iron ore of the Northern
Peninsula of Michigan, and gave the cities on the
shores of the Lakes, wherever fuel could be had, an
invitation to develop the metal industries. The building of railways, the rapid settling of the farming lands
in Southern Michigan, the increasing demands for
agricultural implements, and the growth of cities and
industries in the near by regions stimulated manufactures along many lines.

In Wayne County in 1860 the leading products of
the factories were as follows:[33]

---

33. *Eighth Census, Manufactures,* 272–273. Data for the year
    ending June 20, 1860.

MANUFACTURES OF WAYNE COUNTY FOR 1860.

Product.	Value.	Number of establishments.	Men employed.
Copper smelted	$1,500,000	7	40
Lumber sawed	619,000	43	466
Machinery and steam engines	608,000	12	505
Iron-bar and railroad	585,000	1	300
Leather	380,000	9	108
Flour and meal	314,840	15	35
Liquors, malt	262,000	21	78
Iron, pig	145,000	2	120
Furs	143,000	1	48
Soap and candles	138,000	4	52
Printing (newspaper and job)	136,000	3	135
Boots and shoes	132,000	33	128
Sash, doors, etc	127,000	10	157

Among other articles were saws, clothing, carriages, wagons and carts, marble and stone, cooperage, cigars, and agricultural implements, all above $35,000 in value. Sixty-seven varieties of articles were listed in the report. Most of the factories were small, however, as may be judged from comparison of the number of establishments and persons employed. The iron industries were the largest, employing from forty to three hundred men.

The remarkable showing in the production of copper was due, chiefly, to the enterprise of a few business men of Detroit, but there were geographic factors as well. The existence of copper was known to the French as early as 1660.[34] During the period of British occupation attempts were made to work some of the copper deposits. These attempts, however, were unsuccessful, due mostly to the difficulties of transportation.[35] Active mining dates from 1845. By 1850 there were no less than twenty-three mining

34. *Mich. Hist. Colls.*, XXVII, 628.
35. *Ibid.*, XIII, 51.

companies in the copper region, employing about eight hundred men.[36]   About this time John R. Grout, of Detroit, secured claims to a portion of the copper range, several capitalists from Waterbury, Connecticut, furnished the capital, and in 1850 the "Waterbury and Detroit Copper Company" was organized.   The Copper Country at that time was almost a wilderness. The settled portion of Michigan in 1850 was mostly south of the latitude of the south end of Saginaw Bay.[37]   Since Detroit had connections with Lake Superior by water and was the nearest city to the copper deposits at which any considerable number of workers could be obtained, it was chosen as the site for the smelters.   The works first constructed were crude.   There were a smelter house, a reverberatory furnace, and other accessories.   As the mining interest grew and production increased, the smelter at Detroit was enlarged and improved.   The opening of the St. Mary's Canal in 1855 cheapened the cost of transportation from the mines to the Lower Lakes.   This favored the development of the industry at Detroit. Other works were established at or near Detroit.   In 1860 seven establishments were in existence in Wayne County with an output of $1,500,000.[38]   For many years the smelters at Detroit did a large share of the smelting in the Lakes region.[39]   About 1860 there were seven cities in the United States that had copper smelters.[40]

36. DeBow's *Rev.*, XV, 359.
37. See Population Map, p.
38. *Eighth Census, Manufactures*, 272–273.
39. *Mich. Hist. Colls.*, XXVIII, 650.
40. Hunt's *Merchant's Mag.*, XLII, 433.

The time came, however, after the completion of
the St. Mary's Canal, when people could be induced
to live in the "far away" Copper Country. Smelters
could, therefore, be established near the mines and
lessen expenses of transportation. In 1860 smelters
were erected at Portage Lake. The Detroit smelter
continued to operate, however, until about 1879.[41]

Except for copper, the important industries represented in 1860 were in existence in 1840, the reasons
for which have been suggested.

By 1880 there had been a marked change in the
ranking of the manufactured products of Wayne
County. Some had disappeared from the list of leading products, others which twenty years previous had
occupied only a minor place, or were not represented
at all, now ranked among the leading industries. The
more important products in value were:[42]

MANUFACTURES OF WAYNE COUNTY, 1880

Products.	Establishments.	Value.
Tobacco and cigars	64	$2,716,016
Iron and steel	7	2,498,634
Foundry and machine shop products	27	2,466,355
Men's clothing	33	2,062,182
Flour and grist mill products	28	1,992,219
Slaughtering and packing products	7	1,721,231
Railway car (construction and repairs)	2	1,448,756
Ship building—vessels of all sorts	19	1,215,047
Malt liquors	29	1,157,609

The total product was valued at $33,470,000, or
more than five times the output of the factories of
the county in 1860. The establishments numbered

41. *Mich. Hist. Colls.*, XXVIII, 628, 650; *Eighth Census, Manufactures*, 272, 273; *Tenth Census, Manufactures*, 272.
42. *Tenth Census, Manufactures*, 282. Data for the year ending June 1, 1880.

1088, nearly three times the number in 1860. The establishments had increased in size and in average value of output. Wayne County produced about twenty per cent of the total factory output for the State.[43]

Copper had disappeared from among the list of manufactured products, the smelter having been dismantled and re-erected in the Northern Peninsula, near the mines. The lumber production had declined greatly, the sawmills now being located nearer the source of supply of lumber. The decline had been going on for three or four decades. By 1880 little lumber was manufactured in Wayne County. In 1840 Wayne County produced about six per cent of the output for the State.[44] In 1860 it produced only $619,000 worth out of the $7,000,000 worth sawed in the State, and had only forty-three out of the 927 establishments of the State.[45] In 1880 the mills of Wayne County sawed only $304,015 worth out of the $52,450,000 worth produced in the State, and had only nineteen out of the 1,649 sawmills.[46] From producing about nine per cent of the lumber in 1860, the industry had so declined by 1880 that only about six-tenths of one per cent of the output of the State was produced in Wayne County.[47] As previously stated, the sawmill industry in Wayne County was greatly aided by the excellent facilities for transportation of logs. As the frontier moved northward, mills were

43. Ibid.; Eighth Census, Manufactures, 272, 273.
44. Data from Comp. of Sixth Census, 322 to 333.
45. Eighth Census, Manufactures, 273, 275.
46. Tenth Census, Manufactures, 146, 282.
47. Ibid.

established at the mouths of all the important streams
and the great pine area was tapped. These mills soon
supplanted those of Wayne County. Lumber is more
easily handled than logs. The mills at Detroit, which
had to bear the expense of rafting the logs from the
mouths of the streams of Lake Huron to Detroit, could
not compete with the mills located near the source of
supply, such as those in the Saginaw Valley and along
Lake Huron from the mouth of the Saginaw River
northward.

Considering now the new industries that had become
important, it appears the only geographic reasons for
the great development of the tobacco and cigar industry were, the presence of a growing center of population in Wayne County (which was an important market
in itself) and the excellent facilities for distribution.
Some tobacco was raised in the vicinity for many years
but it was always a minor crop.[48]

In 1840 the output of the tobacco and cigar factories
was valued at $5,000. In 1860 the output increased
to $6,000; but by 1880 the product of the factories
was valued at $2,700,000. In Detroit alone there
were sixty-three establishments, employing 861 men,
227 women, and 154 children. A large number of
establishments were cigar factories in which almost all
the work was done by hand. This was the only
industry at this date that employed large numbers of
women and children.

48. In 1840 Michigan raised 160? pounds of tobacco. Virginia
     the same year produced /5 million pounds and Kentucky
     53 million. In 1860 Michigan produced 121,000 pounds
     and in 1880, 83,969 pounds. (*Twelfth Census, Manu-
     factures*, Pt. III, 640).

The iron and steel industry which by 1880 occupied second rank in value of products and first rank in the magnitude of the plants, was the outgrowth of the start in iron manufacture that had been made previous to 1840.[49]   Since that date there had been a considerable development.   From 1840 to 1850 there was in general little progress in iron manufactures in Michigan, due no doubt to the poor quality of ore and its rapid depletion.   About 1850 beginnings were made in Wayne County in the smelting of the rich iron ores of Lake Superior.   Lake Superior ore was first brought into Southern Michigan in 1846, and tried in a furnace at Jackson, Michigan.   A bar of excellent quality was obtained, the "first iron ever made from Lake Superior ore."[50]   The first shipment of iron ore from the Lake Superior region was in 1850, about five tons being sent to New Castle, Pennsylvania.   After the opening of the St. Mary's Canal, the shipments increased rapidly and the furnaces in Wayne County began to use these ores, but the furnaces in the interior of the State continued to use bog ore.   All these furnaces used charcoal for fuel, as late at least as 1880.   In the Northern Peninsula the abundance of timber for the making of charcoal (and the deposits of iron) attracted the attention of capitalists.   The first forge was erected at Marquette in 1850, and the first pig iron was made in 1850.   By 1880, 23 furnaces had been built in the Northern Peninsula.[51]   In 1880 Michigan was the "first state in the Union in the manufacture of charcoal pig iron,"

49.   See p.
50.   *Tenth Census, Manufactures*, 843, 845.
51.   *Ibid.*

and ranked eighth in the list of iron producing states.[52] At this time there were two rolling-mills in operation in Wayne County, the Eureka at Wyandotte, built in 1853, and the Baugh Steam Forge Company's plant at Detroit, built in 1877.[53] It is reported that Wyandotte was selected as the site for furnaces and rolling-mills "by reason of the heavily wooded tracts in all the neighborhood."[54]

The forests were soon depleted, however, and the production of iron came to depend, in part, upon coal. The situation of Detroit and Wayne County upon the route between the ore deposits and coal deposits was no assurance for the continuation of the manufacture of iron. The blast furnaces came to be located farther east, nearer the markets and nearer the coal deposits, it being easier to handle iron ore than either coal (or coke) or pig iron. Open-pit mining and the improved devices for loading and unloading iron ore have been important factors in bringing this condition about. After 1880 the iron industry declined in importance in Wayne County.

Wyandotte, in Wayne County, has the distinction of having produced the first Bessemer steel in America.[55] Bessemer of England began his experiments in converting cast-iron into steel as early as 1854. In 1856 he endeavored to get patents on the process in the United States, but was confronted by Mr. Kelley, an iron-maker of Pennsylvania, with a claim of priority of discovery. Bessemer lost. The converter, however,

52. *Ibid.*
53. *Ibid.; Mich. Hist. Colls.*, XIII, 370.
54. *Mich. Hist. Colls.*, XIII, 318.
55. *Ibid.*, XXI, 341; *Tenth Census, Manufactures,* 859.

that Kelley used was not like that employed by Bessemer. In a few years the Bessemer Company secured
patents in America. About 1863, Capt. E. B. Ward
and others of Detroit secured control of the patents
of Kelley and organized the Kelley Process Company.
An engineer was sent to England to investigate the
Bessemer process. Upon his return experimental works
were established at Wyandotte, Michigan. A converter of 2.5 tons capacity was constructed, and in the
fall of 1864 Bessemer steel was produced. The use of
Bessemer machinery was in direct violation of the
Bessemer patents. The Kelley Process Company could
not make the steel without the use of the Bessemer
machinery. Arrangements had to be made with the
holders of the Bessemer patents. In 1866 all the
American patents were consolidated. The plant at
Wyandotte continued in operation until 1869.[56] In
the meantime other plants had been started in Wayne
County.

Among the new industries in 1880 were the making
of men's clothing and the meat-packing industries,
both of which are important in most large cities. The
large tailor-shops supplied the local and wholesale
trade of Detroit. The refrigerator car, introduced
about 1875, tended to concentrate meat-packing in the
large cities.

Flouring and gristmilling continued to be important.
The area from which the grains were drawn was much
extended by the settlement of the wheat lands to the
west of the Lakes. Wheat came to be one of the
great bulk cargoes in Lake traffic. Buffalo has been

56. *Tenth Census, Manufactures*, 862.

for many decades the great eastern terminus for the grain trade of the Lakes; but the mills at Detroit, situated on the route between the wheat regions and Buffalo, found it easy to secure wheat to supply their trade. Momentum of an early start, and ability to supply a trade already developed, helped to sustain the industry at Detroit.

In the census report for 1880, statistics for the manufactures of the cities are given for the first time. The total value of the manufactured products for Detroit was over $30,000,000; the number of establishments, 919; the male employees, 12,477; the female employees and children and youths, 1,203. Detroit produced nearly ninety per cent of the manufactures in Wayne County. For the first time adequate data showing the relative importance of the industries of Detroit to those of the country are given. The leading products were as follows:[57]

MANUFACTURES AT DETROIT, 1880.

Product.	Value.	Percentage of product of Wayne County
Iron and steel	$2,499,000	100
Tobacco and cigars	2,409,000	89
Men's clothing	2,056,200	99.7
Foundry and machine shop	1,808,000	75
Meat packing	1,721,000	100
Flour and grist mill	1,650,000	83
Malt liquors	1,144,000	99
Boots and shoes	1,066,000	Practically all.
Printing and publishing	986,000	Practically all.
Bread and bakery	930,000	Practically all.
Ship building	739,000	62

Detroit at this time produced about twenty per cent of the manufactured products of the State. Among the cities of the country it ranked nineteenth in manu-

---

57. *Tenth Census, Manufactures*, 399.

factures and seventeenth in order of population. The cities producing greater amounts of manufactured products were New York, Philadelphia, Chicago, Brooklyn, Boston, St. Louis, Cincinnati, Baltimore, San Francisco, Pittsburgh, Newark, Jersey City, Cleveland, Milwaukee, Buffalo, Providence, Louisville, and Lowell.[58]

By 1909 Detroit had advanced to the sixth city in rank in the United States in value of output of manufactures. It stood ninth in rank of population, show-

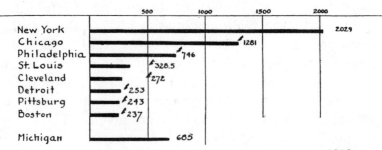

VALUE OF MANUFACTURES OF PRINCIPAL CITIES IN 1909
(Scale of one million dollars)

ing that manufacturing had increased much more rapidly than population, and manufacturing had come to be the chief interest of the city.[59]

The value of all manufactured products amounted to nearly $223,000,000. This was about twice the total output of the factories of the United States in 1810,[60] more than fifty per cent of the output of the country in 1840, and almost equal to the entire output of Michigan in 1889.[61] It was three times the

58.   Ibid., p. xxiv.
59.   See ranking in 1880, p.
60.   Data from Amer. State Papers, Finance, II, 712.
61.   Twelfth Census, Manufactures, Part II, 985.

output of the factories of the city in 1899, and eight times that of 1880.[62] The leading ten products in value were as follows:[63]

MANUFACTURES OF DETROIT, 1909

Automobiles and parts	$59,536,000
Foundry and machine-shop products	18,296,000
Slaughtering and meat packing products	12,850,000
Tobacco (cigars, cigarettes, etc.)	12,773,000
Brass and bronze	12,297,000
Patent medicines	11,558,000
Printing and publishing products	7,291,000
Lumber and timber	6,110,000
Stoves and furnaces	5,676,000
Flour and grist mill products	5,089,000

Automobile and automobile parts constitute nearly 23.5 per cent of the total manufactured products of the city. These products were more than three times the value of foundry and machine-shop products, the next in rank of value. Never before in the development of manufactures at Detroit has one industry dominated so completely the industrial field. In 1860 in Wayne County the copper output was nearly two and one-half times the output of lumber, the next in rank.[64] In 1880 the leading five products ranged in value of output between $1,650,000 and $2,500,000.[65]

In 1909, 38.8 per cent of all the automobiles produced in the United States were built in Michigan, and 14.5 per cent of the capital invested in the automobile industry in the country was invested in Detroit.[66] The automobile industry dates from about 1895. The report of the Twelfth Census does not list automobiles

62. *Tenth Census, Manufactures,* 409.
63. *Thirteenth Census, Manufactures,* IX, 583. Data for the year ending Dec. 31, 1909.
64. See p.
65. See p.
66. *Thirteenth Census, Spec. Rept., Manufactures,* Part II, 270.

among the manufactures of Michigan, but in the United States "automobiles and other horseless conveyances" were manufactured to the value of $4,680,000.[67] In 1904, there were constructed in Michigan 9,125 cars. In 1909, 64,800 machines were constructed and assembled in the State, and valued at $70,360,000; 50,000 of these were built in Detroit alone.[68]

The starting of this industry in Detroit was not purely accidental. It was due largely to the activity of the State in industries allied to that of the automobile industry. Michigan has for a long time ranked high among the States in the manufacture of carriages, wagons, and wheels. In 1900 it was second in rank in the manufacture of "family and pleasure carriages," the output amounting to $7,430,000.[69] The workers and factories producing these products could adapt themselves easily and quickly to the manufacture of automobile bodies and wheels. One writer says,[70] "Detroit, Flint, Pontiac, and Lansing, for the first three years supplied almost all the automobile bodies used in Detroit without the erection of a single additional plant." The opportunities offered for boating had stimulated the manufacture of marine gasoline engines in Michigan. In 1899, the first census at which statistics on this industry were collected, there were 79 establishments in Michigan engaged in the

67. *Twelfth Census* (1900), X, *Manufactures*, Part IV, 310.
68. *Board of Commerce Rept.* (1909), 12.
69. *Twelfth Census*, X, *Manufactures*, Part IV, 311.
70. Stocking in "*The Detroiter*," a publication of the Detroit Board of Commerce, 1913. The main line of thought used here in the discussion of the automobile was suggested by the article by Stocking in this publication.

manufacture of "internal combustion engines." The
product was valued at $268,300.[71] The adaptation of
the marine engine to the propulsion of land vehicles
was not difficult. Foundries and machine shops and
the manufacture of iron and steel have for a long
time been among the important industries in the city.
In 1890 Michigan was eighth in rank among the
States in the manufacture of foundry and machine-
shop products, and ninth in the manufacture of iron
and steel.[72] The city was also well supplied with
factories for the manufacture of copper and brass
wares and easily turned these plants to the manufacturing of copper and brass parts and fixtures needed.
Last among the articles needed were paints and varnishes. For twenty or thirty years these likewise had
been industries of growing importance in the city. In
1890 Michigan was eighth in rank in the United
States in the manufacture of paint, and sixth in rank
in manufacture of varnishes and japans.[73] Starting
with these advantageous elements, success was assured
when Detroit genius devised some of the earliest successful cars. Pioneers in this field, like pioneers in
many other fields, reaped enormous profits. Capital
soon came to stand ready to furnish money to any-
body with definite plans and ideas. The early start
is the most important factor in the development of
the automobile industry in Michigan and Detroit.

The influence of the automobile industry has been
felt in many of the allied trades. The products of

71. *Twelfth Census*, X, *Manufactures*, Part IV, 301.
72. *Eleventh Census, Manufacturing Industries*, Part I, 197, 221.
73. *Ibid.*, 265.
39

foundries and machineshops in the thirty years since 1880 increased from $1,800,000 to over $18,000,000. Bronze and brass which were only of minor value among the products of 1880, by 1909 ranked fifth, with a value of over $12,000,000. The iron and steel industry at Detroit, however, has not advanced in value of output since 1880. In the report of the Tenth Census, iron and steel headed the list with a value of nearly $2,500,000. In 1909 these products stood tenth in rank, with a value of $2,300,000.[74] The developing automobile industry has had little or no influence on this industry, undoubtedly due to the proximity of Detroit to the larger steel producing centers in Ohio and western Pennsylvania.

Both the slaughtering and meat-packing and the tobacco industries have made rapid gains since 1880. Slaughtering and meatpacking has advanced in volume of business 150 per cent within the last ten years. The sales in 1909 were nearly seven and one-half times those of 1880. The local markets in most of the small towns of Michigan have come to depend upon western beef, and many secure their supply from Detroit.[75] As for the tobacco industry the "First Michigan District" ranked eighth among the districts in the United States in value of output. The factories at Detroit make about nine-tenths of all the product of the First District.[76]

The beginning of the pharmaceutical industry, the sixth in rank in the city, goes back to the early drug-

74. *Thirteenth Census, Manufactures*, I, 28.
75. Data from *Tenth Census, Manufactures*, 410; *Thirteenth Census, Manufactures*, 28.
76. *The Detroiter*, Pub. by the Bd. of Commerce, 1913.

stores of Chapin and Hand in the late thirties; although drugs were not manufactured in any great quantity until twenty years later.[77] There seems to be no geographic reasons for the localization of the industry at Detroit. The making of patent medicine is profitable, and capital will readily flow into profitable channels of business. The excellency of the preparations made at Detroit has been an important factor in the development of this industry. As in the automobile industry, the large profits made by the pioneers in the manufacture of drugs induced others to invest capital. Many of the Detroit plants have branches in foreign countries.

The printing industry supplies mainly the local market. The railways radiating from Detroit to many parts of Michigan have stimulated the newspaper business. Rural free delivery has aided much in the expansion of the newspaper business in Detroit.

The manufacture of stoves and ranges had its beginning in the factory of Jeremiah Dwyer in 1861. The first of the large companies was incorporated in 1864; the second large company, the Michigan Stove Company, was incorporated in 1871. The Peninsula Stove Company was organized in 1881.[78] The prominence of Michigan in iron manufactures about the time of the organization of the pioneer companies and the fact that Detroit is a good distributing point are the chief geographic reasons for the growth of the industry in the city.

The seeming increase in the importance of the lum-

77. Leonard, *Industries of Detroit*, 10.
78. *Ibid.*, 9.

ber industry is due to a new basis of classification.   In the previous decades sawed lumber was considered separately.   In the data for 1909 sawed lumber was included with the output of sash, doors, cooperage, interior finish, and all mill work.   Much Canadian lumber is now being worked up in the planing-mills of Detroit.

Detroit has grown in population and in manufactures much faster in the last decade than has the State. From 1900 to 1910 the State increased in population only 16.1 per cent.   Detroit during the decade increased 63 per cent.[79]   In 1899 Detroit made only twenty-eight per cent of the products manufactured in the State; in 1909 it produced thirty-seven per cent. The percentages of the output of the State for the various commodities in which Detroit leads are as follows:[80]

Slaughtering and meat-packing products. . 95.6 per cent.
Brass and bronze. . . . . 88.5 per cent.
Structural and rolling-mill products. 86   per cent.
Patent medicines. . . . . 85.8 per cent.
Tobacco and cigars. . . . . 78.9 per cent.
Fur goods. . . . . 76.1 per cent.
Men's clothing. . . . . 72.9 per cent.
Copper, tin, and sheet iron. . . . . 71.7 per cent.
Stoves and furnaces. . . . . 62.2 per cent.
Automobiles. . . . . 61.6 per cent.
Leather goods. . . . . 54.5 per cent.

In 1810, the first year for which there are data for

79.   *Thirteenth Census, Population,* I, 898.
80.   *Thirteenth Census, Manufactures,* 556, 557.

the manufactures of Detroit, the total value of products turned out was $24.742. This was sixty-seven per cent of the total for the Territory. Detroit at that time was a small settlement of perhaps 750 persons, and except for the settlements in the southeastern part of the Territory, was completely isolated from the remaining portion of the country. It was thirty days distant from New York City, even with the most rapid modes of travel. Michigan Territory contained about 4,700 persons, only a portion of whom were within easy distance of the settlement at Detroit. The majority of the people were French, not much above the hunting and fishing stage in industrial development. For over one hundred years they had been isolated from the factories of Europe and had been accustomed to supplying their own wants from the natural resources about them. A few Americans had come and to them is due the start in manufactures that had been made, but like most emigrants, their purchasing power was exceedingly limited. This was the population that the factories at Detroit at that early date catered to. Poor transportation limited the area from which the raw materials for manufactures could be drawn. The manufacturing plants by necessity, therefore, were primitive in machinery and methods, and their character was determined by the resources of the immediate neighborhood. The average output per establishment was two thousand dollars per year. Only eight kinds of articles are listed as factory products. Grains, fur, hides, and timber were the articles most used in manufacture. There were few establishments in each industry. Only thirteen "factories" were enumerated besides those engaged in the making of woolen goods. Most of the "woolens" was manufactured in the household.

In 1910 the output of the factories of Detroit was valued at over $254,000,000, or ten thousand times the value of output of the factories in 1810. The small settlement of 1810 had grown to a modern city with a population of 466,000 people, or more than six hundred times the population of one hundred years before. Modern transportation facilities have put the factories of the city in touch with every part of the world. Instead of catering to an area of a few thousand square miles and a few thousand people, today many millions of square miles and many tens of millions of people may be reached. It is true that in the larger sphere many cities compete, but in many articles the factories of Detroit have an equal chance with those of other industrial centers. A sphere of commercial control for any city does not exist in an open market. Within the eastern part of Michigan and in parts of Canada in which the factories of Detroit have a great advantage over those of other cities, not only is there a vastly larger population but their needs have been enormously increased, and likewise their purchasing power.

The area from which the raw products may be drawn for the manufactures has likewise been extended enormously and the factories are no longer limited in scope by the resources of the immediate region. The list of products turned out has been increased greatly. With large markets and high purchasing power of the people, large scale industries are made

possible, in which all the best of labor-saving machinery
known to the modern scientific world may be employed.   From a small settlement producing less than
.02 of one per cent of the manufactures of the country,
Detroit in one hundred years has come to be the sixth
city in manufactures, producing about 1.2 per cent
of the total manufactured products of the United
States.[81]

81.   Manufactures of U. S. in 1909 were valued at $20,672,052,000
      (*Thirteenth Census, Manufactures*, 572.)

CHAPTER XIII

FACTORS IN THE GROWTH OF POPULATION AND DEVELOPMENT OF MANUFACTURES—A REVIEW

THE broad geographic factors that have been operative in the growth of population and the development of manufactures at Detroit are associated with its position. It is situated near the eastern edge of the Central Plain of North America, on the largest and most important series of inland waterways in the world, near the entrance to "the Gateways" through the Appalachian Barrier, within easy reach of the copper and iron deposits of the Lake Superior region and the coal of the North Central States, on the border of the most productive agricultural district of the United States, and during the early decades of the nineteenth century had access to large forests of commercial timber. For many decades Detroit enjoyed almost a monopoly of the benefits arising from these important factors; but with the westward migration of population, wealth, and manufactures, many cities have arisen to compete for these benefits. In this competition Detroit, although not the most successful, is to be numbered among the more successful cities of the Lakes region in building up manufactures and attracting and holding people. The elements in the position and environment of Detroit that have favored the concentration of people and manufactures there may be summarized briefly.

In selecting the site for Fort Pontchartrain, the nucleus from which Detroit has grown, the French had two objects in view: first, the checking of the encroachment of the British and Iroquois in the trading territory about the Upper Lakes; and second, the control of the Wabash route. It is evident that many sites on the Detroit River could have been chosen to fulfill these requirements. A post on the site of Fort Malden would have commanded the commerce of the Detroit River quite as well as one at Detroit, and it would have been more effective in controlling the traffic of the Maumee-Wabash route, being nearer the mouth of the Maumee River.

Deep water was not needed for the water traffic of the French. Probably Cadillac gave little or no consideration to the depth of water along the shores; at least there appear to be no records of soundings having been made to determine the best channels. Fortunately, however, for later commercial and industrial development, the Cadillac party selected a site opposite a broad, deep channel. Had a site been chosen on Grosse Isle, or at one of many other points along the west shore of the river, the shallow rocky channel would have been a serious handicap at a later period when the prosperity of the settlement depended on deep-water navigation.

Because of the strategic importance of Detroit, a fort and a garrison were maintained there until 1827. The presence of a military force was an important factor in the early growth of the settlement. Under French rule the post served to hold the British and Iroquois in check and was the stronghold to which the traders brought their furs and about which the settlers gathered for protection. These were the "feudal" days in the history of Detroit. Since it was the only considerable post within a large area, nearly all the French settlers emigrating to the Lakes region settled at Detroit. Under American rule, troops were stationed at Detroit as long as Indian problems and the attitude of the British required. American settlements for the first decade or two were confined to the southeastern part of the Territory partly because of the protection offered by the fort at Detroit against the Indians.

For more than one hundred and fifty years commerce was an effective factor in the growth of Detroit. The position of the post near the east entrance to the Maumee-Wabash trade-route gave it a large share of the Indian trade in parts of Ohio, Indiana, and Illinois. Its location on the Straits gave it a portion of the Indian trade of the Upper Lakes and of the region west and northwest. The strategic and commercial importance of the place during the long period between its founding in 1701 and the time the American frontier reached southeastern Michigan, served to concentrate people at Detroit and make it one of the largest and for most of the period *the* largest settlement in the Lakes region. As population spread westward into the Michigan region and beyond, Detroit, because of its size and its position on the eastern margin of the developing area, on a broad navigable river that connects with Lake Erie, was made the western terminus of most of the lines of both sailing vessels and steamers engaged in the emigrant trade. Thousands of emigrants on their way to interior Michigan entered the Detroit gateway; and before steamers began to make regular trips to the west shore of Lake Michigan, many hundreds if not thousands of emigrants, whose destination was Northern Illinois or Wisconsin, crossed the "Michigan bridge," entering the approaches at Detroit or Monroe. Not a few of these people, attracted by the prospects of Detroit remained to make it their home.

During the era of road-building in Michigan, Detroit, being the largest city on the eastern border toward the best markets of the country, was made the center from which National and Territorial roads were built. Stage-lines and wagon-transportation lines were established along these roads to various parts of the State. Beginning about 1840, lines of railways likewise were constructed radiating out from Detroit, in general along the main wagon roads. These roads and railways gave Detroit almost a monopoly of the external trade of the State, and until the rise of Chicago, of some of the trade of Indiana and Illinois. Through Detroit the grains and wool and other products passed eastward. Manufactured wares and groceries were sent westward. For a time Detroit was the eastern terminus of the Michigan Central Railway from Chicago, the connection with Buffalo being made by steamer during the season of navigation. For many decades, then, Detroit was at a break in transportation on an important east and west traffic route. The break in transportation at Detroit during this period was both mechanical and commercial, to use Cooley's terminology.[1] At a break there is necessarily unload-

1. *Pub. Amer. Econ. Assoc.*, IX, 91, 92.

ing and loading of the commodities from the water-carrier to the land-carrier and vice versa. This involves cartage and storage, labor, and capital, and indirectly, agriculturists, artisans, and merchants. At a commercial break, a break with a change of ownership of goods, there are also involved wholesale merchants, shippers, importers, and bankers.[2] The importance of the break was made greater by the lack of transportation when navigation was closed.

For some thirty or forty years after the Americans took control of the Lakes region, Detroit was the entrepot for a large part of the thinly settled region along the shores of Lakes Huron, Michigan, and Superior. With the westward migration of the people and the rise of cities like Chicago and Milwaukee, Detroit lost most of the trade of the Upper Lakes.

Being the great center of population on the Straits with many lines of railway to the oldest and most densely settled part of Michigan and to the region to the west, when the Great Western Railroad was projected westward from the Niagara region across Canada, Detroit was chosen as the western terminus. The line ended, however, on the east side of the river at Windsor, geographically a part of Detroit. Three car-ferries (after 1867) completed the connection. This railway route from Chicago to Buffalo by way of Detroit became a competitor with the Lake Shore and Michigan Southern Railroad, which runs by way of Toledo and Cleveland. With the construction of through railway lines from east to west, and with the spread of population and the growth of cities to the

2. *Ibid.*

west, Detroit declined in importance as the western terminus of Lake Erie.

During the two or three decades that Detroit and Wayne County were so prominent in copper and pig iron production, the city was one of the chief termini for the iron-ore traffic on the lakes. With the development of the immense bulk-cargo trade in iron and coal, Detroit became only a way-port. The decline of Detroit as a Lake port is only relative, however. While other ports have had their traffic increased eight to ten fold since 1889, that of Detroit has not quite doubled. This relative decline in commerce undoubtedly has had an influence on the relative growth of population; although any effects are difficult to trace, because many other factors have been operative in increasing the population. Long before Detroit lost its relative importance as a commercial port, manufacturing had begun to absorb the attention of capital and labor. For the last fifty or sixty years manufacturing has been the important factor in the growth of population.

The growth in manufactures has kept pace with, and, in some decades, exceeded the growth in population. The early manufactures of Detroit were mainly a response to the abundant raw materials and to the difficulties of access to the eastern markets in which manufactured goods could be purchased. The questions of power and capital were minor considerations, for the early manufactures were chiefly in the household stage of development. The improvements in the means of transportation gave access to a larger variety and amount of raw material and at the same time expanded the market. The flow of capital to the West and the migration of the labor city-ward, which is so characteristic of industrially developing regions, all favored the growth of population and the development of manufactures.

All through the early history of manufacturing at Detroit, the character and variety of the raw materials in the near-by regions were important in determining the character and variety of manufactures. Lumber and wood-working industries, tanneries, woolen mills, hat factories, copper smelters, and iron furnaces were all developed as a response to the resources of the forest, the farms, and the mines. During the last few decades the industries have come to depend less and less on near-by sources for raw materials.

For many decades Detroit and the surrounding region possessed a large store of fuel in the forests. Charcoal was important in localizing copper-smelting and iron manufactures. With the depletion of the forests, coal became the important factor in the localization of industries. Michigan has coal beds under many hundred square miles in the central part of the Southern Peninsula, but the beds are thin and mining relatively expensive. The factories of Detroit, therefore, are dependent on the Appalachian fields for coal. It would seem at first thought that much coal would come to Detroit in Lake vessels, but in 1911 less than 21,000 tons were brought by water.[3] After coal is loaded into a vessel it can be carried a thousand miles about as cheaply as two hundred; Detroit, therefore, is forced to pay nearly as much for Pennsylvania and West Vir-

3. *Monthly Sum. of Com. and Labor*, Dec., 1911, 956.

ginia coal shipped by vessel as Milwaukee, Chicago, or
Duluth, and much more than the coal-shipping cities
of Lake Erie. And since railroad rates tend to equal
those by water under competition, the manufacturers
of Detroit have little advantage in the cost of power
from coal over those of Chicago and Milwaukee and
are at a disadvantage in competition with the manufacturers near the coal fields. Hydro-electric power
has never been a factor in the development of manu-
tures at Detroit and little can be expected from it in
the near future. Some advance, however, has been
made in bringing electric power from Niagara two
hundred miles across Canada. Niaraga power is used
to a limited extent at present in both Windsor and
Detroit. If long-distance transmission ever becomes
more highly developed, larger quantities of Niagara
power may be brought to the factories of Detroit.

Since the development of the steamboat and the
railway in the Lakes region, access to markets, perhaps one of the most important considerations in all
manufactures, has been one of the favorable factors
in the development of manufactures at Detroit. The
central location and transportation facilities of Detroit
give access to markets both east and west. As indicated above,[4] Detroit during the later decades has not
taken advantage of the excellent opportunities offered
by the Lakes and connecting waterways, as outlets for
the products of its factories. The receipts by water
are far in excess of the shipments by water. In 1911
they stood 1,363,400 net-tons for receipts and 169,900
net-tons for shipments. The potential facilities in

4. Page.

water transportation, no doubt, are influential in lowering the freight rates by rail. The railways are at present the chief carriers of the manufactured products of Detroit.

The presence of a large body of skilled workmen never has been, until recently, an important factor in the development of manufactures at Detroit. Until the rise of the automobile industry there were few trades there that served to develop skill in workmanship. Less than a decade ago a company producing computing machines in moving to Detroit was obliged to bring skilled workmen from Connecticut. The automobile industry, however, has been of great value in developing a large body of skilled workmen. The precision required in the making of the best cars is equalled in only a few other trades in a few other regions in the country. The good housing conditions at Detroit, the abundant opportunities for recreation, and the many home-owners among the workmen, however, have contributed to the development of a large body of healthy, competent, and reliable workmen. Such a body of workmen undoubtedly has been a valuable asset in the industrial development of the city.

Capital and enterprise also are important factors in the development of manufactures. The great increase in manufactures in the last decade is to a large extent a result of the great wealth arising from the pioneer enterprises in the automobile industry. The profits were great and most of the dividends were turned back into the industry or into allied industries.

Detroit, at least in recent decades, has depended

entirely on its general advantages to attract industries. Bonuses never have been offered. One of the recent presidents of the Board of Commerce in one of his addresses said,[5] "The most significant feature of the translation of manufacturing plants to Detroit in recent years is that they have come without any of the artificial inducements that have been employed by many booming towns. The city under its charter has no right to grant bonuses nor vote free water nor free sites nor exemption from taxes. The Board of Commerce has never offered these inducements nor has it taken the attitude of promoting stock subscriptions."

In evaluating the various factors, geographic and others, that have been operative in the growth of population and the development of manufactures at Detroit, there seems to be no one factor or set of factors to which the growth can be ascribed. Different factors have been operative at different periods. At no one period has Detroit possessed decided advantages over many other cities on the shores of the Lakes. The remarkable growth indicated in the preceding chapter is by no means characteristic of Detroit alone. Perhaps one of the great factors in the growth of manufactures at Detroit, as in the other cities of the Lakes region in the last one hundred years, has been the westward migration of manufactures, accompanying the westward movement of population. One after another of the natural resources has been developed and depleted. One after another, industries and cities have arisen into prominence. Many have for a time remained on the crest in prominence and then

5. *Rept. of Bd. of Com.* (1910), 12.

declined. Some few industries and some few cities have remained important throughout the entire period. Detroit, along with a few other cities, has had a remarkable growth in population and industries. The future ranking of Detroit is, of course, problematic. The slow but continuous growth, and many factors involved in its present prominence in population and industries, would seem to ensure it for many decades a prominent place among the great cities of the country.

BIBLIOGRAPHY

(Titles abbreviated where possible)

ALBACH, — *Annals of the West*, 1846 to 1857. Pittsburgh, W. S. Hann Press, 1858.

ALVORD, C. W. and BIDGOOD, LEE. *Trans-Allegheny Explorations.* Cleveland, A. H. Clark, Pubs., 1912.

American Antiquarian and Oriental Journal. Chicago, Jameson and Moore, 1878; Salem, Mass., 1878 to 1908; Benton Harbor, Mich., 1909 to date.

American Antiquarian Society, *Proceedings.* Worcester. Semimonthly.

American Economic Association, *Publications of.* Baltimore, 1887 to date.

American Historical Association, *Annual Reports.* New York and London, G. P. Putnam's Sons, 1859 to 1889. Washington, Government Printing Office, 1890 to date.

American Historical Review. 15 vols., New York and London, Macmillan Company, 1895.

American State Papers: Claims, Commerce and Navigation, Indian Affairs, Military Affairs, Miscellaneous, Naval Affairs, Public Lands, from First Congress to 25th Congress, 1789 to 1838. 38 vols., Washington, 1832 to 1861.

ANDERSON, DAVID. *Canada: A View of British American Colonies.* London, 1814.

ANDREWS, ISRAEL D. "Trade and Commerce of British Colonies in America with United States," in *Exec. Doc.* 112. 1st Session, 32nd Congress (1853).

ARMROYD, GEORGE. *A Connected View of the Whole Interior Navigation of United States.* Philadelphia, Carey and Lea, 1826.

ASHE, THOMAS. *Travels in America, performed in 1806.* Newburyport, Mass., 1808.

Atlas of Canada. Canadian Government Publication, 1901.

ATWATER, CALEB. *History of State of Ohio, Natural and Civil.* Cincinnati, Glazen and Shepherd, 1838.

BALDWIN, C. C. "Indian Migrations in America," in *American*

Antiquarian, I. See American Antiquarian Society, *Proceedings*.

BARTON, JAMES L. *Lake Commerce*, 1846. Buffalo, Jewitt, Thomas & Co., 1846.—Letters to Hon. Robert McClelland, M. C., on the importance of the commerce of the Great Lakes.

BEMIS, EDWARD WEBSTER. *Local Government in Michigan and the Northwest*, in J. H. U. Studies in Pol. and Hist. Science, Series I, No. 5. Baltimore, The Johns Hopkins Press, 1883.

BENTON, ELBERT JAY. *The Wabash Trade Route*. J. H. U. Studies in Pol. and Hist. Science, Series XXI, Nos. 1 and 2. Baltimore, The Johns Hopkins Press, 1903.

BENTON, THOMAS HART. *Abridgment of Debates of Congress*, 1789 to 1856. New York, 1857 to 1861.

BESTE, JOHN RICHARD DIGBY. *The Wabash, or Adventures of an English Gentleman's Family in the Interior of America*. 2 vols., London, Huist and Blachett, 1855.

BLANCHARD, RUFUS. *Description and Conquest of Northwest, including the early history of Chicago, Detroit, Vincennes, St. Louis, etc.* Chicago, Cushing, Thomas and Co., 1880.

BLOIS, JOHN T. *Gazetteer of State of Michigan*. Detroit, 1838. (Portions published in *Michigan Pioneer and Historical Collection*, X).

BLOWE, DANIEL. *A Geographical, Historical, Commercial, and Agricultural View of the United States of America, forming a complete Emigrant's Directory*. London, Edwards and Knibb, 1820.

Blue Book of American Shipping (1910). *Marine and Naval Directory of the United States*. Cleveland, 1896 to 1910.

BOGART, ERNEST LUDLOW. *Economic History of United States*. New York, London, etc., Longmans, Green and Co., 1907.

BURNET, JACOB. *Notes on the Early Settlement of the Northwest Territory*. New York, D. Appleton & Co.; Cincinnati, Derby, Bradly & Co., 1847.

BOURINOT, SIR JOHN GEORGE. *Canada under British Rule*, 1760 to 1905. Cambridge, University Press, 1909.

BRADBURY, JOHN. *Bradbury's Travels in the Interior of America*, 1809 to 1811. Cleveland, Ohio, The A. H. Clark Co., 1904.

BREMER, FREDRIKA. *The Homes of the New World*. 2 vols., London, Hall; New York, Harper, 1853.

BRIDGMAN. (See Ensign, Bridgman, and Farming's *Lake and River Guide*.)

BRODHEAD, JOHN ROMEYN. *History of State of New York*. 2 vols., New York, Harper & Bros., 1853 to 1871.

BROWN, SAMUEL R. *The Western Gazetteer or Emigrant's Directory.* Auburn, N. Y., Southwick, 1817.

BRYCE, GEORGE. *The Remarkable History of the Hudson Bay Company.* Toronto, W. Briggs, 1900.

BUCKINGHAM, JAMES S. *The Eastern and Western States of America.* 3 vols., London, Fisher, 1842.

BURPEE, LAWRENCE J. *The Search for the Western Sea.* Toronto, The Musson Book Co., 1908.

BURTON, CLARENCE MONROE. *Cadillac's Village,* 1701 to 1710. Detroit, 1896. *Early Detroit.* Detroit, 1909. *Fort Pontchartrain du Detroit.* Detroit, ——. *A Sketch of Life of La Mothe Cadillac, founder of Detroit.* Detroit, 1895.

BUTTERICK, TILLY. *Voyages* (1812–19) in Thwaites, *Early Western Travels,* VIII. Cleveland, A. H. Clark Co., 1904 to 1907.

CAMPBELL, JAMES VALENTINE. *Outlines of Political History of Michigan.* Detroit, Schober & Co., 1876.

Canada. Navigation, Railways, and Steamboat Lines. Canadian Government Publication, 1912.

Canadian Year Book. Toronto, A. Hewett, 1899 to date.

Census Reports of United States. Reports from 1790 to 1910, inclusive. Washington, Government Printing Office.

CHATEAUBRIAND, FRANCOIS AUGUSTE RENE. *Travels in America and Italy,* 1828. London, H. Coburn, 1828.

CHARLEVOIX, PIERRE FRANCOIX XAVIER DE. *History and General Description of New France.* (Translated, with notes, by J. G. Shea.) New York, J. G. Shea, 1866 to 1872.—Portion in *North American Review,* XLVI.

City. Report on Conference for Good City Government. 1900 to date.

COMAN, KATHERINE. *Industrial History of United States.* New York, Macmillan Co., 1910.

COOK, CHARLES W. "Brines and Salt Deposits of Michigan," in Michigan Geological and Biological Survey's *Publication* 15, *Geological Series* 12.

COLTON, G. W. and C. B. *Map of Michigan* (1869). New York, G. W. & C. B. Colton Co., 1869.

COLTON, G. W. *The Western Tourist and Emigrant's Guide, with a Compendious Gazetteer of States of Ohio, Michigan, Indiana, Illinois, and Missouri* [etc.]. New York, Colton, 1839.—Describes Stage Routes, Canals, Railroads, etc. Editions from 1844 to 1856 have binder's title, Colton's *Western Tourist.*

Commerce and Finance, Monthly Summary of. Bureau of Statistics, Department of Commerce and Labor, Washington D. C.

Congressional Globe, 23rd to 42nd Congress, 1833 to 1873. Washington, 1834 to 1873.

COOLEY, THOMAS McINTYRE. *Michigan, A History of Governments.* Boston, 1895. American Commonwealth Series.

CROGAN, GEORGE. "Crogan's Journal," in Thwaites, *Early Western Travels,* 1748 to 1846, Vol. I.

COX, SANFORD C. *Recollections of Early Settlement of Wabash Valley.* Lafayette, Ind., Lafayette *Courier,* 1860.

DANA, C. W. *The Great West, or the Garden of the World, Its Wealth, Its Natural Advantages, and Its Future.* Boston, Wentworth & Co., 1857.

DARBY, WILLIAM. *Emigrant's Guide to the Western and Southwestern States and Territories,* [etc.]. New York, Kirk and Mercein, 1818.

A Tour from the City of New York to Detroit in Michigan Territory, made between 2nd of May and 22nd of September, 1818. New York, Kirk and Mercein, 1819.

DARBY, WILLIAM and DWIGHT, T., JR. *A New Gazetteer of the United States of America.* Hartford, Conn., Hopkins, 1833.

DAVISON, GIDEON M. *Traveller's Guide through the Middle and Northern States and Provinces of Canada.* 7th edition, Saratoga Springs, 1837.

DAWSON, S. E. North America, I. Stanford's Compendium of Geography. London, Edward Stanford, 1897.

DE BOW, JAMES D. B. De Bow's *Review.* 30 vols., New Orleans and Washington, 1830 to 1867.

DEFEBAUGH, JAMES ELLIOTT. *History of Lumber Industry of America.* Chicago, The American Lumberman, 1906.

Detroit, Directory of. Detroit, J. W. Weeks and Company, 1883.

Detroit Board of Commerce. *Annual Reports.*

Detroit, Manual of City of. Edited by City Clerk, 1912.

Detroit Water Works. *Report of Board of Water Commissioners,* 1853 to date.

Detroit Merchants, Day Books, Ledgers, etc., of. Manuscripts in Detroit Public Library. A few only are here listed:
(a) 1775 to ——— "Petty" Ledger. The sales entered show that a general stock of goods was kept and that rum was in much demand. The homes of purchasers were designated as "up the river," "across the river," "down the river," on "Hog Island," etc.

(b) **1776 to 1778.** Macomb, Edgar, and Macomb. Day Book and Ledger.
(c) **1778 to 1780.** T. B. Barth and Co. "Accounts with Traders of the Upper Country." June 19, 1778 to 1780.
(d) **1781 to 1783.** Alexander Macomb. Day Book.
(e) **1783 to 1785.** James May and Company. Day Book. This manuscript includes the "Adventurer's Journal," a record of transactions at the store known as "The Pinery."
(f) **1798 to 1803.** ————————————. Day Book. Father Richardie's name appears among the purchasers. A general stock of goods was kept but large quantities of gin, brandy, rum, and whiskey were kept.

Detroit Newspapers. The following is a partial list only:
Detroit *Gazette* (W). 1817 to 1830.
Detroit *Courier* (W). December 22 1831 to January 14, 1835.
Detroit *Daily Free Press*. September 28, 1835 to date. Issue not consecutive.
Detroit *Daily Advertiser*. January 11, 1836 to December 30, 1862.
Detroit *Weekly Advertiser*. September 11, 1839 to August 23, 1845.
Detroit *Daily Tribune*. November 19, 1849 to date.
Detroit *Advertiser and Tribune*. (D). January 2, 1863 to December 31, 1877.
Detroit *Post and Tribune* (D). October, 1877 to June, 1884.
Detroit *Evening News*. 1873 to 1905. Published as Detroit *News* from 1905 to date.
Detroit *Journal*. 1884 to date.

Detroiter, The. A monthly published under auspices of Detroit Board of Commerce, September 1910 to August 1912.

DISTURNELL, JOHN. *The Western Traveller, embracing the canal and railroad routes from Albany to Troy to Buffalo and Niagara Falls; also steamboat routes to Detroit and Chicago.* New York, Disturnell, 1844.

Upper Lakes of North America, being a guide from Niagara Falls and Toronto to Mackinac, Chicago, Sault Ste. Marie, passing through Lakes Michigan and Superior, returning through Lakes Huron and St. Clair to Detroit and Buffalo. New York, Disturnell, 1857.

Documents Relating to the Colonial History of the State of New York. 15 vols., Albany, Weed, Parson & Co., Printers, 1853 to 1887. (See also *New York Historical Society Collections*.)

Documentary History of New York. Arranged by E. B. O'Callaghan.   4 vols., Albany, Weed, Parsons & Co., Public Printers, 1849 to 1851.

DODGE, JOHN.   *Narrative of Mr. John Dodge during his captivity at Detroit*, from second edition of 1780.   Introduction by Burton, 1909.

DOUGLAS, JAMES.   *Old France in New World; Quebec in the Seventeenth Century*.   Cleveland and London, Burrows Bros. Co., 1906.

DUNN, J. P.   "French Settlements on the Wabash," in *Indiana Historical Society Publications*, II.

DWIGHT, TIMOTHY.   *A Tour in New England and New York*.   4 vols., New Haven, Conn., T. Dwight, 1821 to 1822.

ELY, RICHARD T.   *The Coming City*.   New York, T. Y. Crowell & Co., 1902.

ENGLISH, WILLIAM HAYDEN.   *Conquest of the Country Northwest of Ohio River*, 1778 to 1783.   Indianapolis and Kansas City, Brown-Merrill Co., 1896.

ENSIGN, BRIDGMAN, and FANNING.   *Lake and River Guide*.   New York, Ensign, Bridgman and Fanning, 1856.

EVANS, ESTWICK.   Evans' Pedestrious Tour, in Thwaites, *Early Western Travels*, VIII.

FAIRLIE, JOHN ARCHIBALD.   *Economic Effects of Ship Canals*. A. A. A., II, Philadelphia, 1898.

FANNING, ——.   *Illustrated Gazetteer of United States*.   New York, Phelps, etc., 1853.   Maps.   (Also see Ensign, Bridgman, and Fanning's *Lake and River Guide*.)

U. S. Dept. Agriculture.   *Farmer's Bulletin No*. 20.

FARMER, SILAS.   *History of Detroit and Michigan*.   Detroit, 1884. *Map and Manual of Detroit*, 1870.   Detroit, 1870.

FAUST, ALBERT BERNHARDT.   *The German Element in United States*.   2 vols., Boston and New York, Houghton, Mifflin Co., 1909.

FERRIS, JACOB.   *The States and Territories of the Great West, their Geography, History, Resources*.   New York, Miller, Orton, and Mulligan; Buffalo, E. F. Bradle, 1856.

FERRIS, EZRA.   *The Early Settlement of the Miami Company*. Indianapolis, The Bowen-Merrill Co., 1897.

FISHER, SWAISON R.   *New and Complete Statistical Gazetteer of United States*, 1853.   New York, 1853.

FLINT, HENRY M.   *The Railroads of the United States, their History and Statistics*.   Philadelphia, J. E. Potter and Co., 1868.

FLINT, JAMES.   *Letters from America, 1818 to 1820*.   Cleveland,

The A. H. Clark Co., **1904**. Reprint of Edinburgh edition of 1822.

FLINT, TIMOTHY. *A Condensed Geography and History of Western States or Mississippi Valley.* 2 vols., Cincinnati, Flint, 1828.
The History and Geography of the Mississippi Valley. Cincinnati, H. Flint, 1833.
Indian Wars of the West. Cincinnati, E. H. Flint, 1833.

Geologic Map of North America. U. S. G. S., Prof. Paper 71.

Geologic Map of Michigan. Pleistocene Geology: The Nellist Map in Michigan Geological Survey, VII, Southern Peninsula; also in *Surface Geology and Agricultural Conditions of the Southern Peninsula of Michigan,* by Leverett and others, Publication 9, Geol. Series 7, Mich. Geol. Surv., 1912.
Northern Peninsula, in Surface Geology of the Northern Peninsula of Michigan, Publication 7, Geol. Series 5, Mich. Geol. Surv., 1911.

[GILMAN, CHANDLER R.]. *Life on the Lakes.* 2 vols., New York, Dearborn, 1836.

Great Lakes (Transportation by Water). *Census Report,* 1907; also *Report of Commission of Corporations,* 1910.

Great Lakes. *Reports of Commissioner of Navigation,* 1910, 1911, 1912, 1913. Washington, Bureau of Commerce and Labor.

Guide Book, No. 5. Canadian Geologic Survey, 1913.—Gives in detail the topographic and geologic features of portions of Georgian Bay. Other books in the same series treat of other areas in Canada.

HASKELL, DANIEL, and SMITH, J. C. *A Complete Descriptive and Statistical Gazetteer of United States of America* (1843). New York, Sherman and Smith, 1843.

HALL, BASIL. *Travels in North America in the years 1827 and 1828.* 3 vols. and Map, Edinburgh, Cadell, etc., 1829.

HALL, JAMES. *Letters from the West.* London, H. Colburn, 1828.
Sketches of History, Life, and Manners in the West. Philadelphia, H. Hall, 1835.
Notes on the Western States. Philadelphia, H. Hall, 1838.
The West, its Commerce and Navigation. Cincinnati, H. W. Derby and Co., 1848.
Romance of Western History. Cincinnati, Applegate and Co., 1857.

HAMILTON, THOMAS. *Men and Manners in America.* Edinburgh, W. Blackwood, 1833.

HARDY, MARY DUFFUS. *Through Cities and Prairie Lands.*

Sketches of an American Tour. New York, R. Worthington, 1881.

HARMON, DANIEL WILLIAM. *A Journal of Voyages and Travels in the Interior of North America.* New York, A. S. Barnes and Co., 1903. First pub. in 1820.

HARNS, THADDEUS MASON. *Journal of a Tour into the Territory Northwest of the Alleghany Mountains* (1803). Boston, Manning and Loring, 1805. Reprint from Boston Ed. in Thwaites, *Early Western Travels,* 1748 to 1846, III.

HARRIS, WILLIAM TELL. *Remarks made during a Tour through the United States of America in the Years* 1817, 1818, 1819. Liverpool, 1819.

HATCH, W. S. *History of War of 1812 in the Northwest.* Cincinnati, 1872.

HENNEPIN, FATHER LOUIS. *A New Discovery of a Vast Country in America.* (See Thwaites.)

HENRY, ALEXANDER (the younger), and THOMPSON, DAVID. *New Light on the Early History of the Greater Northwest.* The manuscript Journals of Alexander Henry (the younger), and David Thompson, 1799 to 1814. Edited by Elliott Cours. New York, F. P. Harper, 1897.

HENRY, ALEXANDER. *Travels and Adventures in Canada and the Indian Territory,* 1760–1776. New York, 1809. A late edition edited by James Bain.

HODGSON, ADAM. *Letters from North America written during a Tour in United States and Canada.* 2 vols., London, Hurst, Robinson & Co., 1824.—Reissued as *Remarks During a Journey through North America,* 1823.

HOSKINS, NATHAN. *Notes upon the Western Country* [etc.]. Greenfield, Mass., Fogg, 1833.

HOWE, HENRY. *Historical Collections of the Great West.* Cincinnati, H. Howe, 1851.
   Historical Collections of Ohio. Cincinnati, Derby, Bradley & Co., 1847; Bradley and Anthony, 1849; R. Clark & Co., 1869.

HINSDALE, BURKE AARON. *The Old Northwest.* New York, T. MacCoun, 1888.

HOLDITCH, ROBERT. *Emigrant's Guide to United States of America* (1818). London, Hone, 1818.

HOPKINS, CYRIL G. *Soil Fertility and Permanent Agriculture.* Boston, New York, etc., Ginn & Co.

HULBERT, ARCHER BUTLER. *Historic Highways.* Vol. VII, is most useful here.—*Portage Paths.* 16 vols., Cleveland, The A. H. Clark Co., 1902 to 1905.

HUBBARD, BELA. *Memorials of a Half Century in Michigan and the Lake Region.* New York and London, G. P. Putnam's Sons, 1888.

HUNT, FREEMAN. *Merchant's Magazine and Commercial Review from 1840 to 1870.* New York, F. Hunt.

Illinois State Historical Society. *Journal.* Springfield, State Printers, April 1908 to date.

Indians. *Handbook of North American Indians.* Bulletin 30, Bureau of American Ethnology. 2 vols., Washington, D. C.

JAMES, JAMES A. "George Rogers Clark and Detroit, 1780 to 1781," in *Mississippi Valley Historical Association Proceedings,* 1910 to 1911.

JENKS, ALBERT ERNEST. "The Wild Rice Gatherers of the Upper Lakes," in *19th Annual Report of Bureau of American Ethnology,* Part 2, 1897 to 1898. Washington, Government Printing Office.

Jesuit Relations and Allied Documents. Edited by Reuben Gold Thwaites. Cleveland, The Burrows Bros. Co., 1896 to 1901.— Travels and explorations of the Jesuit Missionaries in New France, 1610 to 1791.

JONES, DAVID. *A Journal of Two Visits made to Some Nations of Indians on the West Side of the River Ohio, in the Years* 1772 and 1773. New York, reprinted by J. Sabin, 1865.

KINGDOM, WILLIAM, JR. *America and British Colonies. An Abstract of all the most useful Information relative to the United States, Canada,* [etc.]. London, G. & W. B. Whittaker, 1820.

KINGSFORD, WILLIAM. *History of Canada.* 10 vols., Toronto, Rowsell and Hutchinson, 1887.

KNOPP, HORACE S. *History of the Maumee Valley.* Toledo, Mammoth Printing and Publishing House, 1872.

LANMAN, CHARLES. *The Red Book of Michigan, a Civil, Military, and Biographical History.* Detroit, 1871.

LAHONTAN, BARON DE. *New Voyages to North America,* [etc.]. See Thwaites.

LATROBE, CHARLES J. *The Rambler in North America* (1832 to 1833). 2 vols., London, 1835.

LATROBE, JOHN HAZELHURST BONEVAL. *The First Steamboat Voyage on the Western Waters.* Baltimore, J. Murphy, 1871.

LEE, GUY CARLETON. *A History of North America.* Edited by Guy Carleton Lee. 20 vols., Philadelphia, G. Barrie & Sons, 1903 to 1907.

LEES, JOHN. *Journal of John Lees of Quebec, Merchant.* Detroit,

Speaker-Hines Press, for Society of Colonial Wars of State of Michigan, 1911.

LEONARD, J. W. *Industries of Detroit.* Detroit, 1887.

LEVERETT, FRANK. *Outline History of Great Lakes.* Reprint, Michigan Academy of Science, 1910.

LEVERETT, FRANK, and SCHNEIDER, C. F. "Surface Geology and Agricultural Conditions of Southern Peninsula of Michigan." *Publication* 9, Geol. Series 7, Mich. Geol. Surv., 1912.

LIANCOURT, LA ROCHEFOUCAULD. *Travels through United States of North America, the Country of the Iroquois and Upper Canada in the Years 1795, 1796 and 1797.* 2 vols., London, R. Phillips, 1799; French Edition, Paris, Du Pont, 1799.

LONG, JOHN. "John Long's Journal, 1768 to 1782," in Thwaites, *Early Western Travels*, II.

LUCAS, ROBERT. *Journal of War of 1812.* Iowa City, Iowa, State Historical Society of Iowa, 1906.

MACCABE, JULIUS P. BOLIVAR. *Directory of Detroit*, 1837.

MACKENZIE, SIR ALEXANDER. *Voyages from Montreal on the River St. Lawrence and through the Continent of North America to the frozen and the Pacific Ocean, in the Year 1789 and 1793, with Preliminary Account of Rise, Progress, and Present State of the Fur Trade of that Country.* 2 vols., London, Printed for T. Cadell, Jr. and W. Davis, 1802; New York, New Amsterdam Book Co. 1902.

MARTINEAU, HARRIET. *Society in America.* London, Saunders and Otley, 1837.
Retrospect of Western Travels. 2 vols., London, Saunders and Otley, 1838.

MATHEWS, LOIS KIMBALL. *The Expansion of New England, the Spread of New England Settlements and Constitutions to the Mississippi River.* Boston and New York, Houghton, Mifflin Co., 1909.

MAXWELL, ————. *A Run through North America during the Autumn of 1840.* 2 vols., London, H. Colburn, 1841.

MCCARTHY, DWIGHT G. *The Territorial Governors of the Old Northwest.* Iowa City, State Historical Society of Iowa, 1910.

MCCRACKEN, STEPHEN B. *The State of Michigan, embracing Sketches of Its History.* Lansing, 1876.
Detroit in 1900; a Chronological Record of Events, both Local and State during the Closing Year of the Century. Detroit, 1901.

MCKENNEY, THOMAS LORRAINE. *Sketches of a Tour of the Lakes.* Baltimore, F. Lucas, 1827.

McLaughlin, Andrew C. ":The Western Posts and the British Debts," in *Annual Rept. of Amer. Hist. Assoc.*, 1894.

Michigan. Internal Improvements. *Annual Report of Board of Internal Improvements*. State Publishers, 1838.

Michigan Pioneer and Historical Collections. 39 vols., Lansing, Published by State, 1877 to 1915.

Mitchell, John. *The Present State of Great Britain and North America with regard to Agriculture, Population, Trade, and Manufactures, Impartially Considered.* London, T. Becket, 1767.

Mitchell, John J. *Detroit in History and Commerce.* Detroit, Rogers and Thorpe, 1891. A Compilation of the History, Mercantile, and Manufacturing Interests of Detroit.

Mitchell, D. W. *Ten Years in United States.* London, 1862.

Mitchell, Samuel A. *Principal Stage, Steamboat, and Canal Routes in the United States. An Accompaniment to Mitchell's Traveller's Guide.* Philadelphia, Mitchell and Hinman, 1834. Several editions. Name varies.

Compendium of all the Internal Improvements of the United States. Philadelphia, Mitchell and Hinman, 1835.

Moore, Charles. *The Northwest Under Three Flags.* New York, Harpers, 1900.

Morrison, John Harrison. *History of American Steam Navigation.* New York, W. F. Sametz & Co., Inc., 1903.

New York Historical Society, *Collections.* New York, printed for society, 1868 to date.—Annual.

New England Magazine. Boston, J. N. McClintock & Co., 1884 to date.

Niles, Hezekiah. *Weekly Register.* 75 vols. and 3 nos. of vol. 76, Baltimore, 1811 to 1849. Title varies.

North American Review. Boston, Wells and Lilly, 1815 to 1877; New York, D. Appleton & Co., 1878 to date.

Palmer, Friend. *Early Days In Detroit.* Detroit, Hunt and James, 1906.

Peck, John Mason. *A New Guide for Emigrants to the West, containing Sketches of Ohio, Indiana, Illinois, Missouri, Michigan, with Territories of Wisconsin and Arkansas and Adjacent Parts.* Boston, Lincoln and Edwards, 1831; Gould, etc., 1836; Kendall and Lincoln, 1837.

Phelps, ——, and Squires, ——. *Traveller's Guide and Emigrant's Directory through the States of Ohio, Illinois, Indiana, and Michigan.* New York, Phelps and Squires, 1836.

Plumb Ralph G. *History of the Navigation of the Great Lakes,*

1911.—Commission on Railways and Canals.   Hearing of Commission of the Great Lakes.

Pontiac Area.   United States Soil Survey, Bureau of Soils, *Fourth Report*, 1902.—Field operations.

POOR, HERVEY V.   *Manual of the Railroads of the United States, Street Railway and Traction Companies, Industrial and Other Corporations, and Statements of Debts of United States*, [etc.]. New York and London, H. V. and H. W. Poor, 1880.
Sketches of the Rise and Progress of the Internal Improvements and of the Internal Commerce of the United States, with a Review of Charges of Monopoly and Oppression made against Railroad Corporations.   New York, H. V. and H. W. Poor, 1881.

PORTIER, P.   *Huron Mission of Detroit.   Account Book of Father Peter Portier*, S. J., 1733 to 1751, translated and annotated by Richard R. Elliott.   Detroit, 1891.

RENARD, C.   *Official Report made by Mr. Dubuisson to Governor General of Canada of War of 1812.*   Detroit, 1845.

RINGWALT, JOHN LUTHER.   *Development of Transportation Systems in United States.*   Philadelphia, Railway World Office, 1888.

ROBERTS, ROBERT E.   *Sketches of Detroit, Past and Present.*   Detroit, 1855.
Sketches and Reminiscences of City of Straits and Vicinity.   Detroit, 1884.

ROGERS, JAMES EDWIN THOROLD.   *The Economic Interpretation of History.*   New York, G. P. Putnam's Sons; London, T. F. Unwin, 1889.—Lectures delivered in Oxford.

ROGERS, ROBERT (Major).   *A Concise Account of North America, of the Interior or Western Parts of the Country upon the Rivers St. Lawrence, the Mississippi . . . . , and the Great Lakes.*   London, printed for Author, 1765.

ROOSEVELT, THEODORE.   *The Winning of the West.*   6 vols., New York and London, G. P. Putnam's Sons, 1900.

ROSS, ROBERT, and CATLIN, GEORGE B.   *Landmarks of Wayne County and Detroit.*   Detroit, 1898.

RUPP, ISRAEL DANIEL.   *The Geographical Catechism of Pennsylvania and the Western States.*   Harrisburg, Pa., Winebrenner, 1836.

SCHOOLCRAFT, HENRY R.   *Narrative Journal of Travels from Detroit Northwest through the Great Chain of American Lakes to the Source of the Mississippi River in the Year 1820.*   Albany, 1821.

The American Indians. Their History, Conditions, and Prospects, from Original Notes and Manuscripts. Rochester, Wanzer, Foot and Co., 1851.

Information Respecting the History, Conditions, and Prospects of the Indian Tribes of the United States. Bureau of Indian Affairs, Published by authority of Congress. Philadelphia, Lippincott, Grambo & Co., 1851 to 1857.

SCOTT, JOSEPH. *The United States Gazetteer, containing an Authentic Description of the Several States, their Situation, Extent, Boundaries, Soil, Produce, Climate, Population, Trade, and Manufactures.* Philadelphia, F. & R. Bailey, 1795.

SHELDON, (Mrs.) ELECTRA M. *The Early History of Michigan from the First Settlement to 1815.* New York, 1856.

SHERZER, WILLIAM H. "Geological Report of Monroe County" (1900), in *Michigan Geological Survey*, Vol. VII, Pt. I.
"Geology of Wayne County," in Michigan Geological and Biological Survey, Publication 12, Geol. Series 9.

SLOCUM, CHARLES ELIHU. *History of Maumee River Basin from the Earliest Account to its Organization into Counties.* Defiance, Ohio, the author, 1905.

SPARKS, JARED. *The Writings of George Washington.* New York, Harper and Bros., 1847 to 1848.

SQUIRE, ——. See Phelps and Squire. *Traveller's Guide and Emigrant's Directory through the States of Ohio, Illinois, Indiana, and Michigan.*

Statistical Atlas of United States. Eleventh and also Twelfth Census.

STEELE, OLIVER G. *Steele's Western Guide Book and Emigrant's Directory.* Buffalo, Steele, 1835. Earlier edition known as *Emigrant's Guide* published in 1832.

STRICKLAND, WILLIAM PETER. *Old Mackinaw, or the Fortress of the Lakes, and its Surroundings.* Philadelphia, J. Challen & Son; New York, Carlton and Peter, 1860.

SWAN, LANSING B. *Journal of a Trip to Michigan in 1841.* Rochester, Humphrey, 1904.

TANNER, HENRY S. *The American Traveller, or Guide through United States.* Philadelphia, author, 1834.
A Brief Description of the Canals and Railroads of the United States. Philadelphia, author, 1834. Reissued as a *Description of the Canals and Railroads.* New York, Tanner and Disturnell, 1840.

TANNER, JOHN. *A Narrative of the Captivity and Adventures of*

J. Tanner during Thirty Years Residence among the Indians of the Interior of North America. Prepared by Edwin James. New York, 1830.

THOMAS, DAVID. *Travels Through the Western Country in Summer of 1816.* Auburn, N. Y., Rumsey, 1819.

THWAITES, REUBEN GOLD. *New Voyages to North America, by the Baron de Lahontan.* Reprinted from English edition of 1703. Introduction, notes and index by Reuben Gold Thwaites. Chicago, A. C. McClurg & Co., 1905.

Father Marquette. New York, D. Appleton & Co., 1902.

A New Discovery of a Vast Country in America by Father Louis Hennepin. Reprint from the second London issue of 1698. Introduction, notes and index by Reuben Gold Thwaites. Chicago, A. C. McClurg & Co., 1903. (See Hennepin.)

How George Rogers Clark Won the Northwest, and Other Essays in Western History. Chicago, A. C. McClurg & Co., 1903.

France in America, 1497 to 1763. New York and London, Harper and Bros., 1905.

Toledo Area. United States Soil Survey. Bureau of Soils, *Fifth Report,* 1903.—Field operations.

TURNER, FREDERICK JACKSON. "Character and Influence of the Fur Trade in Wisconsin," in Wis. Hist. Soc., *Proceedings,* 1889. Also in J. H. U. Studies in Hist. and Pol. Science, Series IX. Baltimore, The Johns Hopkins Press, 1891.

TUNNELL, GEORGE G. "Statistics on Commerce of Lakes (1898)," in 55th Congress, 2nd Session, *House Doc.,* 277.

TUTTLE, CHARLES R. *General History of State of Michigan.* Detroit, 1873.

UTLEY, HENRY MUNSON, and CUTCHEON, BYRON M. *Michigan, a Province, Territory, and State.* New York, The Publishing Society of Michigan, 1906.

VOLNEY, C. F. *A View of the Soil and Climate of United States of America.* Translated from the French. London, J. Johnson, 1804.

WALKER, AUGUSTUS. "Early Days on the Lakes." From manuscript records of Capt. Augustus Walker. Buffalo Historical Society, *Publications.* Buffalo, 1902.

WALKER, CHARLES IRISH. *The Northwest During the Revolution.* Address before Wisconsin State Historical Society, 1871. Madison, Atwood and Culver, State Printers, 1871.

Water Supply and Irrigation Papers, U. S. G. S., No. 182. Washington, Govt. Printing Office, 1906.

WEBER, ADNA FERRIN. *The Growth of Cities in the Nineteenth Century.* New York, published for Columbia University by ·Macmillan Co., 1899.

WEEKS, J. W. *Directory of Detroit.* Detroit, J. W. Weeks & Co., 1883.

Washtenaw County, History of, and Biographies of Representative Citizens. Chicago, C. C. Chapman & Co., 1881.

WELD, ISAAC, JR. *Travels through the States of North America and the Provinces of Upper and Lower Canada during the Years 1795, 1796, and 1797.* 2 vols., fourth edition, London, 1800.

WILLIAMS, MEADE CREIGHTON. *Early Mackinaw. A Sketch, historical and descriptive.* 3rd edition, St. Louis, Brischart Bros., 1901.

WILSON, WOODROW. *A History of the American People.* New York and London, Harper & Bros., 1902.

WINSOR, JUSTIN. *Narrative and Critical History of America,* Edited by Justin Winsor. 8 vols., Boston and New York, Houghton Mifflin & Co., 1884 to 1889.

Cartier to Frontenac, or Geographic Discoveries in Interior of North America. Boston and New York, Houghton Mifflin & Co., 1894.

Wisconsin Geologic Survey. *Atlas,* Vol. II, 1877.

Wisconsin State Historical Society, *Collections.* Vols. I to XIX. Madison, Wis., 1854 to 1910.

WORCESTER, JOSEPH E. *Gazetteer of United States.* 2nd edition, Andover, Flagg and Gould, 1818.

INDEX

INDEX

Agriculture, in Detroit region in 1788, 121; in 1812, 133

Albany, founding of, 27; commodities shipped from, 27; favorable location of for fur trade, 27; area tributary to, 28, 36

Albach, *Annals of the West*, 323

Alleghany, *trans-explorations of*, 323 (Alvord and Bidgood)

Alleghany Mountains, *tour northwest of*, 330 (Harns)

Allouez, Claude, on Lake Superior, 29; founded LaPointe de Esprit, 29

Alvord and Bidgood, see trans-Alleghany explorations

America, *narrative and critical history of*, 337 (Winsor); *new discovery of vast territory in*, 330 (Hennepin); *travels in, and Italy*, 325 (Chateaubriand)

Americans assume control, 128

American Antiquarian and Oriental Journal, 323

American Antiquarian Society, *Proceedings* of, 323

American Economic Association, *Publications* of, 323

American Fur Company, 140, 182

American Historical Association, *Annual Reports*, 323

American Historical Review, 323

American People, *history of*, 337 (Wilson)

American State Papers, 323

Amherstburg and Sandwich compete with Detroit, 130

Anderson, David, *Canada: A view of British American Colonies*, 323

Andrews, Israel D., *Trade and Commerce of British Colonies in America*, 323

Annals of the West, 323 (Albach)

Antiquarian, American, 323

Area of Detroit at various decades, 170

Armroyd, George, *Interior Navigation of United States*, 323

Ashe, Thomas, *Travels in North America*, 323

Astor, John Jacob, founds American Fur Company, 140

Atlas of Canada, 323

Atwater, Caleb, *History of State of Ohio*, 323

Automobile industry, 303-306

Baldwin, C. C., *Indian Migrations in America*, 323

Baltimore and Ohio Railroad, 262

Bars at mouths of rivers, 232

Batteaux, 207; Cadillac used, 208; on Lake Erie, 208

Bed rock of Great Lakes region, 5; influence on topography of Lakes, 5-8; map of, 34; relation to origin and location, and shape of Lakes, 6

Bemis, Edward Webster, *Local Government in Michigan and the Northwest*, 324

Benton, Elbert Jay, *The Wabash Trade Route*, 324

Benton, Thomas Hart, *Abridgment of Speeches in Congress*, 324

Bessemer steel, made at Wyandotte, 299-230

Beste, John R. D., *The Wabash*, 324

INDEX

Captivity of John Dodge, *narrative of*, 328 (Dodge)

Car-ferry, 275

Carrying agents, see Great Lakes, Shipping, etc

Cartier in estuary of St. Lawrence, 21

Cascade Point, canal at, 236

Census Reports, 325; figures on manufactures, 281, 283; figures on population, 170, 196; figures for 1763-1796, unreliable, 98; of Detroit for 1773, 96; for 1779, 100

Central Railroad of Michigan, 264-268

Channels across Mississippi-St. Lawrence divide, influence of, 10; position of Detroit with respect to, 11

Chartres, Fort, settlement at, 80

Chateaubriand, Francois, A. R., *Travels in America and Italy*, 325

Charlevoix, Pièrre Francois X., *History and General Description of New France*, 325

Cheap goods, Charlevoix quoted on, 36; influence of in winning Indian trade, 36; reasons why British could offer, 37

Chicago, boat line to, from New Buffalo, 270; treaty of, 171; reduces jobbing trade of Detroit, see Jobbing center; portage, see Portage

Chippewa Portage Company, builds tramway at "Soo," 250

City, *report on conference for good city government*, 325; of Straits, *sketches and reminiscences of*, 334 (Roberts); planning at Detroit, 198; *growth of in nineteenth century*, 337 (Weber)

Clark, George Rogers, *How George Rogers Clark Won the Northwest*,

336 (Thwaites); prevented from attacking Detroit, 98; takes forts in Illinois Country, 98

Clinton River, bars at mouth, 160; drowned at mouth, 159; government improvement of, 160; navigable near mouth, 106; settlement on, 149; used by British for harbor, 160; water power on, 159

Coal, source of, at Detroit, 318

Cod fisheries, discovery of on Grand Banks, 21

Colden, discusses portages, 10; favors prohibiting settlers from trading with Indians, 95; favors sending settlers to Detroit, 95

Colleges and seminaries at Detroit, 183

Colonies, *American and British*, 331 (Kingdom)

Colton, G. W. and C. B., *Map of Michigan*, 325; *Western Tourist and Emigrants Guide*, 325; map copied from, see Maps

Coman, Katherine, *Industrial History of U. S.*, 326

Commerce, lake, 324 (Barton); *Statistics of*, 336 (Tunnell); with Montreal, 75; and Navigation, *American State Papers*, 323; of Detroit, 1796, 126; eras of lake, 204, and Finance, *Monthly Summary of*, 326

Congress grants military reserve, 178

Congressional Globe, 326

Cook, Charles W., *Brines and Salt Deposits of Michigan*, 326

Cooley, Thomas McIntyre, *Michigan, a History of Governments*, 326; quoted on banks, 187

Copper smelting, 293, 296

Corn, grown in Detroit region, 62

Coteau de Lac, canal at, 235

in 1849, 268; railroads in Michigan in 1857, 267; railroads in 1869, 269; interurban lines centering at Detroit, 276

Malden, Fort, controlled mouth of river, 133

Markets, access to, 319

Marquette, Father, 336 (Thwaites)

Marquette and Joliet, voyages of, 29 (n. 29)

Martineau, Harriet, *Society in America*, 332

Mathews, Lois, *Expansion of New England*, 332

Maumee River basin, *History of*, 335 (Slocum)

Maumee Valley, *History*, 331 (Knapp)

Maxwell, *A Run through North America*, etc., 332

May, James, describes Detroit, in 1778, 99

Merchants, Montreal, send petition to retain posts, 102

Miami Company, *early settlement of*, 328 (Ferris)

Michigan, *a Province, Territory, and State*, 336 (Utley and Cutcheon); *early history of*, 335 (Sheldon); *Gazetteer of*, 324 (Blowe); *general History of*, 336 (Tuttle); *Internal Improvements, Report of*, 333; *journal of a trip to*, 335 (Swan); map of, 325 (Colton); *outlines of political history of*, 325 (Campbell); *the State of*, 332 (McCracken)

Michigan, Lake, improvements on, 23

Michigan Pioneer and Historical Collections, 333

Michigan Stove Company, 307

Michigan United Railway, 278

Michillimackinac (Mackinaw), captured by agents of Northwest Company, 136; center of American Fur Company, 140; missionaries at, 203; Northwest Company petitions to retain, 140; location of, 140 (n. 53); rendezvous of traders and missionaries, 203; settlers at, 80

Migrations of Indians in America, 323 (Baldwin)

Mill at Detroit, 54

Mineral resources of Detroit region, 166

Mississippi Valley, *geography and history of*, 329 (Flint)

Mitchell, John, *Agriculture, Population, Trade, and Manufactures of Great Britain and United States*, 333

Mitchell, John, *Detroit in History and Commerce*, 333

Mitchell, Samuel, *Principal Stage, Steamboat, and Canal Routes in U. S.*, 333; *Compendium of Internal Improvements in U. S.*, 333

Mohawk River, Erie Canal in Valley of, 245; outlet for Detroit commerce, 243

Moore, Charles, *The Northwest under Three Flags*, 333

Money, lack of, 188; cut money, 188

Moraine, altitude of at Detroit, 155; Detroit located on, 155; moraines in Detroit region, 151; more important ones in Great Lakes region, 9; origin of, 155; served to locate Fort Pontchartrain, 156

Morrison, John, *History of American Steam Navigation*, 333

Mortgages, against settlers (1740), 73

Navigation, on Huron River, 160; on Clinton, 160; *interior, of U. S.*,

People, character of, in 1764, 84

Peripheral location of Lakes region, effects of, 91

Perry's Fleet, delayed in fitting out, 138

Pharmaceutical industry, 306-307

Phelps and Squires, *Traveller's Guide and Emigrant's Directory*, 333

Plains, geographic influence of, 1

Plumb, Ralph, *History of the Navigation of Great Lakes*, 333

Pontchartrain, Fort, *du Detroit*, 325 (Burton); described, 81

Pontchartrain reviews situation at Detroit, 59-60

Pontiac and Grand River Road, see Grand River Road

Pontiac area, *U. S. soil survey*, 334

Pontiac, attacks Detroit, 88; reasons for hostility of to British, 85

Poor, Henry, *Manual of Railroads of U. S.*, 334

Population, by decades, 170; cosmopolitan, 121, 131, 194; distribution of in Lakes region in 1810, 132; effects of increase in Michigan on Detroit, 174; factors in growth, 312,322; factors in slow growth, 1800-1810, 171; factors in rapid growth since 1830, 171; foreigners appear in, 181; foreign in 1850, 188; foreign in 1860, 194; foreign in 1880 and 1910, 196; growth rapid, 1749-1755, 79; at Detroit in 1707, 55; in 1736, 71; in 1805, 131; in 1810, 131; in 1850, 188; increase by decades, 170; increase of from 1830 to 1840, 177; maps showing distribution of in 1820, 133; nativity of in 1850, 1880, 1910, 196; growth retarded in early period, 56

Portages of Great Lakes region, 9; Colden's remarks regarding, 10

Portier, *Account book of, at Huron Mission*, 334

Post, importance of Detroit, in 1768, 92

Posts, *western, and British debts*, 333 (MacLaughlin)

Presents, requisition list of, to Indians, 116

Printing industry, 307

Property, value of increasing, 181

Public buildings in 1837, 182, 183

Public lands, *American State Papers*, 322

Quebec, founding of, 25; favorable elements in location of, 26; political center of New France, 26; *in seventeenth century*, 328 (Douglas)

Quebec Act, retarded settlement of Detroit, 94

Railroads, centering at Detroit, 182; Detroit and St. Joseph, 181; Detroit and Pontiac, 182, 262, 265; economic effects of, 273; extending from Detroit in 1885; from Detroit to-day, 271; growth of in Michigan, 272; leading westward, 272; map of, 268, 269

Railroads, *of U. S.*, 328 (Flint); *manual of*, 334 (Poor)

Raisin River, government improvements on, 160

Receipts and shipments, Diagram of, at lake ports, 229, 230

Retention of Lake posts, 111; reasons for, 103-104; Montreal Merchants petition to retain, 102, 112; boundary proposals regarding, 112

Richardie, mission near Detroit, 73; transactions at mission store, 73-75 (n. 73-75)

Settlers, accused of being lazy
(1730), 70; advances to, in 1748,
77
Sewage system, 183
Simcoe induces settlers to leave
Detroit, 128
Sheldon, Electra M., *Early History
of Michigan*, etc., 335
Sherzer, William H., *Geologic Re-
port of Monroe County*, 335;
Geology of Wayne County, 335
Ship Canals, *economic effect of*,
328 (Fairlie)
Shipbuilding, history of, 222-223,
280-281
Shipments and receipts, see Receipts and shipments
Shipping, *American Blue Book of*,
324; at various lake ports, 224;
owned at Detroit, 182, 224, 235
Slaughtering and meatpacking, 306
Slocum, Charles, *History of Maumee
River Basin*, 335
Society, democratic at Detroit, 147;
in America, 332 (*Martineau*)
Soils, methods of judging, by early
settlers, 165; of Black Swamp,
162; of clay knolls and ridges,
163-164; of Detroit region, 160,
161; sands and gravels, 164; of
kames and eskers, 164; of till and
lacustrine plains, 162; of valley
bottoms, 165
Soil and Climate of U. S., *a view of*,
336 (Volney)
"Sole market" idea, influence of in
America, 23
Southern Railroad, 264, 271
Sparks, Jared, *The Writings of
George Washington*, 335
Squires, see Phelps and Squires
Stage coach lines, 25, 260; map of,
in 1849, 268
Statistical Atlas of U. S., 335

Steamboat, *first on Western Waters*,
331 (Latrobe)
Steamboats, improvements, 220;
lines of, 225, 226; on Lake Erie,
173; Chippewa, 218; Henry Clay,
218; Superior, 218
Steam navigation, *history of Ameri-
can*, 333 (Morrison); beginnings
of, 131
Steam shipping, growth of, 218;
growth in tonnage of, 219; de-
cline in number's of vessels, 219
Steele, Oliver G., *Western Guide
Book*, etc., 335
Stoney island, quarry worked on,
83, 168
Stoves and ranges, 307
Strickland, William Peter, *Old
Mackinaw*, 335
Structure of city, changes in, 199
Suburbs, location of, 198
Superior, Lake, growing trade on,
250; improvements on, 233;
visited in 1629, 203
Supply trains, to Detroit, cut off,
136
Swamps, in Detroit region, 156,
deterred settlement, 158
Swan, Lansing B., *Journal of a Trip
to Michigan*, 335
Tanner, Henry S., *The American
Traveller*, 435
Tanner, John, *A Narrative of Cap-
tivity*, etc., 335
Tanning industry, 287, 288
Thomas, David, *Travels through
Western Country*, etc., 336
Thwaites, Reuben G., various
works, 336
Tidal waters of Hudson River, see
Hudson River
Till plain, elevation of, 152; extent
of, 151; location of, Detroit on,
151; origin of, 153; width oi fn

eastern Michigan, 152

Titles, of land in Detroit region, classes of, 129

Tobacco, grown in Detroit region, 180; industry, 297

Toledo area, soil survey, 336

Treaty at Detroit, see Detroit

Tour, *An American, sketches of,* 330 (Hardy); Evans' *Pedestrious,* 328; *from city of New York to Detroit,* 326 (Darby); *of Lakes, sketch of,* 332 (McKenney); *of New England and New York,* 328 (Dwight); *remarks during, through U. S.,* 330 (Harris)

Tourist, *Western,* 325 (Colton)

Trade of Montreal, threatened by Iroquois, 14

Traders, Dongan sends, to Upper Lakes, 48; first English, to Upper Lakes, 30; required to buy licenses, 66, 68

Trading posts of American Fur Company, 141

Trails, Indian, from Detroit, 82, 253; map of, 257

Trans-lake routes, on Lake Erie, 7

Transactions, typical at Richardie's mission store, 73 (n. 73-74)

Transportation, importance of break in, 316; facilities of Detroit, 181, 200, 247; *development of, in U. S.,* 334 (Ringwalt)

Travels, *in America,* etc., 323 (Ashe); *in the States and Canada,* 337 (Weld); *narrative journal of,* 334 (Schoolcraft)

Traveller's Guide, 326 (Davidson); *and Emigrant Directory,* 333 (Phelps and Squires); *The American Traveller,* 335 (Tanner); *The Western Traveller,* 327 (Disturnell)

Treaties, Chicago (1821), 171; Detroit (1807), 171; Greenville

(1795), 171; provisions of treaty of 1783, 101

Trent River route, see Portages

Tonnage, see Shipping

Tonty takes charge, 68

Topography, influence of bed rock on, 5-8; influence of glaciation on, 8-10; local, of Detroit region, 151-159

Toronto Channel, see Portages

Towns at mouths of rivers owe early start to fur trade, 141

Troops, withdrawal from Detroit, 61

Tunnel, under Detroit River, 275

Turnpikes, map of, 257

Upper Lakes of North America, *Guide to,* 327 (Disturnell)

Vaudreuil, approves settlement at Detroit, 58

Vessels, steel, specialization in type of, 221

Vessels, sailing, British build, 212; built in Detroit, 213; first American on Lakes, 215; French build, 211; on Lakes in 1870, 1880, 1890, 1900, 216; private, excluded from Lakes, 213

Village, *Cadillac's,* 325 (Burton)

Vincennes, settlers at, 80

Voyages, 325 (Butterick)

Wabash, *the, or adventures of an English gentleman's family in interior America,* 324 (Beste); portage, settlement at, 80; *Trade route,* 324 (Benton); *Valley, recollection of early settlement of,* 326 (Cox)

Walk-in-the-Water, first trip, 172; described, 216, 217; Darby describes, 231; movements of discussed, 218; reduces time of travel, 172; trip to Mackinaw, 173

Washtenaw County, *history of,* 337